Cognitive Behavior Therapy with Children in Schools (PGPS-154)

Pergamon Titles of Related Interest

Cartledge/Milburn TEACHING SOCIAL SKILLS TO CHILDREN: Innovative Approaches, Second Edition

Conoley/Conoley SCHOOL CONSULTATION: A Guide to Practice and Training

Maher/Zins PSYCHOEDUCATIONAL INTERVENTIONS IN THE SCHOOLS: Methods and Procedures for Enhancing Student Competence

Plas SYSTEMS PSYCHOLOGY IN THE SCHOOLS

Wielkiewicz BEHAVIOR MANAGEMENT IN THE SCHOOLS

Related Journals

(Free sample copies available upon request)

CLINICAL PSYCHOLOGY REVIEW
JOURNAL OF SCHOOL PSYCHOLOGY

PERGAMON GENERAL PSYCHOLOGY SERIES

Cognitive Behavior Therapy with Children in Schools

Jan N. Hughes
Texas A&M University

PERGAMON PRESS

New York • Oxford • Beijing • Frankfurt
São Paulo • Sydney • Tokyo • Toronto

U.S.A.	Pergamon Press, Maxwell House, Fairview Park, Elmsford, New York 10523, U.S.A.
U.K.	Pergamon Press, Headington Hill Hall, Oxford OX3 0BW, England
PEOPLE'S REPUBLIC OF CHINA	Pergamon Press, Room 4037, Qianmen Hotel, Beijing, People's Republic of China
FEDERAL REPUBLIC OF GERMANY	Pergamon Press, Hammerweg 6, D-6242 Kronberg, Federal Republic of Germany
BRAZIL	Pergamon Editora, Rua Eça de Queiros, 346, CEP 04011, Paraiso, São Paulo, Brazil
AUSTRALIA	Pergamon Press Australia, P.O. Box 544, Potts Point, N.S.W. 2011, Australia
JAPAN	Pergamon Press, 8th Floor, Matsuoka Central Building, 1-7-1 Nishishinjuku, Shinjuku-ku, Tokyo 160, Japan
CANADA	Pergamon Press Canada, Suite No. 271, 253 College Street, Toronto, Ontario, Canada M5T 1R5

First edition 1988

Library of Congress Cataloging-in-Publication Data

Hughes, Jan N., 1949–
Cognitive behavior therapy with children in schools.
(Pergamon general psychology series; 154)
Bibliography: p.
Includes index.
1. Behavior modification. 2. Behavior therapy for children.
3. School psychology. I. Title. II. Series. [DNLM: 1. Behavior Therapy—in infancy & childhood. 2. Cognition—in infancy & childhood. WS 350.6 H893c] LB1060.2.H84 1988 372.11'024
87-7274

British Library Cataloguing in Publication Data

Hughes, Jan N.
Cognitive behavior therapy with children in schools. —
(Pergamon general psychology series; 154).
1. Cognitive therapy for children. 2. Problem children —
Education
I. Title
371.94 RC505.C6

ISBN 0-08-034326-0 Hardcover
ISBN 0-08-034325-2 Flexicover

Printed in Great Britain by A. Wheaton & Co. Ltd, Exeter

To Jim for his confidence
in me, patience,
and support

Contents

Acknowledgments

Chapter 8 was co-authored by Lisa A. Moore and me. Ms. Moore is a doctoral student in the school psychology program at Texas A&M University. I consider Lisa Moore to be the first author for chapter 8.

I wish to express my appreciation to Kim Schultz, Rebecca Kocurek, Peggy Locke, and Sharon Sidoti for their secretarial assistance during the various phases of this project.

Jan N. Hughes

Introduction

School psychologists, counselors, and other specialists who are responsible for treating children's emotional and behavioral problems in schools require assessment and intervention strategies that are effective, consistent with the philosophy and goals of the schools and with the roles of school professionals, and feasible. Many cognitive-behavioral approaches to assessment and intervention meet these requirements and therefore they offer the school mental health specialist a theoretical and practical framework for helping children who display emotional and behavioral problems.

Cognitive behavior therapy represents a merging of cognitive and behavioral treatment approaches. Rather than discarding behavioral assessment and intervention strategies that have demonstrated their utility with educationally relevant problems, the cognitive-behavioral school psychologist adopts a broadened behavioral framework that permits a focus on children's cognition (i.e., thoughts and thinking processes) as well as behavior.

The purpose of this book is to provide an integrative, empirical account of selected cognitive-behavioral approaches to promoting children's emotional and behavioral adjustment in the schools. Three criteria were used to select assessment and intervention practices for inclusion in this integrative account. First, the use of the procedure with children with behavior problems similar to those of children for whom the procedure is recommended is supported by empirical evidence. Second, the theoretical rationale for the procedure is consistent with cognitive-behavioral theory. Third, the procedure is practical in school settings. Regarding the last point, schools offer possibilities as well as constraints, and the effective change agent maximizes the possibilities inherent in schools while minimizing the constraints. If, on the one hand, change agents attempt directly to replicate a procedure developed in a hospital or laboratory setting in a school setting, they will tend to view setting differences as obstacles. If, on the other hand, change agents attempt to accommodate the procedure to the uniqueness of the school setting, they will view differences as opportunities as well as constraints.

Procedures based only on operant or classical conditioning paradigms are excluded from this account. This decision does not reflect a devaluation of these approaches. On the contrary, it is recognized that operant approaches in the schools have achieved considerable success. Rather, this decision is based on the availability of several excellent sources of behavior modification in the schools (e.g., Witt, Elliott, & Gresham, 1987).

The first chapter provides a historical and conceptual overview of the field of cognitive behaviorism. First, cognitive-behavioral approaches are discussed in light of the distinction between philosophical behaviorism and methodological behaviorism. Second, streams of influence on contemporary cognitive behavior therapy are reviewed. Third, a brief overview of behavior modification in school is provided. The chapter concludes with a discussion of promises and pitfalls attendant on cognitive-behavioral approaches in schools.

The remaining two chapters in the first section focus on cognitive-behavioral assessment. Chapter 2 provides a theoretical treatment of the topic, and chapter 3 reviews specific assessment strategies.

Each of the six chapters in the second section focuses on a specific clinical population. Each chapter discusses relevant definitional and conceptual issues and reviews specific assessment and intervention practices. Because the book is written for the practitioner who expects practice recommendations to be supported by psychological science, the theoretical and empirical bases for recommended assessment and intervention practices are critically reviewed, limitations of applications are noted, and important areas for future research inquiry are delineated. Recommended assessment and intervention practices take into account both the constraints and the possibilities inherent in school settings.

Chapter 10 discusses school-based prevention research. A rationale for cognitive-behavioral prevention approaches is suggested, and examples of cognitive-behavioral prevention efforts representing each of three prevention approaches are reviewed.

SECTION I

FOUNDATIONS

1 Historical and Conceptual Overview

COGNITIVE BEHAVIOR THERAPY AND METHODOLOGICAL BEHAVIORISM

The term cognitive behavior therapy (CBT) encompasses a diverse assemblage of models and strategies for assessing and treating an individual's performance. An apt description of the field of CBT is provided by Keogh and Hall (1984) who liken CBT to a rapidly expanding city that greedily extends its boundaries to annex suburbs. Despite the diversity that characterizes CBT, three broad theoretical assumptions underlie CBT approaches. First, a person's thoughts, images, perceptions, and other cognitive mediating events affect behavior. A corollary assumption is that a specific focus on a person's cognitions is an effective strategy for changing performance. The second assumption is that individuals are active participants in their own learning. Rather than being passive recipients of environmental influences, individuals to a considerable degree create their own environments. A third assumption of CBT is the requirement that the utility of cognitive constructs in behavior change efforts must be empirically demonstrated. That is, cognitions are subjected to scientific investigation and objective methods of inquiry and must demonstrate utility in predicting behavior. These three assumptions characterize a variety of clinical procedures that are subsumed under the term cognitive behavior therapy.

Several attempts have been made to define cognitive behavior therapy (Hobbs, Moguin, Tyroler & Lahey, 1980; Urbain & Kendall, 1980; Wilson, 1978). Kendall and Hollon's definition of CBT reflects the view that CBT is a broadened, evolutionary form of behavior therapy. "It is a purposeful attempt to preserve the demonstrated efficiencies of behavior modification within a less doctrinaire context and to incorporate the cognitive activities of the client in the efforts to produce therapeutic change" (Kendall & Hollon, 1979:1). Cognitive behavior therapy attempts to preserve methodological behaviorism, while accommodating recent developments in several areas of experimental psychology, especially cognition, development, language, motivation, and learning.

The distinction between methodological behaviorism and metaphysical behaviorism is important (Mahoney, 1974). Metaphysical behaviorism, also referred to as radical behaviorism, is a theory of human behavior that denies the existence of mental phenomena. Watson (1924), the principal figure in formulating metaphysical behaviorism, considered thought, images, and ideas as improper subjects for scientific inquiry and proclaimed the supremacy of the environment in determining individual differences in behavior. Methodological behaviorism, however, does not limit the content of psychological inquiry to overt behavior, but it requires that psychological theories and constructs be subjected to scientific inquiry. A hallmark of behavior therapy has been its close ties to experimental psychology and its allegiance to the scientific method. As American psychology turned cognitive (Dember, 1974), behavior therapists began to incorporate cognitive constructs into therapy procedures and empirically evaluate the clinical utility of these procedures. As Wilson (1978) noted, this marriage of behavior therapy and cognitive experimental psychology was inevitable, given the historic ties between behavior therapy and experimental psychology. Rather than being a retreat to mentalism, CBT represents a triumph of methodological behaviorism, a view of behavior as influenced by multiple and interactive determinants, and an expanded range of strategies for changing behavior.

This evolved behavioral paradigm did not emerge fully articulated overnight. Rather, developments in several research and applied fields over a period of two decades shaped and continue to shape contemporary behavior therapy. A brief summary of these events helps not only to define CBT but also to clarify its relationship to traditional behavior modification approaches with children.

HISTORICAL ANTECEDENTS OF COGNITIVE BEHAVIOR THERAPY WITH CHILDREN

The Cognitivization of American Psychology

In 1960 Hebb was one of the first psychologists to discern a paradigmatic shift in the science of psychology:

> In the psychology revolution, the second phase is now getting under way. The first banished thought, imagery, volition, attention, and other seditious notions. The sedition of one period, however, may be the good sense of another. These notions relate to a vital problem in the understanding of man, and it is the task of the second phase to bring them back (p. 736).

Hebb's forecast concerning the reemergence of phenomena outside the behaviorist paradigm that had dominated psychology since Watson's 1924 text was entirely accurate. Important to this reemergence was the publication in 1967 of Neisser's text, *Cognitive Psychology*, which provided the first comprehensive summary of the rapidly expanding research in cognitive processes such as attention, memory, problem-solving, imagery, self-referent speech, and attributions. In a seminal article in 1974, Dember proclaimed the revolution complete when he asserted "Psychology has gone cognitive" (p. 161). Among those events that contributed to the cognitive revolution, Dember included research in language learning, memory, perception, and motivation. An operant analysis had proven inadequate to the task of explaining language acquisition. The view that language learning is more than a set of stimulus-response chains acquired according to the principles of operant and classical conditioning gained acceptance in American psychology. Research on memory demonstrated that the efficient storage and retrieval of information require active strategies by the learner. Research on human perception demonstrated that basic perceptual processes are affected by the perceiver's affective and cognitive state. This research supported the view that the physical properties of a stimulus may be a less important determinant of its effect on an individual's behavior than is the individual's perception of the stimulus, a perception influenced by the person's expectancies, motives, and affective state. Succinctly stated, "an individual responds—not to some *real* environment—but to a *perceived* environment" (Mahoney, 1974:5).

Similarly, experimental psychologists studying motivation were confronted with the inadequacies of the Hullian view of drive states as departures from a physiological state of homeostasis. The new look in motivation that Dember (1965) articulated deemphasized the drive-reducing aspects of stimuli and emphasized the information properties of events. In this view, the rewarding property of an event depends on how an individual perceives it rather than on its drive-reducing properties.

An experimental psychologist, Dember (1974) concluded that the behavioral model that had characterized American psychology for four decades could no longer accommodate research findings in basic experimental areas. He admonished psychologists for confusing methodological purity (i.e., methodological behaviorism) with conceptual barrenness (i.e., metaphysical behaviorism). The results of this confusion were twofold: "First, it deprived psychology of most of its interesting problems. Second, S-R theorizing proved inadequate to the task [of explaining human behavior]" (p. 162).

Social Learning Theory

Perhaps the single most important event in the ontogenesis of CBT was Bandura's theory of observational learning. Whereas other research findings and theories were important to the development of CBT, in the sense that they contributed to a critical mass of data that could not be explained by S-R models of human performance, Bandura's 1969 book, *Principles of Behavior*

Modification, provided a comprehensive and integrative explanation of human behavior that incorporated principles of operant conditioning and classical conditioning. Bandura's social learning theory was a learning theory explanation of behavior. This fact, combined with Bandura's impeccable credentials as a vigorous experimentalist, gave him a voice in the behavioral camp. Yet, Bandura turned Watson's brand of behaviorism on its head. Rejecting a unidirectional view of the effects of the environment on the individual, Bandura viewed the person-environment relationship as a reciprocal influence process.

> Psychological functioning, in fact, involves a continuous reciprocal interaction between behavior and its controlling conditions. Although actions are regulated by their consequences, the controlling environment is, in turn, often significantly altered by the behavior. . . . Persons, far from being ruled by an imposing environment, play an active role in constructing their own reinforcement contingencies through their characteristic modes of response (Bandura, 1969:46).

During the 1960s Bandura and his colleagues conducted a series of experiments on modeling and on factors that influence learning through observation. This research demonstrated that children and adults learn through observing others, that such learning does not depend on reinforcement to the observer or to the model, and that individuals not only learn new responses but also learn standards for self-reinforcement (Bandura, 1969). Bandura postulated four subprocesses involved in observational learning: attentional processes, retention and covert rehearsal, motor reproduction processes, and incentive and motivational processes. Each of these processes involves the learner as an actively thinking participant in his or her own learning. "Observers do not function as passive videotape recorders which indiscriminately register and store all modeling stimuli encountered in everyday life" (p. 143). Instead, observational learning is a complex, multiprocess phenomenon.

Although even a summary of Bandura's social learning theory is outside the scope of this book, a brief overview of the role of attentional and incentive processes involved in observational learning will serve to illustrate the place of symbolic thought (cognition) in Bandura's explanation of modeling effects.

Attention

Repeated exposure to modeling stimuli does not guarantee the learner will acquire the modeled response. Therefore, the acquisition of matching responses to those of a model cannot be explained simply on the basis of associative learning. Attention to the relevant modeling cues is necessary, and attention is determined by characteristics of the observer, characteristics of the model, incentive conditions, and the saliency of modeling cues.

Bandura investigated each of these determinants. For example, model characteristics that influence attention to modeling cues include the model's competence, status, age, sex, and social power. Bandura concluded that individuals selectively attend to models who possess characteristics that signify differential probabilities of reinforcement. Thus, observers' expectancies concerning reinforcement (outcome expectancies) affect their attention to modeling displays.

Incentives

Social learning theory provides a mediational interpretation of the effect of reinforcing consequences on behavior. According to an operant, nonmediational theory of learning, consequences act directly and automatically to strengthen preceding responses. In this view, consequences increase the habit strength of responses through a "stamping in" process. Skinner (1971) succinctly stated this unidirectional view of the determinants of behavior: "A person does not act upon the world, the world acts upon him" (p. 211). In the operant view, awareness of consequences is not necessary for learning. If awareness occurs, it is a by-product of conditioning rather than a precondition for learning. According to social learning theory, the influence of consequences on behavior is determined largely by cognitive processes. That is, reinforcement is not an automatic strengthener of behavior but a source of information and an incentive. Consequences serve as antecedent events through an individual's awareness of the reinforcement contingencies. Therefore, an individual engages in behaviors that have been reinforced because the individual is aware of the probability of reinforcement.

In 1977 Bandura synthesized his views of human thought and behavior in an already classic text, *Social Learning Theory*. In explaining the central tenet of social learning theory, reciprocal determinism, Bandura stated that personal factors, environmental factors, and behavior all operate as "interlocking determinants of each other" (p. 10). The reciprocal determinism view emphasizes the role of symbolic processes in learning, the self-regulatory aspect of behavior, and the interdependence of personal and environmental influences.

The Role of Expectancies

Regarding symbolic processes, Bandura distinguished between two types of expectancies that influence behavior: efficacy expectations and outcome expectations. Efficacy expectations refer to persons' estimates that they can successfully engage in a specific behavior. An outcome expectancy is a person's belief that a given behavior will result in certain outcomes (rewards or punishers). There are multiple determinants of both types of expectancies. These expectancies, in turn, influence an individual's behavior. A goal of many therapies is a change in efficacy or outcome expectations or both. For example, providing a dog-phobic child with a model of a fearful child overcoming his or her fear and interacting in playful ways with dogs may change the child's efficacy expectations ("I could do that, too") and outcome expectancies ("Playing with dogs is safe"). Researchers (e.g., Vallis & Bucher, 1986) have demonstrated that self-efficacy expectations predict behavior change resulting from treatment.

Self-Regulatory Processes

Bandura observed that much human behavior is performed in the absence of immediate external reinforcement and is under the control of self-reinforcement rather than external reinforcement. Primarily through vicarious reinforcement and observational learning, people learn to set standards of behavior for themselves and respond to their own actions in self-rewarding or self-punishing ways. Bandura interpreted many behavior disorders as resulting from faulty self-reinforcement mechanisms. For example, an anxious but perfectionistic girl may have learned strict standards for self-reinforcement by observing her parents' self-reinforcement practices and by being directly rewarded both for achieving high standards and for establishing strict performance standards.

Interdependence of Personal and Environmental Influences

Persons' expectations affect their behavior, and the outcome of their behavior affects their expectations in a reciprocal influence process. For example, aggressive children expect others to react with hostile intent toward them. This expectation causes the aggressive child to act aggressively. Others respond to the child's aggressive behavior with counteraggression, strengthening the child's initial expectation. "Aggressive children thus create through their actions a hostile environment, while children who favor friendly modes of response generate an amicable social milieu" (Bandura, 1977:198).

Recent experimental evidence supports this reciprocal deterministic view of the causes of children's aggressive behavior. In a series of studies, Dodge and his colleagues (Dodge & Frame, 1982; Dodge, Murphy, & Buchsbaum, 1984; Steinberg & Dodge, 1983) demonstrated that aggressive children expect their peers to respond toward them with hostile intent. Furthermore, their aggressive behaviors are a direct function of their perceptions of peers' hostile intent. The implication of this interdependence of personal and environmental influences is that a focus on the individual or the environment is likely to contribute less to an understanding of behavior or to efforts to change behavior than is a focus on the person-behavior-environment interrelationships.

Clinical Implications

Not only did Bandura serve as an important bridge between learning theorists and cognitive psychologists, but also he bridged the gap between experimental and clinical psychology. In applying principles of social learning theory to clinical problems, Bandura significantly influenced the practice of behavior therapy. With children, Bandura investigated the relative efficacy of self-monitored and externally imposed reinforcement systems on task performance (Bandura & Perloff, 1967), the transmission of self-reinforcement processes (Bandura & Kupers, 1964), the therapeutic effectiveness of modeling on phobias (Bandura, Grusec, & Menlove, 1967), and the influence of models on children's moral judgments (Bandura & McDonald, 1963). Today, self-monitoring, self-reinforcement, and modeling are common ingredients in CBT programs applied to a wide range of children's problems. The chapters in Section II provide numerous examples of interventions derived from social learning theory.

Self-Control

The idea that an individual's cognitions (i.e., thoughts) influence behavior was accepted by Skinner (1953). His and others' initial explanations of self-control processes were exclusively operant. Thoughts were subvocal responses that ultimately were under external influence. In a classic paper on self-control processes, Homme (1965) posited that thoughts ("coverants of the mind") are subject to the same laws of learning as are overt behaviors. He suggested procedures for applying principles of operant conditioning to the modification of coverants. Homme described the technique of coverant control as it applied to cigarette smoking. First, the client makes a list of self-statements that refer to the aversive aspects of smoking. Second, the client selects a reinforcer. When the client experiences the urge to smoke, he engages in the self-statements, such as "Smoking makes my breath smell terrible," and "I'll die of lung cancer if I smoke." On engaging in these coverants, the client delivers the self-reinforcement.

Several self-control therapies were developed in the 1960s and early 1970s, usually as treatments for habit control problems (Goldfried & Merbaum, 1973; Thoresen & Mahoney, 1974). In addition to modifying self-statements through operant conditioning principles, self-control included procedures to teach persons to systematically arrange environmental antecedents and consequences to modify their own behavior. Thus, obese individuals were instructed to modify the stimulus conditions associated with eating. For example, they were instructed to take a walk at a time when they would normally be eating, to restrict eating to one room, and to rid the house of foods that require little effort to prepare. Similarly, they were instructed to reward themselves for engaging in the desired behaviors and for achieving established subgoals (Stuart, 1967).

Although early explanations of self-control procedures were operant, self-control provided an entry point for behaviorists into the realm of covert mental processes (Kendall & Hollon, 1979). By the early 1970s, the idea that behavior was controlled, at least in part, by cognitions had taken root in behavior therapy. During the 1970s conceptualizations of self-control became more cognitive, often resulting in a lively debate within behavior therapy (Bandura, 1976; Catania, 1975; Goldiamond, 1976; Mahoney, 1976).

A useful framework for organizing the burgeoning research on self-control was provided by Kanfer. Kanfer (1970; Kanfer & Karoly, 1972) distinguished three types of self-control processes: self-monitoring, self-evaluation, and self-reinforcement. Viewing these processes as interrelated, Kanfer applied an information-processing analysis to self-control. In this view, a person's self-monitoring serves as a feedback loop, providing the individual with information that is compared against performance standards. When the observed response matches the performance standard, the individual provides self-reinforcement. In Kanfer's view, the individual is an active participant in the learning process.

The therapist's role in self-control therapy is one of educator and motivator in helping the individual to initiate a behavior change program. The therapist teaches the child or adolescent how, when, and where to engage in various cognitive strategies to effect a behavioral change (McReynolds, Morris, & Kratochwill, in press).

Therapists applying self-control to children's fears have taught children to engage in specific self-verbalizations in the fearful situation. In an early study on the clinical utility of self-control therapy with children, Kanfer, Karoly, and Newman (1975) instructed children who were afraid of the dark to say to themselves, "I am a brave boy (girl). I can take care of myself in the dark." Compared with control children, children so instructed exhibited less fear of the dark in a behavioral analogue test.

Self-Instructional Training

One way individuals control their own behavior is through self-instruction. Although self-instructional training (SIT) is a type of self-control, its theoretical antecedents are different from those of self-control. Luria (1959, 1961) and Vygotsky's (1962) developmental theories of the functional relationship between language and behavior provided the theoretical underpinnings for Meichenbaum's early work in SIT (Meichenbaum & Goodman, 1971). Vygotsky (1962) described a developmental progression in language control over behavior from talking aloud, to internalized talking, to silence. Luria (1961) experimentally investigated developmental changes in children's ability to regulate their behavior by adult verbalizations and then by their own self-verbalizations. Luria also documented a shift in the nature of self-verbalizations from verbalizations that function to slow down behavior to verbalizations that semantically guide behavior. Meichenbaum was also influenced by Mischel's (1974) research on self-mediated cognitive strategies, particularly strategies used to help children cope with frustration during delay-of-gratification tasks.

In an often-cited study, Meichenbaum and Goodman (1971) taught impulsive second-grade children how to use self-instructions to slow themselves down and to think through problems. Their program consists of five stages. First, an adult model performs a task, such as completing a maze or coloring a design, while instructing himself or herself aloud. The self-statements include statements that identify the problem, label alternative solutions, evaluate solutions, choose one solution, monitor implementation of the solution, correct errors, and provide self-reinforcement. For example, in a task that required copying geometric designs, the examiner performed the tasks while self-instructing aloud, as follows:

> Okay, what is it I have to do? You want me to copy the picture with the different lines. I have to go slowly and carefully. Okay, draw the line down, down, good; then to the right, that's it; now down some more and to the left. Good, I'm doing fine so far. Remember, go slowly. Now back up again. No, I was supposed to go down. That's okay. Just erase the line carefully. . . . Good. Even if I make an error I can go on slowly and carefully. I have to go down now. Finished. I did it!

In the second stage, the child performs the task while receiving verbal instructions from the adult. In the third and fourth stages, the child performs the task, first pronouncing the self-statements aloud and then whispering them. Finally, the child performs the task while using covert self-instructions. Early in training, the tasks are simple perceptions. As the child masters self-instruction, the tasks become more complex.

Kendall and Braswell (1985) review 15 years of research on self-instructional training for impulsive and hyperactive children. They note that newer, effective training procedures teach children general versus specific types of self-instruction, include problem-solving training, and combine SIT with behavioral contingencies.

Cognitive Development

Another stream of influence on contemporary CBT is research on children's development of increasingly effective cognitive learning strategies. These research findings suggest that young children and problem learners do not spontaneously engage in cognitive mediation strategies; however, they can produce these strategies when provided instruction in their use. Children who do not spontaneously generate memorial strategies but who can produce and benefit from these strategies when instructed to use them are referred to as having a production deficiency (Keeney, Canizzo, & Flavell, 1967). Even when these children are induced to engage in memorial strategy with a resultant improvement in learning, they discontinue use of the strategy when the inducement, or demand for strategy production, is removed. Subsequent research on children's metamemorial strategies focused on children's knowledge and understanding of their own memory system and their knowledge of strategies that aid in memorization. Brown (1975) referred to these metamemorial processes as "knowing about knowing" and "knowing how to know." Problem learners may either lack effective memorial strategies or fail to apply the strategy. An active research field developed in cognitive training with mentally retarded and learning-disabled students (Keogh & Hall, 1984; Ryan, Weed, & Short, 1987; Whitman, Burgio, & Johnston, 1984; Wong, 1985). The purpose of this training is to teach children how to monitor their use of memorial strategies and how to apply more effective memorial strategies.

Cognitive Therapy

Cognitive therapy is based on the assumption that persons' emotional and behavioral reactions (e.g., hostility and depression) are the result of their interpretations of events and not the result of the events themselves. The two most influential cognitive therapy proponents are Ellis (1962, 1973) and Beck (1976). Whereas therapies developed by Ellis and Beck attempt to alter persons' irrational self-statements, beliefs, expectancies, and interpretations of events, Ellis focuses on specific irrational statements that presumably underlie a range of emotional and behavioral problems, while Beck focuses on general cognitive errors (e.g., overgeneralization and logical inconsistencies) that characterize the thinking of depressed persons.

Although cognitive therapies share characteristics with both self-control therapy and self-instructional training, their conceptualization of the relationships among thought, behavior, and emotion is strictly cognitive. Ellis's ABC conceptualization of human functioning is a linear model instead of an interactive one. Some activating event in the environment (A) triggers a client's relevant beliefs (B). The client's emotional and behavioral consequences (C) result directly from these beliefs.

Beck's theory is less explicit regarding the casual relationships among events, thoughts, and emotions. In Beck's theory, depressed persons have a systematic negative bias in their thinking, which causes them to have a negative view of themselves, the future, and the world. They filter events through these negative cognitive schemata, which results in a distorted and overly pessimistic interpretation of reality, which results in the affective states and behavioral symptoms characteristic of depression.

Although Ellis provides data on the effectiveness of rational-emotive therapy (RET) (Ellis, 1977), both his methodology and his conclusions regarding the almost miraculous success of RET have seriously been challenged (Eschenroeder, 1982; Mahoney, 1977). However, several researchers have documented the effectiveness of Beck's cognitive therapy with depressed adults (Rush, Shaw, & Khatomi, 1980; Rush & Watkins, 1981).

Because cognitive therapy, whether patterned on Ellis or Beck's approach, depends largely on the client's ability to engage in philosophical disputation, logical analysis, and abstract thinking, it is not developmentally appropriate for children. However, related therapies that attempt to alter children's beliefs and expectancies have been developed. One type of belief that has been the focus of such interventions is attributional style. Attributional style refers to a person's preferred causal explanations for performance (Palmer & Rholes, in press).

In separate investigations, differences in attributional styles between depressed and nondepressed children (Friedlander, Philips, & Morrison, 1981; Kaslow, Rehm, & Siegel, 1984) and between mastery oriented and helpless children (Diener & Dweck, 1978; Dweck & Reppucci, 1973) were demonstrated. Similarities in attributional styles of depressed children and children who do not persist in the face of failure (helpless children) led researchers to develop attribution retraining programs. These programs (Dweck, 1975) attempt to increase children's tendencies to attribute success to their ability (an internal and stable cause) and failure to their effort (an internal but unstable cause).

Problem-Solving Approach to Adjustment

Beginning in the early 1970s, George Spivack, Myrna Shure, and their colleagues at the Hahnemann Medical College and Hospital in Philadelphia began an extensive research program on the assessment and treatment of children and adolescents' interpersonal cognitive problem-solving (ICPS) skills (Shure & Spivack, 1978; Spivack, Platt, & Shure, 1976; Spivack & Shure, 1974). This research supports the view that deficits in specific problem-solving skills underlie a range of behavioral disorders. Spivack, Shure, and their associates as well as researchers in other institutions developed programs to teach ICPS skills to children and adolescents, generally with positive results. (This research is reviewed in chapter 10. For additional reviews see Urbain & Kendall, 1980, and Urbain & Savage, in press). Typically, problem-solving training is combined with other interventions, including modeling, behavior rehearsal, and self-instructional training (e.g., Camp, Blom, Herbert, & Van Doorninck, 1977; Feindler, Marriott, & Iwata, 1984). Consequently, its unique contribution to outcomes cannot be evaluated.

Social Cognition

A final stream of influence on contemporary CBT is research on children's social cognition. Children's ability to infer others' intentions accurately in social interaction, their ability to take the role of another person, their knowledge of socially effective strategies, and their motivations in social interactions determine their social behavior, which in turn affects others' reactions to them. Research on the social/cognitive correlates of peer acceptance (Dodge & Murphy, 1984; Putallaz & Gottman, 1982) has led to an information-processing view of social behavior (Dodge & Murphy, 1984; Hughes & Hall, 1987). Accordingly, socially competent behavior is viewed as resulting from a complex, sequential process of accurately interpreting ("reading" or "decoding") social cues, generating and evaluating responses, implementing the selected response, and monitoring performance. This view of socially competent behavior suggests the need to assess children's relevant cognitive processes as well as overt social behaviors and to design interventions that attempt to remediate cognitive as well as behavioral deficiencies.

BEHAVIOR MODIFICATION IN THE SCHOOLS

Because behavior modification procedures frequently are combined with cognitive-behavioral procedures, the reader should have some familiarity with the principles of behavior modification. The following chapters assume this familiarity. For the reader who lacks a working knowledge of behavior modification principles, a brief overview of behavior modification principles and procedures, which are frequently combined with more cognitively oriented procedures, will be provided subsequently herein.

Behavior modification, or applied behavior analysis, is an approach to changing behavior that involves the systematic application of a set of principles, especially those of operant conditioning, derived from learning theory. During the 1960s educators embraced the new behavior technology, and legions of behavior modifiers descended on the schools. The enthusiasm educators felt for behavior modification was largely a result of its demonstrated effectiveness with a wide range of children's problems, including academic problems such as reading, handwriting, and task completion and social and behavioral problems such as aggression, shyness, and school avoidance (O'Leary & O'Leary, 1972). Applied first to institutionalized children with severe handicaps (Bijou, 1966; Lovaas, 1968), behavior modification was soon recognized as an important behavior management tool for regular classroom teachers (Alberto & Troutman, 1982; Becker, Englemann, & Thomas, 1971; O'Leary & O'Leary, 1972). In 1968 a new journal, *Journal of Applied Behavior Analysis*, was inaugurated to publish the burgeoning empirical studies on the educational and therapeutic applications of behavioral principles. As evidence of the effectiveness of operant conditioning and classical conditioning procedures with a wide range of problems accumulated, schools clamored to offer behavior modification workshops to teachers. As greater attention was focused on the influence of antecedent stimuli on behavior, the term applied behavior analysis replaced behavior modification, and educators were urged to assess and alter task and setting conditions as well as consequences.

Paradoxically, the early success of applied behavior analysis in schools caused many educators to reject it when their unrealistically high expectations for it proved false. Often their training in behavior modification was inadequate, and they learned just enough to implement poorly conceptualized behavior modification programs. Lacking the theoretical basis for the procedures, they were unable to make needed alterations in programs, based on a continuous evaluation of the program's effectiveness. Furthermore, evangelical behavior modifiers were not cognizant of the culture of schools (Sarason, 1981). Therefore, their recommendations were not congruent with many realities of schools. Teachers resisted behavior modification programs that interfered with their teaching, restricted their ability to attend to a group of children, made excessive demands on them, and were inconsistent with their values, goals, and philosophies (Abidin, 1975). These early behavior modifiers ignored influences on child performance that could not be observed and counted, and then they used the jargon of the research laboratory to explain everyday concepts.

The late 1970s and early 1980s witnessed a more critical attitude on the part of educators toward behavior modification. As a result of this more mature evaluation of behavior modification, extreme proponents and opponents of behavior modification are less visible in schools today, and behavior modification principles have become an accepted, staple part of a teacher's armamentarium for modifying children's behavior.

The next section summarizes the principles of applied behavior analysis in schools. The reader well-versed in applied behavior analysis may choose to skip this section.

Principles of Applied Behavior Analysis

Positive Reinforcement

This involves presenting a reward to a child after the child performs a specific desired behavior. If that behavior occurs more frequently after the reward, positive reinforcement has occurred. A reinforcer, or reward, is defined in terms of its effect on the behavior it follows. A reinforcer is something (a stimulus) that, when administered contingent on a behavior, increases the frequency of that behavior. What is a reinforcer for one child may not be a reinforcer for another child, because different children react differently to such potential reinforcers as adult praise and bubble gum. Allowing a child 5 extra minutes of free time when he or she completes an assignment with 80 percent accuracy is an example of positive reinforcement. It is important that the positive reinforcer be contingent on the specific desired behavior. That is, if the behavior occurs, then the reinforcer is given. If the behavior does not occur or does not occur at the specified level or frequency, then the reinforcer is not given. Sometimes teachers and parents will inadvertently reinforce undesired behaviors. For example, when children get out of their seats, the teacher calls out the children's names. If the out-of-seat behavior occurs more frequently, the teacher's calling out the child's name is a reinforcer for that child. When reinforcement is used, the reinforcement can follow every appropriate behavior (continuous reinforcement schedule) or only a portion of the appropriate behaviors (intermittent reinforcement). Continuous reinforcement results in a quick initial increase in the rate of the reinforced behavior, and intermittent reinforcement results in maintenance of the behavior change when the behavior is no longer being reinforced.

When a behavior that has been followed by a reinforcer in the past no longer is reinforced, *extinction* has occurred. Often the immediate result of extinction is a temporary increase in the previously reinforced behavior. If a teacher who has attended to a child's temper tantrums begins to ignore the temper tantrums, the child is likely to increase the frequency and duration of tantrum behavior; however, if the teacher continues to ignore the tantrums (and there are no other reinforcers that follow the tantrums, such as peer attention), the tantrums should decrease in frequency.

Negative Reinforcement

This, like positive reinforcement, is a procedure for increasing the rate of a desired behavior. In negative reinforcement, some unpleasant event (stimulus) is terminated following the desired behavior. For example, a teacher tells students that children who complete their assignments at 85 percent accuracy will be relieved of their homework assignment.

Punishment

Punishment is a process in which the consequences of a behavior reduce the future rate of that behavior. There are three types of punishment procedures. In the application of an unpleasant consequence, a behavior is followed by some unpleasant stimulus, such as extra work, a verbal reprimand, or physical punishment. In response cost, a teacher removes a reinforcer contingent on a specified behavior. Children may lose 5 minutes of recess each time they hit or shove. In *time-out*, the child is denied the opportunity to participate in positive reinforcement for a specified time contingent on a specified undesired behavior. Requiring a child to sit on a bench at recess when playing roughly or to sit on a mat during art are examples of time-out.

When a child has learned to say "red" only to colors in the red spectrum, the response of saying "red" is under the *stimulus control* of the color red. This control is established by reinforcing the correct response and/or punishing the incorrect response. The reinforcer may be praise or a star. The punisher may be "no" or an X on the paper. When the child learns to respond differently to the color red and to all other colors, this shows *discrimination learning*. The child who goes to the cookie box when mother is occupied on the telephone has also mastered a discrimination learning task. Going to the cookie box is reinforced with a cookie when mother is on the phone. When mother is not on the phone, she either prevents the child from getting a cookie or reprimands the child.

Shaping

Shaping involves reinforcing improvement in behavior. For example, a child may work only three math problems during a 30-minute period. The teacher would like the child to work 15 problems. (It is assumed the teacher has determined that the problems are at the appropriate level of difficulty for the child.) If reinforcement were made contingent on the child working 15 problems, reinforcement would not occur because the goal behavior is too difficult for the child at this time. Instead, the teacher establishes a series of steps between the current level of performance and the goal behavior and applies differential reinforcement at each step. Only if the child performs the behavior at or above the behavioral criterion at the operative step in the hierarchy does the child receive the reinforcer. When the child is consistently successful at one step, the next step is operative, and the child's behavior must meet or exceed the criterion for reinforcement at that step.

Task Analysis

Task analysis, a procedure similar to shaping, involves specifying the prerequisite behaviors to successful performance of a given task. Many instructional tasks are composed of several smaller steps that occur in a specific order. Often the difficulty of the task is the reason the child is having difficulty mastering the task. A *skill hierarchy* breaks a complex skill, such as two-digit multiplication, into sequential steps in which each step is a prerequisite to the next higher step in the hierarchy. Skill hierarchies exist in all areas of human learning, including reading, penmanship, dressing, and eating. Task analysis is a useful tool for selecting what skill to teach. Shaping procedures involve the application of reinforcement and extinction to teaching the selected skill.

Prompting

Prompting involves the use of additional cues to increase the probability the child will respond appropriately to the discriminative stimulus. These extra cues increase the saliency of the discriminative stimuli and are phased out as soon as the behavior is under the control of the discriminative stimulus. Prompts may be visual, verbal, or physical. The first-grade teacher who places pictures with letters of the alphabet is using visual prompts to increase the probability that the child will make the correct letter-sound association. The phasing out of prompts involves gradually decreasing the saliency of the prompt.

Systematic Desensitization

Whereas the foregoing principles are based on operant conditioning, desensitization is based on the classical conditioning paradigm. In classical conditioning, a response is elicited by antecedent stimuli through an associative learning process. At first, some stimulus (unconditional stimulus) automatically elicits a response (unconditional response). For example, a feather tickling the nose causes a person to sneeze. A loud noise elicits a startle reaction. The feather and noise are unconditioned stimuli and elicit an automatic response. After a neutral stimulus (e.g., a tone) is repeatedly presented just before the onset of the unconditioned stimulus, the neutral simulus, when presented alone, elicits the response. When the unconditioned response occurs in response to the conditioned stimulus alone, it is referred to as the conditioned response.

Watson and Rayner (1920) used classical conditioning principles to condition a 9-month-old infant to be afraid of a white rat. The fear was conditioned by first pairing the presentation of a neutral stimulus, a white rat, with a loud noise. The innate startle response to a loud noise was conditioned to the white rat. One of the first clinical applications of learning theory involved classical conditioning. Jones (1924) applied classical conditioning to eliminate young Peter's (age 2 years 10 months) fear of furry objects. This was accomplished by presenting a furry object (rabbit) to Peter. Peter was gradually exposed to the rabbit while engaging in a relaxing response, eating. If Peter showed signs of distress, the rabbit was moved further away. Eventually, Peter was able to play fearlessly with the rabbit. Contemporary clinical use of classical conditioning principles with children involves a gradual increase in the intensity of the feared stimulus while the child is relaxed. Typically, gradual exposure is combined with modeling and reinforcement (Begelman & Hersen, 1971). The presentation can be actual or imagined, as in systematic desensitization.

Limitations of Applied Behavior Analysis in the Schools

Even as research demonstrating the effectiveness of applied behavior analysis in the schools continued to accumulate rapidly in the 1970s and 1980s, researchers and educators were becoming increasingly aware of the limitations of traditional behavioral approaches. These limitations, which prompted behaviorally oriented special educators and school psychologists to broaden their behavioral framework, are summarized briefly.

Often the behavioral changes resulting from reinforcement programs did not persist when the external reinforcement was removed (Walker, Greenwood, Hops, & Todd, 1979). Additionally, behavioral changes were limited to specific behaviors and did not generalize to situations in which the behavior had not been reinforced (Kuypers, Becker, & O'Leary, 1968; Meichenbaum, Bowers, & Ross, 1968; O'Leary, Becker, Evans, & Saudargas, 1969). The failure of operant strategies to produce durable (Birnbrauer, Wolf, Kidder, & Tague, 1965; Kuypers et al., 1968) and generalizable behavioral change prompted researchers, educators, and clinicians to supplement strategies that depend on external control with approaches that attempt to modify a child's knowledge, expectancies, and self-controlling responses.

Reinforcement programs placed excessive demands on teachers. Individual contingency programs require teachers to make major shifts in their pattern of attending to children (Abidin, 1975). Recording the frequency or duration of specific behaviors, a frequent requirement in behavior modification interventions, is difficult for classroom teachers who are continuously responsible for groups of 20 to 25 children. Another practical problem of individual reinforcement programs is the reaction of other children to the program.

Furthermore, the behaviors selected for change in behavior modification programs too often were not socially consequential for the child (Wolf, 1978). Socially consequential behaviors are those that are related to socially valid outcomes, such as peer acceptance, learning, or teacher evaluation, or that increase the child's participation in the natural community of reinforcers. For example, often behavior modification programs successfully changed the target behavior (e.g., on-task behavior) but did not result in a concomitant increase in academic responding (Ayllon & Rosenbaum, 1977;

Ferritor, Buckholdt, Hamblin, & Smith, 1972; Marholin & Steinman, 1977). Too often target behaviors are selected on the basis of the ease with which they can be measured or the convenience of adult caretakers. Winnett and Winkler (1972:501) described the pupil produced by behavior modification programs in regular classrooms as one:

> who stays glued to his seat and desk all day, continuously looks at his teacher or his text (workbook), does not talk to or in fact look at other children, does not talk unless asked to by the teacher, hopefully does not laugh or sing (at the wrong time), and assuredly passes silently in the halls.

Certainly this caricature of the child taught with behavior modification techniques is an exaggeration. Nevertheless, the target behavior paradigm lends itself to change efforts that focus on circumscribed, nontransportable, and socially inconsequential behaviors (Kazdin, 1985; Kratochwill, 1985). A recent critique of target behavior selection in published social skills training studies (Hughes, 1986) revealed that the skills targeted for training in behavioral training programs tend to be selected on nonempirical grounds. For example, there is no evidence that specific assertion skills (eye contact, speech duration, and assertive content) frequently taught in behavioral social skills training are related to peer acceptance or teacher ratings or that they increase a child's probability of engaging in positive social interactions.

Another limitation of contingency management, or reinforcement, programs is the possible deleterious effect of extrinsic rewards on a child's intrinsic motivation. If children perform activities for external rewards, they may attribute their behavior to the external reward rather than to their intrinsic interest in the activity. Thus, they will be less likely to choose that activity when the external rewards are removed. There is some experimental support for this interpretation (Lepper & Greene, 1975; Lepper, Greene, & Nesbitt, 1973). Additionally, external rewards may reduce a child's sense of self-determination and personal competence (Deci, 1975). Many questions remain as to the effect of extrinsic rewards on motivation, and the issue is more complex than it first appears. Whether external rewards reduce intrinsic motivation depends on several factors, including what behaviors are rewarded, whether the external rewards are used in a contingent manner, and the child's initial interest in the activity (Bandura, 1977). In a recent study comparing the effects of external and self-administered rewards on a normally high base-rate behavior, external rewards decreased the children's rate of and interest in the reinforced activity. However, the same amount of self-reward did not result in decreased rate or interest (Margolis & Mynatt, 1986). These researchers interpreted their findings in terms of children's greater sense of self-determination and internal locus of casualty in the self-reward condition. One implication of research on the effect of external rewards on intrinsic motivation is the importance of considering the effect of reward on children's attributions for their performance.

The search for alternatives to reinforcement programs for improving task performance of hyperactive children was further spurred by research demonstrating that external reinforcement disrupts the performance of hyperactive children. Some children demonstrate an increase in impulsivity and a decrease in their attention to academic tasks under conditions of external reinforcement (Douglas, 1975; Douglas & Parry, 1983; Firestone & Douglas, 1975; Parry & Douglas, 1983). Although these deleterious effects can be minimized through careful attention to the obtrusiveness and timing of the reinforcers, these studies demonstrate the need to consider idiosyncratic responses to reinforcements and to carefully monitor the effects of the program on children's cognitive style and accuracy as well as on overt motor behaviors.

A final limitation of behavior modification is the tendency to treat topographically similar overt behaviors the same. The maxim, "behavior is behavior," may lead to ineffective interventions that do not address the different cognitive mediators of behavior. As McFall (1982) and Hughes and Hall (1987) posit, two individuals may exhibit the same overt behavior, but the causes of that behavior may differ, and this difference requires different interventions. Consider two boys who behave aggressively on the playground. One boy's aggressive behavior is a result of his tendency to attribute hostile intentions to peers' behaviors toward him. This boy is responding to his distorted perception of a hostile environment. A successful intervention program will need to help him interpret others' behaviors more accurately. The second boy's aggressive behavior is a result of his belief that aggression "pays off." A successful intervention will need to change his outcome expectancies, possibly through teaching problem-solving, consequential thinking and evaluation, and contingency management. Coie and Dodge (1986) refer to these two types of aggressive children as reactive aggressive and instrumentally aggressive.

PITFALLS AND PROMISES OF COGNITIVE BEHAVIOR THERAPY

Cognitive behavior therapy is neither a panacea for treating children's behavioral and emotional problems nor a completely novel therapeutic and child management approach. Rather, it represents an expanded behavioral paradigm that shows considerable promise for helping children. Whether CBT achieves its promise will depend greatly on whether its proponents avoid certain pitfalls. One pitfall is an uncritical acceptance of any new technology, an acceptance based on the belief that change is progress and new is better. Traditional behavioral approaches in the schools have demonstrated their utility across a wide range of problems and are still the treatment of choice for many problems. Often the greatest benefit of the newer cognitive-behavioral approaches will result from efforts that combine these approaches with behavioral approaches. Such combined approaches capitalize on the initial improvement obtained with behavioral programs while altering a person's sense of competence (self-efficacy), which promotes greater durability of treatment gains (Collins, Rothblum, & Wilson, 1986).

Although there is some evidence of greater generalization and durability of behavioral changes resulting from CBT, this evidence is far from conclusive. Just as behaviorists realized that generalization must be programed into change efforts, cognitive-behaviorists are investigating factors that enhance generalization across behaviors, settings, and tasks (Wong, 1985). The claim that CBT results in greater generalization is overly broad and empirically unjustified.

A final pitfall of CBT in schools is the cost effectiveness of CBT interventions. Many CBT interventions involve intensive and expensive child training. Their superiority over behavioral approaches, when demonstrated, must be weighed against their greater cost in terms of time, resources, effort expended, and efficiency (Wong, 1985). The need to consider cost efficiency is related to the need to specify the "active" ingredients in multicomponent CBT interventions. Eliminating training components that do not significantly contribute to treatment effectiveness will result in more efficient programs that, in turn, will increase the probability that schools will allocate the necessary resources for the program.

On the promise side of this equation, CBT approaches are congruent with a preventive orientation to children's adjustment and learning. Its emphases on competence versus remediation of dysfunctional behaviors and on self-regulatory mechanisms versus external control extend its impact to all children, not just to abnormal children. Although the value of prevention has been well stated by many educators and mental health specialists for decades, empirically based preventive approaches have not been very evident in schools. The final chapter in this book reviews preventive approaches based on cognitive behavioral principles and procedures. In this regard, programs that teach problem-solving skills to regular education children provide empirical evidence of the value of a preventive approach to mental health in the schools.

Finally, the educator/consultant role of the therapist in CBT is consistent with the training of many school professionals (Brown, Pryzwansky, & Schulte, 1987; Conoley & Conoley, 1982). Kanfer (1970:336) describes the role of the cognitive-behavioral therapist:

> The therapist serves as a consultant and expert who negotiates with the client in how to go about change and to what end. The interactions are future oriented in that the focus on the development of general repertoires for dealing with problem situations.

The role of the teacher as motivator, model, instructor, and coach in cognitive-behavioral interventions is also consistent with teachers' roles and with their emphases on teaching children "life skills" and on enhancing children's autonomy and competence. Rather than modifying children's behavior through external contingencies, the teacher instills in children general self-control and problem-solving strategies for handling a wide range of future problem situations.

2 Issues in Cognitive-Behavioral Assessment

Mischel (1981:484) described what he referred to as the cognitive-social learning approach to assessment:

> The focus in this approach shifts from trying to compare and generalize about what different individuals "are like" to assessing what they *do*—behaviorally and cognitively—in relationship to the psychological conditions in which they do it. The focus shifts from describing situation-free people with broad trait adjectives to analyzing the specific interactions between conditions and the cognitions and behaviors of interest.

This description highlights two key characteristics of cognitive-behavioral assessment. First, the emphasis on performance rather than on presumed underlying dispositions aligns cognitive-behavioral assessment with behavioral assessment. However, a distinguishing feature of cognitive-behavioral assessment is its dual focus on two types of performance, both cognitive and behavioral, and their interrelationships. It is assumed that what a person does cognitively influences and is influenced by what a person does behaviorally. For example, a child's task-irrelevant and anxiety-provoking self-talk in testing situations affects the child's ability to respond correctly to test items. The child's poor performance on tests increases the child's tendency to engage in self-defeating self-talk.

A second key characteristic of cognitive-behavioral assessment is the emphasis on situation-specific cognitions and behaviors. A person's cognitions are viewed not as global traits but as subjective interpretations of experience or as particular ways the person processes information. Although some cognitive events and processes demonstrate high cross-situational consistency, these cognitions are assessed in particular contexts. For example, rather than assessing a child's global self-concept, the psychologist assesses the child's self-efficacy expectations for influencing social interactions with peers (Wheeler & Ladd, 1982).

Some cognitive processes of interest to the cognitive-behavior therapist may demonstrate high cross-situational consistency. For example, an individual's tendency to respond impulsively instead of engaging in cognitive mediation may affect the child's performance in a number of different tasks. Nevertheless, cognitive impulsivity is assessed in relation to specific task requirements and refers to the individual's task approach rather than to an underlying personality trait. Thus, it is viewed as modifiable.

COMPARISONS WITH TRADITIONAL AND BEHAVIORAL ASSESSMENT

In the premier issue of the *Journal of Behavioral Assessment*, Hartmann, Roper, and Bradford (1979) compared traditional and behavioral assessment on several dimensions. Table 2.1 summarizes these differences. It is instructive to compare cognitive-behavioral assessment with both traditional and behavioral assessment, using these same dimensions.

Assumptions

Cognitive-behavioral assessment, like behavioral assessment, focuses on what a person *does*, cognitively and behaviorally, rather than on what a person *has*, in terms of underlying personality constructs. Like the traditional assessor, the cognitive-behavioral assessor looks within the individual for causes of behavior. However, these causes are viewed as cognitive mediating processes and events that are the result of a lifetime of learning and interpreting one's experiences. Furthermore, these cognitions are viewed as modifiable through the same reciprocal influence process that accounts for their development. Eschewing both the behaviorist view of behavior as a function of the environment and the psychodynamic view of behavior as a function of person variables, the cognitive behaviorist views behavior, person variables (i.e., thoughts and feelings), and the environment as forming a mutual influence system.

Implications

Behaviors and cognitions are viewed as important samples of performance in their own right and not just as signs of an underlying cause. Because some cognitive processes and events have good temporal and cross-situational stability, the historical origin of these processes is of concern. However, the search for historical predecessors is usually directed to the recent past rather than to the distant past. For example, experiences with uncontrollable failure affects a person's expectancies for future controllability.

The level of cross-situational consistency expected by cognitive behaviorists falls somewhere between the low consistency predicted by behaviorists and the high consistency expected by trait psychologists. The

Table 2.1. Differences Between Behavioral and Traditional Approaches to Assessment

	BEHAVIORAL	TRADITIONAL
I. Assumptions		
1. Conception of personality	Personality constructs mainly employed to summarize specific behavior patterns, if at all	Personality as a reflection of enduring underlying states or traits
2. Causes of behavior	Maintaining conditions sought in current environment	Intrapsychic or within the individual
II. Implications		
1. Role of behavior	Important as a sample of person's repertoire in specific situation	Behavior assumes importance only insofar as it indexes underlying causes
2. Role of history	Relatively unimportant, except, for example, to provide a retrospective baseline	Crucial in that present conditions are seen as a product of the past
3. Consistency of behavior	Behavior thought to be specific to the situation	Behavior expected to be consistent across time and settings
III. Uses of data	To describe target behaviors and maintaining conditions	To describe personality functioning and etiology
	To select the appropriate treatment	To diagnose or classify
	To evaluate and revise treatment	To make prognosis; to predict
IV. Other characteristics		
1. Level of inferences	Low	Medium to high
2. Comparisons	More emphasis on intraindividual or idiographic	More emphasis on interindividual or nomothetic
3. Methods of assessment	More emphasis on direct methods (e.g., observations of behavior in natural environment)	More emphasis on indirect methods (e.g., interviews and self-report)
4. Timing of assessment	More ongoing; before, during, and after treatment	Pre- and perhaps posttreatment, or strictly to diagnose
5. Scope of assessment	Specific measures and of more variables (e.g., of target behaviors in various situations, of side effects, context, strengths as well as deficiencies	More global measures (e.g., of cure or improvement) but only of the individual

Source: D. P. Hartmann, B. L. Roper, and D. C. Bradford, "Some Relationships Between Behavioral and Traditional Assessment," *Journal of Behavioral Assessment, 1*, 4. Copyright 1979 by Plenum Publishing Company. Reprinted by permission.

view of behavior as determined by variables in the environment (highly changeable) and within the person (moderately changeable) accounts for this middle position on performance consistency. Meichenbaum and Cameron (1981) suggest that cognitive assessment targets should be those higher level cognitive processes that are central to the person and have high cross-situational consistency. They cite a pattern of "negative self referent ideation" when confronted with a stressor as an example of a higher level, or more general, cognitive process. Meichenbaum and Cameron suggest that rather than assessing a person's situation-specific self-statements when confronting a stressor, assessors should assess this cognitive pattern, or schema, which consists of three types of self-statements: (1) statements about self rather than about the task; (2) statements about the negative consequences of task failure; and (3) statements that focus on explanations for failure and that are emotionally arousing rather than statements that focus on remedies for improving performance. Certainly a determination of the optimal level of specificity of cognitive assessment targets requires additional research investigation.

Uses of Data

Data on cognitive processes and events are used for the same purposes as data collected in both behavioral and traditional assessment. In particular assessment situations, one or more purposes will take priority. Like behavioral data, cognitive assessment data are used to describe deficient performance, to select treatment targets, and to evaluate and revise treatment. For example, a teacher or therapist might assess a child's tendency to respond impulsively to cognitive tasks without first thinking through the problem and selecting a task approach. On the basis of assessment results, the child's cognitive impulsivity might be selected as a treatment target. Like traditional psychometric data, cognitive assessment data are used to diagnose individuals and to describe general processes that have high temporal and cross-situational consistency. For example, children's self-reported perceptions of themselves, the world, and the possibility of future happiness can make a meaningful contribution to the diagnosis of depression. A pattern of viewing oneself, the world, and the future negatively (the "negative triad") characterizes depressed individuals and is moderately stable across time and situations.

An additional purpose of cognitive-behavioral assessment is to test the functional relationship between cognitive mediating events and behavior. A finding that improvement on behavioral targets is associated with improvement on cognitive targets, following a cognitive-behavioral intervention, would support the view that cognitive and behavioral targets are functionally related.

Other Characteristics

Because cognitive variables cannot be observed directly, cognitive assessment always involves inference. When a child responds quickly to a perceptual task and makes many errors, the psychologist has observed the child's latency and error rate but not the child's cognitive impulsivity or self-control. These are constructs inferred from behavior (Kagan, 1966). Similarly, a psychologist asks a child questions about future rewarding and punishing events and infers the child's hopelessness (Kazdin, French, Unis, Esveldt-Dawson, & Sherick, 1983).

Therefore, the psychologist interested in a child's cognitions relies on indirect assessment approaches, such as interviewing, measuring task performance, and asking children to report on their own "private thoughts." Diener and Dweck (1978) assessed children's attributions for a failure experience by directly asking, "Why do you think you had trouble with these problems?" Although asking children to report their own thoughts may appear to be a direct approach, inference is still required, because there may not be a perfect correspondence between the child's reported causal explanation and the child's subjective causal attributions. Similarly, "think aloud" approaches (Diener & Dweck, 1978) that require children to verbalize what they are thinking while performing a task do not yield direct information on children's self-talk. The act of translating private thoughts to words for public consumption may alter a child's naturalistic self-talk.

Idiographic versus Nomothetic Approaches

Cognitive-behavioral assessment procedures employ both idiographic and nomothetic comparisons. When emphasis is placed on describing an individual's relevant expectancies, explanations, and thought patterns, data are used to make intraindividual (idiographic) comparisons. The idiographic approach examines changes within the individual resulting from treatment as well as the relationship between an individual's thinking and behavior. The child clinical interview is well designed for investigating an individual's unique patterns of thinking, feeling, and behaving. Nomothetic approaches, however, permit comparisons between persons and are essential to between-group experimental designs. Studies that examine differences between two groups (e.g., differences in perspective-taking ability between delinquent and nondelinquent boys) require nomothetic assessment approaches.

Timing of Assessment

Cognitive-behavioral assessment data tend to be collected before and after intervention rather than continuously during intervention. Typically, a child is selected for treatment based, at least in part, on the child's below-average performance on tests of the target cognitions and behaviors. Following treatment, these same measures are readministered to determine the outcomes of the intervention. One reason cognitive measures are not taken continuously throughout treatment is possible practice effects on many cognitive task measures. The problem of practice effects is demonstrated by studies finding improvement from pretest to posttest on cognitive task performance measures for control group children who receive no treatment (e.g., Kendall & Wilcox, 1980). Compounding the problem of repeated measurement in cognitive assessment is the lack of alternative forms for many cognitive tests.

RELEVANCE OF PSYCHOMETRIC STANDARDS TO COGNITIVE BEHAVIORAL ASSESSMENT

Norms

Age norms are especially important in cognitive behavioral assessment because children at different ages typically perform differently on many cognitive assessment measures. For example, as children grow older, they become more reflective, their social cognition improves, their purposeful deployment and self-monitoring of learning strategies increase, and their ability to coordinate multiple perspectives improves. Therefore, knowledge of age-expected performance on cognitive measures is essential to identifying deficient performance. As Roberts and Nelson (1984) point out, scores on many cognitive tests cannot be interpreted outside a developmental context. For example, a reflective or impulsive score on the Matching Familiar Figures Test (Kagan, Rosman, Day, Albert, & Phillips, 1964) can be determined only in relation to a child's age, because children's performance on this test becomes more reflective with age.

Reliability

To the extent that a measure is reliable, it is free of measurement error. Measurement error introduces error into procedures for selecting children for treatment, reduces the experiment power of statistical analyses, and reduces the chance of documenting functional relationships between cognition and behavior. Evidence of consistency of performance across time (test-retest reliability), across items (internal consistency), and across raters (interrater reliability) is just as relevant to evaluating cognitive measures as to evaluating trait measures.

Validity

The issue of validity is central to the evaluation of any cognitive assessment instrument. Because the targets of our assessment efforts cannot be observed directly, evidence that our assessment instruments measure the psychological constructs they purport to measure is critical. There are several approaches to obtaining evidence of a test's validity. One of the most frequently used approaches is correlating test scores with external criteria with which test scores are expected to covary (criterion-related validity). For example, scores on a paper-and-pencil measure of children's self-reported assertion should correlate with teacher ratings of behavioral assertion. The external criterion is often membership in some known group. For example, children receiving inpatient treatment for depression should score higher on a self-report scale of hopelessness than children receiving inpatient treatment for other psychiatric disorders. Evidence of the construct validity of a measure is provided by experimental studies that observe the effect of some environmental manipulation on test scores. For example, experience with uncontrollable failure is expected to result in a shift in children's locus of control from internal to more external.

The multitrait-multimethod model of construct validation (Campbell & Fiske, 1959), originally applied to trait assessment, is very applicable to cognitive-behavioral assessment. The convergent validity of assessment methods is established when two or more dissimilar methods of measuring the same variable yield similar results. For example, if teacher ratings of self-control and task performance measures of self-control yield similar results, the construct validity of both measures is strengthened. Divergent validity is established when two or more similar methods of measuring different variables yield different results. For example, if teacher ratings of self-control and teacher ratings of peer relationship problems yield dissimilar results, the construct validity of each instrument is strengthened. The convergent-discriminant validity model helps sort out measurement results that are due to the measurement method rather than to the trait (or construct) the test purports to measure.

It is important for cognitive-behavioral assessors to employ multiple measures of their constructs and to examine evidence of convergent and discriminant validity. Reynolds and Stark (1986) provide an example of this approach to construct validation of self-control measures. Reynolds and Stark note that self-control training studies have proliferated during the last 15 years with few attempts to compare different measures of self-control. The measures they compared included teacher and parent ratings of behavioral self-control on two instruments, teacher and parent ratings of hyperactivity, a task performance measure of cognitive impulsivity, and a child self-report measure of self-control. According to the cognitive behavioral theory of self-control, deficiencies in cognitive impulsivity lead to overt behavioral deficits in self-control. Self-control training programs attempt to remediate cognitive impulsivity by teaching children to use covert verbal self-instructions to mediate their behavior. According to this view, measures of cognitive impulsivity and measures of behavioral self-control should be related, because they stem from the same deficiency.

Reynolds and Stark (1986) found that within groups of raters (i.e., parents or teachers) correlations on the three rating scales were very high. The correlations across raters were low, which may reflect low cross-situational consistency in behaviors. The task performance measure (Matching Familiar Figures Test, Kagan et al., 1964) did not correlate with any of the other measures. The authors concluded that the Matching Familiar Figures Test measures cognitive impulsivity, whereas the rating scales measure overt behavioral excesses. The lack of convergence between the cognitive and behavioral measures of self-control suggests that the instruments do not adequately operationalize the construct "self-control." The authors suggest that cognitive self-control and behavioral self-control are different constructs and recommend that both measures be included as outcome measures in self-control intervention studies.

OUTCOME ASSESSMENT ISSUES IN COGNITIVE BEHAVIOR ASSESSMENT

Multiple Outcome Measures

Cognitive-behavioral therapies attempt to bring about behavioral change by modifying the deficient cognitive processes and events assumed to underlie dysfunctional behaviors. To evaluate cognitive-behavioral interventions adequately, treatment outcome measures should include both cognitive and behavioral targets. If only behavioral targets are assessed, the mechanism of change cannot be determined. For example, a child's behavioral self-control may decrease after self-instructional training, but unless measures of the child's cognitive impulsivity also show improvement, it cannot be concluded definitively that the behavioral improvement resulted from greater cognitive self-control. Similarly, if delinquent adolescents who receive training in perspective-taking ability and problem-solving demonstrate greater improvement on teacher ratings of behavioral adjustment, it cannot be concluded that this improvement was mediated by changes in the target cognitions unless those cognitions improve from pretest to posttest.

Unfortunately, several cognitive-behavioral researchers have employed exclusively behavioral outcome measures. For example, Graziano, Mooney, Huber, and Ignasiak (1979) and Graziano and Mooney (1980) used self-instructional training to reduce severely fearful children's fear of the dark. The intervention included relaxation training (lie down and relax), positive imagery (imagine a pleasant scene), and instructions to engage in coping self-talk when in the dark ("I am brave. I can take care of myself when I am in the dark"). Children earned tokens for practicing these strategies as well as for "fearless" nights. Outcome measures included parent report of fearless nights. Children in both studies improved as a result of the treatment. Unfortunately, given the multicomponent nature of the treatment and the lack of measures of cognitive change, it is impossible to evaluate the role of self-talk in producing behavioral improvement.

Goodwin and Mahoney (1975) used exclusively behavioral measures to evaluate the effectiveness of cognitive modeling with impulsive, aggressive boys. Treated boys viewed a filmed model coping with taunts by instructing himself with statements such as, "I'm not going to let them bug me." The therapist pointed out the model's private thoughts and actions, and the boys were asked to remember as many of the coping statements as they could. Treatment outcomes were assessed by observing children's responses to verbal taunts in a taunting game and their classroom behavior. Although treatment resulted in behavioral self-control (i.e., fewer aggressive behaviors), it cannot be concluded that self-verbalizations accounted for the boys' nonaggressive response to taunting following treatment, as no data on the boys' reported use of self-talk was obtained. Alternative explanations for the behavioral improvement include habituation effects and effects of modeling other than those effects attributed to cognitive modeling. That is, the boys may have imitated the model's overt, calm behavior without imitating the model's self-verbalizations.

Several social skills training studies based on social learning theory employed exclusively behavioral and sociometric outcome measures (Csapo, 1983; Edelson & Rose, 1982; Gresham & Nagle, 1980; Ladd, 1981; Oden & Asher, 1977). These researchers are to be commended for assessing specific target behaviors as well as socially valid measures of the impact of change (i.e., peer acceptance ratings). Nevertheless, changes in social cognition that may have mediated the behavioral changes cannot be determined from their outcome measures. For example, Oden and Asher (1977) used a coaching procedure to teach four social skills to low accepted third- and fourth-grade children. The coaching procedures included instructions, modeling, structured practice opportunities, and self-evaluation of performance. Trained children improved relative to controls on sociometric measures. However, without measures of children's social-cognitive processes, the degree to which the coaching procedure modified cognitions that mediate social behaviors cannot be determined.

Asher and Renshaw (1981), in analyzing the components of the coaching procedure used by Oden and Asher (1977), suggest tha the effectiveness of coaching may be due in part to its influence on children's goal construal processes. The experimenter in the Oden and Asher study imposed goals such as making friends and being helpful on the hypothetical stories used in training. Thus, children may have been influenced to focus on these prosocial goals rather than on other goals such as winning a game or avoiding a situation. Additional social-cognitive processes that coaching interventions may affect include "metacognitive" skills such as self-monitoring of strategy implementation and strategy effectiveness, self-reinforcement practices, self-efficacy expectancies, and outcome expectancies.

Determining Treatment Mechanisms

Designs that compare the effects of different treatment components on both cognitive and behavioral targets help answer questions related to treatment mechanisms. Kendall and Wilcox (1980) compared the effectiveness of two types of self-instructional training with a response cost contingency and an attention control condition in producing changes on measures of cognitive impulsivity and behavioral self-control. Training was conducted with 33 non-self-controlled children. Outcome measures included the Matching Familiar Figures Test (Kagen et al., 1964), Porteus Mazes (Porteus, 1955), and two teacher rating scales of self-control. Training occurred in six 30- to 40-minute individual sessions held twice weekly. Self-instructional training was similar to that used by Meichenbaum and Goodman (1971), which involves cognitive modeling of effective self-instructions. One group received conceptual self-instructions, and one group received concrete self-instructions. Conceptual self-instructions are stated more generally and apply across different tasks, whereas concrete self-instructions refer to the specific training task. Control children received practice with the training materials but did not receive self-instructional training or response cost. All three groups had improved results on the Matching Familiar Figures Test and Porteus Maze, probably due to practice effects. Teacher blind ratings of treated children's self-control improved at posttest, relative to control children. Only children receiving conceptual self-instructional training maintained their behavioral improvement at follow-up assessment 1 month after treatment. The relative superiority of conceptual self-instructions over concrete self-instructions supports the view that the self-instructional component accounted for behavioral gains.

Establishing Functional Relatedness

In addition to measuring both cognitive and behavioral targets and comparing treatment components, researchers should attempt to determine the functional relatedness of cognitive and behavioral measures. For example, Urbain and Kendall (1981) investigated the functional relationship between improved social-cognitive skills and improved social behavior. Urbain and Kendall randomly assigned 44 aggressive and impulsive children to one of three treatment groups: an interpersonal problem-solving group, a perspective training group, and a behavioral contingency group. Outcome measures included performance measures of social perspective training and social problem solving and teacher ratings of impulsivity-aggressiveness. Although no between-group differences were found, improvement on the social-cognitive tasks correlated significantly with improved teacher ratings. Thus, children who gained the most on cognitive measures improved the most on teacher ratings. Similarly, Shure (1979) provided evidence of a direct link between improved problem-solving performance and behavioral adjustment. Specifically, those preschool children who improved the most on measures of alternative thinking after training were the same children whose behavior improved according to teacher ratings.

Specifying and Impact Level Assessment

Finally, outcome assessment procedures should include measures at both the specifying and impact assessment levels (Kendall & Morrison, 1984). Measures at the specifying level identify exactly what did or did not change as a result of treatment. Specific behaviors are most effectively assessed through naturalistic observations, and specific cognitions are assessed by task performance measures. The Matching Familiar Figures Test (Kagan et al., 1964) and Children's Means-End Problem Solving (MEPS) Test (Shure & Spivack, 1972) are examples of specifying measures. Measures at the impact level assess the impact of treatment on the perceptions of parents, teachers, peers, and others in the natural environment as well as on other socially consequential outcomes, such as academic achievement. If treatment results in changes in target skills with no accompanying change in the child's impact on significant others, the treatment may have changed an inconsequential, or socially invalid, behavior. Conversely, if treatment results in improved peer acceptance or teacher perceptions with no documented improvement in specific measures, the treatment was beneficial. However, we are left wondering what exactly it was that changed to produce the positive impact.

3
Cognitive Assessment Strategies

Several excellent sources of information on conducting behavioral assessments are available (e.g., Ciminero, Calhoun, & Adams, 1977; Ollendick & Hersen, 1984). Although a consensus exists on the recommended behavioral assessment procedures, a generally accepted technology of cognitive assessment for cognitive behavior therapy does not yet exist. For this reason, this chapter focuses on cognitive assessment strategies, rather than giving equal attention to both cognitive and behavioral assessment strategies.

In this chapter several strategies for assessing what children *do cognitively* are reviewed. These strategies attempt to assess a broad spectrum of children's cognitions, including their understanding of significant events and people in their lives, expectancies for their own and others' behavior, goal construal processes, problem-solving abilities, perspective-taking ability, causal explanations for positive and negative events, irrational thought patterns, and self-regulatory mechanisms. This incomplete listing of the targets of cognitive assessment strategies gives some hint as to the complexity and richness of cognitive assessment.

Next, three cognitive assessment approaches are reviewed: the child interview, self-report questionnaires, and task performance measures. The major advantages and limitations of each approach are summarized briefly and examples of their application in cognitive behavior therapy are provided. Specific assessment strategies with particular relevance to one or more clinical problems are reviewed in greater detail in the chapters in Section II on specific child problems.

CHILD CLINICAL INTERVIEW

Purposes of the Interview

The purpose of the diagnostic child interview is to learn the child's subjective definition of experience and perceptions of significant persons and events in his or her life. Succinctly stated, if a therapist wants to know what or how a child is feeling and thinking, the therapist must ask the child.

The child is the expert on his or her subjective experience and perceptions of important persons and events.

The Child Clinical Interview is based on two assumptions. First, children's interpretations of their experiences affect their reactions to their environment, including their interpersonal behaviors, goal striving, and mastery. Second, children are capable of communicating complex affective and intellectual experiences in the context of the clinical interview. Whether the child succeeds in effectively communicating these subjective experiences depends largely on the interviewer's skill in accommodating his or her interview approach to the child's cognitive, linguistic, and psychosocial developmental levels. Even children as young as 3 years of age are able to communicate important thoughts and feelings to the interviewer *if* the interviewer is cognizant of the child's developmental levels and makes the necessary modifications. Use of concrete props to present questions, rephrasing questions to reduce their complexity and their threat, and permitting alternative options such as pointing, moving doll figures, or talking for a puppet are examples of the types of modifications that may be necessary. In addition to knowledge of child development and specific child interviewing skills, the interviewer must also possess a genuine respect for children as active problem solvers who are attempting to make sense out of their experience.

Although the child interview is uniquely well suited for obtaining information on a child's subjective experience, it is poorly suited for other assessment purposes. For example, the interview is less likely to yield accurate factual information on a child's behavior than are teacher behavior ratings or direct observation. Additionally, because parents and teachers' perceptions of children's behavior are the basis for referral for special services, their inclusion in child assessment is critical. Finally, if we are interested in a child's cognitive performance, a performance test such as Chandler's Bystander Cartoons (Chandler, 1971) may yield more accurate information. Thus, the child interview is best employed as part of a multimethod assessment.

The importance of integrating data from a child interview with other assessment data is illustrated in the following example. A 10-year-old girl was referred to the school psychologist for social withdrawal. The psychologist asked the girl's teacher to rate the child's social interactions with a rating scale designed for this purpose. The psychologist observed the child's social interactions during lunch, recess, and a small group discussion during class. Data from the teacher rating and observation were consistent in describing a shy youngster who rarely initiated social interactions and who responded only minimally to classmates' interactions. Her peers were not negative to her, but they made few social overtures to her. These data confirm a social withdrawal problem, but they do not shed light on *why* the child avoids social interaction. During an interview, the psychologist asked the girl questions about peer relations. The child revealed that she believed she "isn't very good" at joining in and having fun. Furthermore, she reported that she was afraid she would embarrass herself, that the other children would laugh at her, and that she could not stand it if they laughed at her. These expectancies for her own performance and for others' reactions to her kept her from actively participating in classroom social interactions. Consequently, these self-efficacy and outcome expectancies were targeted in a cognitive-behavioral intervention.

Although the clinical interview is an important component in adult assessment, it has been underutilized in working with children. There are at least two reasons for the interview's low priority in child clinical assessment. First, children's responses to the open-ended, general questions typically used in adult interviews tend to be brief, vague, and confused. Second, because children do not usually refer themselves for help, they may not perceive that a problem exists, or they may define the problem differently from the problem as conceptualized by the referring adult. Thus, the child may not expect that therapy will help him or her, and motivation to participate in the interview may be low.

Both of these limitations can be minimized considerably through special child interviewing approaches. For example, a child may give a vague or otherwise inadequate answer to the general question, "How do you feel about school?" The same child might provide a competent answer to a series of specific questions like the following: "What part of the school day do you look forward to the most?" "If you could change one thing about your teacher, what would you change?" The interviewer can help to engage the youngster's cooperation by discussing the reason for the referral with the child, respecting the child's thoughts and feelings and putting the child at ease.

Developmental Implications

The interviewer's general approach and specific strategies depend in part on the child's developmental level. Children at different ages differ in language competence, person perception, understanding of social relationships, ability to think logically, abstract thinking ability, ability to look at situations from multiple and differing perspectives, and in many other ways that have implications for conducting the child interview. Recently, Hughes (in press–c) and Bierman and Schwartz (1987) discussed developmental considerations in interviewing children. This section will highlight a few of these developmental considerations and their implications for interviewing children.

Language Competence

Children's vocabulary and syntax develop rapidly during the years 2 to 6. Nevertheless, even 6- and 7-year-old children have not mastered all the rules of language usage and may have difficulty expressing themselves. The use of concrete referents for questions, the incomplete sentence and story format, and drawings help the young child communicate affective and cognitive experiences.

Children are able to give more competent answers to questions when the questions occur in a natural context and are accompanied by pictures or manipulatives. For example, if the interviewer is interested in the child's ideas about sex-role typing, the interviewer might present pictures of toys and a girl and a boy doll and ask the child which toys the girl would choose to play with. Similarly, a psychologist interviewing a young boy about situations that make him angry could present a picture of an "angry thermometer" with readings from 0 degrees (cool) to 212 degrees (boiling mad). Next, the interviewer describes anger-producing situations varying in intensity and asks the boy to point to the thermometer reading that indicates how angry he feels in the situations described. As a final example, an interviewer interested in a shy girl's self-talk in the context of social interactions might present a picture of a girl standing off to the side of some children playing with a frisbee. The interviewer says the girl is thinking about playing but cannot decide whether to join in the game or not. What do you think the girl might be thinking?

Another interview strategy for overcoming language problems is the use of incomplete sentences and stories. The child is asked to complete a sentence, such as "Sometimes at night I worry that . . ." or "The best thing about school is. . . ." The incomplete sentence format allows the interviewer to introduce different content, and children find it easier to complete a sentence than to formulate their own complete response to the interviewer's questions. The incomplete story technique is similar. For example, the therapist is interested in an aggressive child's knowledge of ways to resolve conflicts and expectations for interpersonal conflict. The therapist tells a story about two children disagreeing over whether to play Monopoly or baseball and asks the child to complete the story. After the child's completion, the interviewer asks if what the story child did was the best thing to do, was it what he or she would do, what other things could the story child say or do, and what might happen next if the story child did those things.

Many children are capable of communicating their feelings and perceptions of others and of important events through the medium of art. Chalk, a chalkboard, colored markers, and paper are the only materials needed. Drawings can help children express their affective experiences. For example, the interviewer might ask a child to pick a card with a feeling word written on it and then to draw a picture of that feeling. The child's pictures can be used in several ways. The child can point to the picture that expresses how he or she feels about different experiences and people. The child and therapist can take turns acting out a feeling in a game of charades, and the other person must guess the portrayed feeling. The child can take the pictures home and write on the back of each picture a time when he or she experienced that feeling during the week.

All-or-None Thinking

Young children's perceptions of people tend to be global and undifferentiated, and they have difficulty viewing people as having both good and bad qualities. This all-or-none characteristic of their perception of people is probably a result of their cognitive inability to consider and compare multiple aspects of situations simultaneously. This all-or-none thinking makes it difficult for young children to recognize and accept their own bad or angry feelings or behavior. The 6-year-old girl does not believe she can both be a good girl and pinch her baby sister. Thus, 6-year-olds may deny a wrong doing even when confronted with overwhelming evidence of their culpability. For the same reason, the young child finds it difficult to admit negative feelings. Yarrow (1960) described several ways a child interviewer can phrase questions to reduce their perceived threat and to enable children to admit negative feelings and behaviors. (1) Suggest that other children might feel the same way. For example, "All girls sometimes get mad at their parents. What kinds of things make you feel mad?" (2) Present alternatives, all of which appear to be equally acceptable. "Do you think Mom expects too much of you, or do you think she expects about the right amount, or too little?" (3) Choose words that soften an undesirable response or that make it appear more acceptable. Instead of asking the child if he hits, ask him "If a boy in your class teases you, do you punish him so he stops or do you let the teacher know about it?" This example represents giving two alternatives that sound about equal in acceptability and phrasing negative behavior (tattling) in a more acceptable light (let your teacher know). (4) Assume the child engages in negative behaviors instead of requiring the child to admit to negative behavior. For example, ask a child, "All children sometimes feel angry with their parents. When you feel angry at your father, how do you let him know you are angry?" If this question is too complex, the interviewer can follow up with, "Some kids tell their parents with words that they are angry, and some kids do something that lets their parents know they are angry. Which way is it with you?" (5) Permit the child to express positive feelings before negative feelings. For example, ask children what they like about school before asking them what they dislike. Similarly, ask children what their mothers do that pleases them before asking what their mothers do that displeases them.

In addition to being global and undifferentiated, children's person perceptions tend to be concrete, and their descriptions of others focus on external characteristics such as clothes, possessions, the color of their hair, and size. Children's descriptions of people rarely mention personal traits, and if any personal traits are mentioned, they are global and highly evaluative (e.g., "She is very nice."). Thus, the interviewer will obtain little meaningful information on the young child's perceptions of a person's individual characteristics from asking the child to describe what he or she likes about the person. If the child's perceptions of others are desired, the interviewer might play the "Guess Who?" game with the child. In this game, the interviewer shows the child pictures of the people about whom the interviewer wishes to obtain the child's perceptions. The interviewer asks the child to point to the one who is often grumpy, smiles a lot, reads stories to you, has a hot temper, hugs you a lot, and so forth.

Personality Development

The interviewer must be aware of psychosocial developmental stages and match the interview approach to the child's developmental level. Young children (approximately aged 3 to 8) are eager for adult approval. The desire for approval can pose an obstacle to the interview because the child may give answers based on the child's perception of what would please the interviewer. The interviewer must guard against this tendency by avoiding leading questions and by being careful not to present one alternative to a question as more desirable.

The grade-school child is interested in competition and mastery and will not be won over as easily as the younger child. Rapport is based less on friendly exchanges and more on the interviewer's ability to convey respect for the youngster's autonomy and identity. The interviewer should explain the purpose of the interview in more detail, emphasizing the importance of having the child's point of view. "No one else can tell me how you think or feel about things, so it is very important that I talk with you, and not just with your parents, your teacher, or anyone else." Quiet acceptance and nonthreatening questions about age-appropriate interests and issues such as school, sports, and television programs are likely to put grade-school children at ease and gain their cooperation. The interviewer can capitalize on the child's developmentally normal mastery concerns by taking a task-oriented interview approach. To capitalize on grade-school children's concern with competition, the interview might be conducted around or after a game of Connect Four or Uno.

Interviewing Approaches

Child interview approaches differ in several ways, including the amount of structure provided by the interviewer, the use of toys, puppets, and other communication aids, and the question-asking format. The choice of an approach depends on the purpose of the interview and the developmental status of the child as well as on other factors. Next, four interview approaches are briefly described: diagnostic play interviews, open-ended interviews, semistructured interviews, and structured diagnostic interviews.

Diagnostic Play Interview

This approach is especially helpful in interviewing younger children for whom play is a natural medium of expression and whose ability to verbally reason about their problems is limited. This approach provides the least amount of structure for the child. Greenspan (1981) offers guidelines for conducting the diagnostic play interview as well as numerous case studies and interview excerpts demonstrating this approach. The interviewer makes a variety of toys and drawing materials available to the child. Toys that encourage dramatic play and permit the child to enact important events and current concerns are preferred. The interviewer invites the child to play and maintains an interested but nondirective interview style. The interviewer observes the child's selection of play materials and notes themes that characterize the child's play. If a child's play has a common theme, the interviewer hypothesizes that that theme (e.g., dependency, keeping secrets, denying negative feelings, control of emotions, jealousy, and fear of losing a loved one) is an important concern for the child. The interviewer responds empathetically to the child's verbalizations and behaviors and gently probes areas of clinical concern.

For example, a depressed 6-year-old girl continued to draw happy pictures that had something sad in them too. For example, she drew a rainbow with storm clouds and a heart with the words "I love you," a tear, and a black flower. The girl had been unable to discuss her sad feelings about the divorce and subsequent changes in her life. The interviewer referred to the pictures as happy-sad pictures and commented that, "Sometimes we feel happy and sad." The girl denied the sad part of the pictures and called them happy pictures. The therapist continued to remark on both the happy and sad aspects of the pictures, commenting that sad feelings are OK too. Feeling understood and accepted, the child began to draw sad pictures and to talk about her sad feelings, including the guilt she felt about her father leaving home.

A particularly dramatic example of the use of toys to help a child communicate complex affective experiences is provided by 4-year-old Susie, who attended a Head Start program. Susie was referred to the school psychologist for pervasive unhappiness and occasional self-injurious behavior. Susie's mother had been killed 1 year earlier in an accident involving an automobile. Susie and her mother were in their car when Susie's mother stopped the car and got out to get her mail at a rural mailbox. Somehow, the car shifted out of "park" and backed over Susie's mother, killing her. Efforts by her father and teachers to get Susie to talk about the incident had been unsuccessful. During the second diagnostic play interview, Susie enacted an automobile accident with toy cars, including police and ambulance cars. She used the telephone to call the doctor (the therapist) to tell her what had happened. Whenever Susie got too afraid while telling her story, she hung up the phone, saying she had to go cook supper. In bits and pieces Susie retold the event and disclosed that the naughty girl in the car was bad and got out of her car seat. The telephone continued to be a communication vehicle for Susie to talk to the therapist about her mother's death and her feelings of responsibility for the accident.

Open-Ended Interview

In this approach, the interviewer asks the child open-ended questions. The way questions are phrased and the use of concrete referents depend on the developmental level of the child. The advantages of the open-ended interview include the opportunity to learn how children see their problems and to observe children's ability to reason about their problem. It also establishes a reciprocal system of communication that can facilitate subsequent therapy (Bierman & Schwartz, 1987). It is an especially useful approach with grade-school children and adolescents. For example, when interviewing a 12-year-old aggressive child, the interviewer asks questions intended to elicit the child's perceptions of peers, understanding of the reasons for frequent conflicts with peers, ability to generate flexible solutions, goal construal processes, and ability to accurately label others' intentions toward him or her. "What happened that caused you and Tim to fight? What do you think Tim wanted to happen? What did you want to happen? If you wanted that, what are some other things you could have said or done?" The interviewer might discover that the child misattributes accidental peer provocation to hostile intent, does not know constructive ways for solving conflicts, or holds the irrational belief that "Boys who let others shove them around are worthless scum and deserve what they get." These cognitive deficiencies, distortions, and beliefs could be targets for a cognitive-behavioral intervention.

Semistructured Interview

Semistructured interviews can be standardized or nonstandardized. In the nonstandardized semistructured interview, the interviewer presents the child with stories or sentences to complete. Through the selection of the content of stories and sentences, the interviewer exerts control over the content of the interview. A sample dialogue, patterned after Bierman and Schwartz (1987) from an interview with a 9-year-old boy having difficulty with completing school work, illustrates the semistructured interview.

Psychologist: OK. Today we're going to make up some stories together. I'll read the story and you fill in the blanks. OK? The first story is about a child at school. The child is working on math sheets. He gets to a hard problem. The child. . . . What should I say here?
Child: He raises his hand for help.
Psychologist: OK. He raises his hand for help. The teacher is busy and cannot come right away. So the boy. . . .
Child: Tries to solve the problem.
Psychologist: The boy tries to solve the problem. He works hard at it for a few minutes. Finally. . . .
Child: The teacher comes and helps.

In this example, the psychologist learned that the child believes effort does not pay off. His low persistence may be partly a result of his failure expectation and belief that greater effort will not result in success.

The Interpersonal Understanding Interview (IUI) is a standardized, semi-structured interview used to assess a child's level of interpersonal understanding. In a series of longitudinal studies beginning in 1973 (Gurucharri, Phelps, & Selman, 1984; Selman, 1980), Selman and his colleagues at Judge Baker Child Guidance Clinic documented developmental changes in social understanding in normal populations and differences in developmental patterns between clinical and normal samples. The IUI presents children with interpersonal dilemmas and uses a semistructured interview to assess a child's ability to coordinate multiple social and psychological perspectives. This ability is referred to as social perspective taking (a construct similar to but not identical to role taking) and is at the core of social intelligence, according to Selman (1980). "Social perspective taking includes a developing understanding of how human points of view are *related* and *coordinated* with one another and not simply what social or psychological information appear to be like from an alternative individual's perspective as in the construct of role taking" (p. 22). A different dilemma is used to measure a child's level of social perspective taking in each of four domains: individual, friendship, peer group, and parent-child. Within each domain, Selman (1980) specified a set of issues that appear to be intrinsic to the understanding of that particular relationship. In the friendship domain, these issues are formation of friends, trust, jealousy, intimacy, conflict resolution, and termination. Five levels of perspective taking (from egocentric to societal) are applied to issues within each domain. The result is an issue by level analysis within each domain.

The dilemma for the friendship domain interview involves a child who has to decide between keeping a date with an old friend or accepting a fun invitation with a new child. Each of the six issues in the friendship domain is the basis for a series of intensive questions about the dilemma and about the subject's beliefs and experiences around the issue. In a standard but open-ended interview, the subject is asked to think carefully and express his or her understanding about friendship issues. The interviewer probes the responses to clarify the subject's meaning and to identify the developmental level that characterizes the child's understanding of the concepts within each issue. The basic unit of analysis in the scoring system is the issue concept. Each issue within a domain is scored in terms of the levels of interpersonal understanding it represents. A detailed, 400-page manual provides computational procedures for obtaining a quantitative score for each interpersonal domain (Selman, Jaquette, & Bruss-Saunders, 1979).

Selman (1980) presents evidence of the IUI's reliability and validity. Interrater reliabilities for each domain range between 0.82 and 0.97 and average 0.91 (Gurucharri et al., 1984; Selman, 1980). There is strong coherence or synchrony in a child's level of understanding across the four separate interviews, and this synchrony is not the result of rater or interviewer bias (Selman, 1980). Reported test-retest reliability is adequate. Selman also presents extensive evidence of the construct validity of the interviews. Of critical import to the use of the test in child clinical assessment is its ability to discriminate normal and socially deviant children. Selman presents evidence that children with low levels of interpersonal understanding, relative to peers, are likely to be rated low on peer acceptance and on teacher evaluations of social adjustment; however, high levels of interpersonal understanding are not predictive of popularity or teacher perceptions of social strengths (Selman, 1980). It seems that the ability to integrate multiple social and psychological perspectives in interpersonal situations is necessary but not sufficient for adequate social functioning. Gurucharri and colleagues (1984) found that emotionally disturbed youths, relative to normal youths, progressed more slowly through the stages of interpersonal understanding based on interviews in the friendship and peer relations domains. Furthermore, there was a relationship between the level of interpersonal understanding and self-reported resolutions to interpersonal conflicts, with higher levels of interpersonal understanding associated with more sophisticated conflict resolution. Uphoff, Smith, and Stewart (1983) found a relationship between social perspective-taking scores on the friendship interview and the naturally occurring behaviors of behaviorally disordered children.

Although the IUI offers a reliable and valid interview methodology for understanding a child's social reasoning, a disadvantage of the IUI is the time-consuming nature of the method and the level of skill required of interviewers. Thus, its primary use will remain in research rather than in clinical child assessment.

Structured Diagnostic Interviews

Several structured diagnostic interviews have been developed during the last decade. The primary purpose of the structured diagnostic interview is to diagnose the presence and severity of psychopathology. In this approach, the child is asked questions about the presence or absence of symptoms (e.g., I get into lots of fights). The child's ability to reason about problems is not assessed with this approach. The diagnostic interview is essentially a list of questions covering target behaviors and symptoms. Although all interview schedules are structured, some permit flexibility on the part of the interviewer in phrasing and sequencing questions and in deciding when and how to probe the child's response. The more flexible interview schedules, like the Child Assessment Schedule (CAS; Hodges, Kline, Stern, Cytryn, & McKnew, 1982) permit the clinician to exercise considerable judgment in scoring children's responses. Highly structured interview formats, like The Diagnostic Interview Schedule for Children (DISC; Edelbrock, Costello, Dulcan, Kalas, & Conover, 1985) were developed to minimize clinical judgment required and are used primarily for research and epidemiological studies rather than for individual child clinical assessment. Highly structured interview schedules typically include parallel parent forms, and research has focused on comparing child and parent forms (Herjanic & Reich, 1982; Edelbrock et al., 1985).

Although most child interview schedules cover a broad range of child psychopathology, some schedules were developed for specific clinical populations. For example, the Interview Schedule for Children (Kovacs, 1982), discussed in greater detail in chapter 7, assesses depressive symptoms.

The Child Assessment Schedule (CAS; Hodges, Kline, Stern, Cytryn, & McKnew, 1982) is intended to assist in the formulation of diagnostic impressions rather than to yield specific diagnoses. The child's answers are qualitatively analyzed in order to select treatment targets and to develop a treatment plan. The authors note that child interviewing skills are important and that the child should experience the interview as an informal discussion about various aspects of his or her life. Example questions are provided in Table 3.1. Rather than attempting to obtain a yes/no answer to questions about symptoms, the interviewer attempts to elicit the child's phenomenological world. Developed for clinical use with children between the ages of 7 and 12, the CAS consists of 75 questions covering 11 content areas. In addition, the interviewer rates 53 items immediately following the interview. The CAS is scored in terms of 11 content areas and 9 symptom complexes (Table 3.2). A total score based on the number of symptoms is also obtained. Consistent with its purpose of facilitating understanding of a child's problems, the CAS permits considerable flexibility on the part of the clinician in phasing and sequencing questions, skipping sections, and probing and scoring responses.

Interrater reliability for the total symptom score is good ($r = 0.90$), whereas the reliability coefficient for the 11 content areas and 9 symptom complexes is somewhat low ($r = 0.73$ and 0.69, respectively). Evidence of criterion-related validity, demonstrated by comparisons between CAS total

Table 3.1. Sample Items from Child Assessment Schedule

		False (or no)	True (or yes)
Worries and Concerns			
Many children worry about different things, what do you worry about?	Denies any worries	____	____
	Reports considerable worry	____	____
	If applicable: check all that apply to areas of concern.		
	a. Excessive worry about natural disaster (e.g., fire, flood, storms, dark) or external concerns (i.e., lose job)	____	____
	b. Worry about family members	____	____
	c. Worry about self	____	____
Do you worry about yourself or people in your family—like your mom and dad?	If true: check all that apply to content and target of worry.		
	a. Worries that a family member is or will become sick	____	____
	b. Worries that a family member will die	____	____
	c. Worries that parents will argue (verbal)	____	____
	d. Worries that parents will fight (physical)	____	____
	e. Worries about marital separation or divorce (i.e., that a family member will leave)	____	____
	f. Worries about parents' mental health (e.g., loneliness, depression, sensitivity) or says he does activities to help alleviate these problems or symptoms	____	____
	g. Other, specify____________	____	____

Source: K. Hodges, J. Kline, L. Stern, L. Cytryn, and D. McKnew, "The Development of a Child Assessment Interview for Research and Clinical Use," *Journal of Abnormal Child Psychology, 10,* 178–179. Copyright 1982 by Plenum Publishing Co. Reprinted by permission.

score and three other indicators of psychopathology, is good. Scores on the CAS discriminate between groups of children differing in levels of pathology and correspond to maternal report of child behavior problems. Furthermore, the relevant scales on the CAS correspond to scores on self-report measures of anxiety (Hodges, McKnew, Cytryn, Stern, & Kline, 1982) and depression (Kovacs & Beck, 1977).

SELF-REPORT QUESTIONNAIRES

The use of self-report questionnaires with children had a low priority in child clinical assessment for the same reasons the child interview has been deemphasized and underutilized. Children's reports of their own behavior have been viewed as highly suspect. The low levels of agreement between children's self-reported behaviors and objective measures of their behavior

Table 3.2. Content Areas and Symptom Complexes Scored from the Child Assessment Schedule (CAS)

Content Areas
School
Friends
Activities
Family
Fears
Worries
Self-Images
Mood
Somatic Concerns
Expression of Anger
Thought Disorder
Symptom Complexes
Attention Deficit with Hyperactivity
Attention Deficit without Hyperactivity
Undersocialized Conduct Disorder-Aggressive
Undersocialized Conduct Disorder-Unaggressive
Socialized Conduct Disorder
Separation Anxiety
Overanxious
Oppositional
Depression

Source: Hodges et al., "The Development of a Child Assessment Interview for Research and Clinical Use," *Journal of Abnormal Child Psychology, 10,* 181. Copyright 1982 by Plenum Publishing Co. Adapted by permission.

convinced behaviorally oriented clinicians to exclude self-report questionnaires from their assessments. When children's self-reports and observed behaviors were inconsistent, the self-report data were viewed as inaccurate and invalid. Two trends account for the increased emphasis on self-report instruments in child assessment. First, children's perceptions of their experiences are considered valuable in their own right and not just as a proxy for observational data. If a child reports feelings of depression, anger, or loneliness, these subjective affective experiences are clinically significant. To exclude children's perceptions from the assessment process unnecessarily narrows our focus to observable behavior and external contingencies and ignores the role of cognitive events in influencing behavior. Second, data from self-report measures can be valuable in planning interventions. For example, it is expected that children's self-perceptions of their problem affect their motivation to participate in treatment. Children's cognitions also act as independent variables, predicting which children will respond best to different treatments. Bugental, Whalen, and Henker (1977) found that impulsive and hyperactive children's scores on a measure of locus of control predicted the differential effectiveness of two interventions. Children who believed they exercised little control over school success and failure (external locus of control) tended to benefit more from a social reinforcement program, whereas children who believed they exerted considerable control over success and failure (internal locus of control) benefited more from a self-control program. Bugental et al. (1977) stated: "Change strategies (behavioral management, educational programs, psychotherapy, medical intervention) have implicit attributional textures which interact with the attributional network of the individual to influence treatment impact" (p. 881).

Another example of cognitions as independent variables is provided by Evers-Pasquale and Sherman (1975; Evers-Pasquale, 1978). Socially withdrawn children viewed a modeling film intended to increase children's social interaction rates. The authors proposed that children's differential responsiveness to the film was a result of individual differences in the reward value placed on peer contact. Children were classified as peer-oriented or non-peer-oriented based on a self-report measure of the reward value of peers. As predicted, after viewing the film, peer-oriented children increased their rates of social interaction significantly more than did non-peer-oriented children.

Self-report questionnaires are used differently in cognitive-behavioral assessment and in traditional or behavioral assessment. In traditional child assessment, self-report questionnaires are grouped into scales, and scores are obtained for each scale. These scores are interpreted as indicators of underlying personality traits. When behaviorally oriented clinicians use self-report measures, they ask children to report on their behavior. Some of these behavioral measures ask children to self-monitor countable behaviors that could be observed by others (Finch & Rogers, 1984).

Self-report measures used by cognitive-behavioral clinicians attempt to assess specific perceptions of experience rather than global self-perceptions. The self-report data are combined with data from different sources to develop a more complete understanding of the referral problem. As Atkeson and Forehand (1978) state, when data from different sources are inconsistent, they should be viewed as complementary rather than competitive. The task for the clinician is to integrate these data into an individual model of child functioning that serves as a guide for selecting treatment targets and developing and evaluating treatment plans.

Child self-report measures have proliferated at a phenomenal rate in recent years. One reason for this growth is the tendency for each researcher to develop a new measure of the specific perception under investigation rather than to conduct systematic research on existing measures. This tendency is illustrated in research on children's casual attributions. As Fielstein et al. (1985) point out, the various measures of attributional style in children differ in the content of the vignettes, in whether only failure or success and failure vignettes are used, in the types of attributions measured (skill, luck, or task difficulty), and scoring procedures.

A second reason for this proliferation is the trend for self-report measures to assess specific versus general perceptions. For example, the following six questionnaires assess different aspects of children's interpersonal relationships. The Loneliness Scale (Asher, Hymel, & Renshaw, 1984) assesses a child's perceptions of loneliness (e.g., I am often lonely), social adequacy (e.g., I'm good at working with other children), and peer status (e.g., I have lots of friends). The Self-Efficacy Scale for Peer Interaction (Wheeler & Ladd, 1982) measures children's perceptions of their ability to enact prosocial verbal persuasive skills in specific peer situations. The Children's Action Tendency Scale (Deluty, 1979) assesses children's perceptions of their typical behavior in conflict situations.

The Friendship Questionnaire, a self-report measure developed by Bierman and McCauley (1987), assesses children's perceptions of the quality and quantity of their peer interactions. The Friendship Questionnaire yields scores on 3 factors: positive interactions, negative interactions, and the extensiveness of a child's peer network. Finally, the Network of Relationships Inventory (Furman & Buhrmester, 1985) requires children to rate the relevance of 14 qualities to each of 5 relationships (parent, grandparent, teacher, friend, and sibling).

Self-report instruments can be grouped according to the type of child perception they assess: perceptions of subjective affective experience, perceptions of own behavior, and subjective interpretations of significant events and people in their lives.

Instruments that attempt to assess children's subjective affective experience include the revised Manifest Anxiety Scale (Reynolds & Richmond, 1978), the Test Anxiety Scale for Children (Sarason, Davidson, Lighthall, Waite, & Ruebush, 1960), the Children's Depression Inventory (Kovacs, 1983), and the Children's Inventory of Anger (Nelson & Finch, 1978).

Children's perceptions of their own behavior are the focus of the Children's Assertive Behavior Scale (Michelson & Wood, 1982), the Children's Action Tendency Scale (Deluty, 1979), and the Children's Perceived Self-Control Scale (Humphrey, 1982).

Finally, numerous instruments evaluate children's interpretations of significant events and people in their lives. These tests are the hallmark of cognitive-behavioral assessment because they assess cognitive mediating responses that are assumed to directly affect performance in specific situations. They include the Locus of Control Scale (Nowicki & Strickland, 1973), measures of self-efficacy for social interaction (Ollendick, Oswald, & Crowe, 1986; Wheeler & Ladd, 1982), tests of attributional style (Crandall, Katovsky, & Crandall, 1965; Dweck, 1975; Fielstein et al., 1985), and the Network of Relations Inventory (Furman & Buhrmester, 1985).

In the chapters on specific child problems in Section II, several self-report measures are reviewed and their contribution to a multimethod assessment is evaluated. In this chapter, three self-report measures representing the three different types of child perceptions are briefly discussed to illustrate the advantages and limitations of the self-report methodology.

Children's Depression Inventory

The most widely used self-report measure of depression in children in the Children's Depression Inventory (CDI; Kovacs, 1983). Like many child cognitive assessment measures, the CDI is a downward extension and revision of an adult questionnaire, in this case the Beck Depression Inventory (Beck, Ward, Mendelson, Mock, & Erbaugh, 1961). Recommended for use with children 8 to 17 years of age, the CDI consists of 27 items. Each item requires the child to select from one of three sentences the sentence that best describes the child's current feelings. These sentences represent nondepressed, mildly depressed, and severely depressed symptoms and are scored 0 to 2, for a maximum total score of 54. The following two items illustrate the item format of the CDI.

I am sad once in a while
I am sad many times
I am sad all the time

I do most things OK
I do many things wrong
I do everything wrong (Kovacs, 1983).

Results of several studies support the conclusion that the CDI is a reliable instrument. (See Finch & Rogers, 1984, for a review.) Because the CDI is frequently used in making a diagnosis of depression and in evaluating treatment, its ability to discriminate between depressed and nondepressed children is critical. Several researchers have investigated the discriminant validity of the CDI, with mixed results. The CDI discriminates samples of depressed and normal children (Kovacs, 1980/1981) as well as samples of depressed or nondepressed emotionally disturbed children (Asarnow & Carlson, 1985; Kazdin, Colbus, & Rodgers, 1986; Lobovits & Handal, 1985). However, CDI scores did not correlate with therapists' or peers' ratings of depressive symptons (O'Brien, 1982; Saylor, Finch, Baskin, Furey, & Kelly, 1984).

The classification accuracy of the CDI is relatively low. Asarnow and Carlson (1985) found the CDI's sensitivity (true positive rate) to be 54 percent and overall classification accuracy of 71 percent with a sample of hospitalized psychiatric children. That is, using cutoff scores on CDI that yield the maximum accuracy, 71 percent of children were accurately classified as depressed or nondepressed. A sensitivity rate of 54 percent means that 46 percent of children diagnosed as depressed were not classified as depressed by the CDI. Lobovits and Handal (1985), using optimal cutoff scores on CDI, report sensitivity of 76 percent and overall classification accuracy of 88 percent with an outpatient sample of children ages 8 to 12. Finally, Kazdin, Colbus, & Rodgers (1986) report sensitivity to be 61 percent and overall accuracy of 59 percent with severely disturbed inpatient children.

Although the use of the CDI by itself yields relatively poor concordance with psychiatric diagnoses of depression, when used with other child-completed and parent-completed questionnaires, the CDI improved diagnostic accuracy above that yielded by reliance only on parent-completed scales (Kazdin, Colbus, & Rodgers, 1986). The authors concluded that the use of multiple measures from one source (i.e., children or a parent) does not greatly enhance classification accuracy for depression over that achieved by single scales. However, the use of a battery of child- and parent-completed scales can yield a relatively high degree of classification accuracy.

Children's Action Tendency Scale

The Children's Action Tendency Scale (CATS) (Deluty, 1979) measures a child's tendency to respond aggressively, assertively, or submissively in interpersonal conflict situations. Assertion is defined as the ability to express in a nonhostile manner thoughts and feelings while not violating the rights of others. Unassertive behavior can take one of two forms: aggression or submission. In developing the CATS, Deluty took care to "unbind" aggression from assertion. Toward this end, Deluty employed a forced-choice pair comparison format. The CATS consists of 13 items. Each item presents an interpersonal conflict and three pairs of responses to that conflict. From each pair, the child selects the response that best characterizes what he or she would typically do in that situation. Each of three responses (aggressive, assertive, and submissive) is paired with each of the other two responses. The item format is illustrated by the following item.

> You're standing in line for a drink of water. A kid your age and size walks over and just shoves you out of line. What would you do?
>
> (a) Push the kid back out of line.
> (b) Tell them, "You've no right to do that."
>
> (a) Go to the end of the line.
> (b) Push the kid back out of line.
>
> (a) Tell them, "You've no right to do that."
> (b) Go to the end of the line. (Deluty, 1979).

The CATS yields three subscores: aggressive, assertive, and submissive. Reported test-retest, split-half and internal consistency reliability coefficients indicate moderately high reliability (Deluty, 1979; 1981a,b; Scanlon & Ollendick, 1986). Because the CATS attempts to measure a child's assertive behaviors, CATS scores should correspond with others' reports of aggressive, assertive, and submissive behaviors or with naturalistic observation of behavior. Evidence suggests CATS scores are correlated with teachers' and peers' perceptions of aggressive behaviors (Deluty, 1979; Scanlon & Ollendick, 1986). Although the CATS is successful at unbinding aggressive from assertive children, it is less successful at separating submissive and assertive children (Scanlon & Ollendick, 1986). Therefore, the CATS is useful in identifying aggressive children and in selecting conflict situations to which a child reports responding aggressively.

Self-Efficacy and Outcome Expectancy Questionnaires

Two scales developed by Ollendick and his colleagues (Ollendick, 1984; Ollendick, Oswald, & Crowe, 1986; Ollendick, Crowe, & Oswald, 1986) exemplify self-report questionnaires that attempt to assess children's situationally specific beliefs assumed to mediate their social behaviors. Both the Self-Efficacy Scale for Social Skills in Children and the Outcome Expectancy Questionnaire (Experimental Scale) are explicitly based on Bandura's social learning theory. Self-efficacy is defined as a person's expectation that he or she can perform the specific behaviors required for a desired outcome. Self-efficacy expectancy can be distinguished from outcome expectancy, defined as the person's belief that a specific behavior will, in fact, lead to a certain outcome (i.e., reinforcement). A person might believe a certain response would lead to a positive outcome but have little confidence that he or she could perform the specific required behaviors. Alternatively, a person might believe he or she could successfully perform specific behaviors but believe those behaviors would not result in positive reinforcement or would result in punishment. Tables 3.3 and 3.4 present the first four items from both the Self-Efficacy Scale and the Outcome Expectancy Questionnaire. The Self-Efficacy Scale is moderately reliable (alpha coefficient = 0.75). Test-retest coefficients for periods of over 6 months and 1 year are low ($r = 0.37$ and 0.32, respectively; Ollendick, Oswald, & Crowe, 1986). There are no published data on the reliability of the Outcome Expectancy Scale. Scores on the Self-Efficacy and Outcome Expectancy Scales are strongly positively related ($r = 0.61$; Ollendick, Crowe, & Oswald, 1986), suggesting the constructs are not independent. To date, only limited data on validity are available. In an initial validation study, children nominated by teachers as withdrawn scored significantly lower on the Self-Efficacy Scale than did children nominated as aggressive or popular (Ollendick, Crowe, & Oswald, 1986). Also, aggressive and withdrawn children had significantly lower expectancies that social behaviors would result in positive outcomes.

Table 3.3. Example Items from the Children's Self-Efficacy Questionnaire for Social Skills

DIRECTIONS: Listed below are a number of situations in which you might find yourself. First, indicate whether or not you would be able to do what is asked of you, *if you tried your best*. Then, indicate how sure you are of being able to do it. There are no right or wrong answers.

1. Can you start up a conversation with someone your age whom you have just met?

yes _____ no _____

How sure are you that you could start up the conversation?

1	2	3	4	5
Not sure at all	Probably not	Maybe	Probably	Really sure

2. When someone your age wants you to do something that you do not want to do, can you tell them you do not want to do it?

yes _____ no _____

How sure are you that you could tell them "no"?

1	2	3	4	5
Not sure at all	Probably not	Maybe	Probably	Really sure

3. Can you go up to a group of children your age who are playing a game and ask them if you can play with them?

yes _____ no _____

How sure are you that you could ask them if you could play with them?

1	2	3	4	5
Not sure at all	Probably not	Maybe	Probably	Really sure

4. When someone your age does a good job at something, can you tell them they did a good job and congratulate them?

yes _____ no _____

How sure are you that you could congratulate them?

1	2	3	4	5
Not sure at all	Probably not	Maybe	Probably	Really sure

Source: T. H. Ollendick, *The Children's Self Efficacy Questionnaire for Social Skills-Children(R)*. Unpublished test. Virginia Polytechnic Institute and State University, Blacksburg, Va. Adapted by permission.

Initial results of these two scales are promising. An important direction for future research on these scales is the role of self-efficacy and outcome expectancies as mediators of behavior change in social skills training studies (Ollendick, Oswald, & Crowe, 1986). Do children's self-efficacy and outcome expectancies change as a result of cognitive-behavioral interventions, and do these changes mediate improvement on other measures, such as social interaction, teacher ratings, and sociometric measures?

TASK PERFORMANCE MEASURES

A wide variety of tasks have been used to assess children's performance on specific cognitive skills. Because cognitive mediating processes of interest cannot be directly observed, a child's performance on tasks that are assumed to require the relevant skill is observed and scored. The most frequently used task performance measures in cognitive behavior therapy with children are the Matching Familiar Figures Test (MFFT; Kagan et al., 1964) and Shure and Spivack's (1972) children's Means-End Problem Solving (MEPS)

Table 3.4. Example Items from the Children's Outcome Expectancy Questionnaire (Experimental Scale)

DIRECTIONS: Listed below are a number of situations that you might find yourself in with other boys and girls. Read each situation first and then indicate whether the other child would do what you expected him or her to do. There are no right or wrong answers.

1. If you went up to someone your age whom you didn't know and said "Hi," will that child start to talk with you?

1	2	3	4	5
Definitely not	Probably not	Maybe	Probably so	Definitely so

2. If someone your age asks you to do something but you don't want to do it and so you say "no," will that child stop asking you and leave you alone?

1	2	3	4	5
Definitely not	Probably not	Maybe	Probably so	Definitely so

3. If you went up to a group of children your age who were playing a game and you asked if you could play with them, will they say "sure" and let you play with them?

1	2	3	4	5
Definitely not	Probably not	Maybe	Probably so	Definitely so

4. If you tell someone your age they did a good job, will they accept your compliment and say "thanks"?

1	2	3	4	5
Definitely not	Probably not	Maybe	Probably so	Definitely so

Source: T. H. Ollendick, *Children's Outcome Expectancy Questionnaire—Experimental Scale*. Unpublished test. Virginia Polytechnic Institute and State University, Blacksburg, Va. Adapted by permission.

Test. The MFFT, described in detail in chapter 8, is a 12-item match to sample task in which the child is shown a single picture of a familiar object and is instructed to select from an array of six variants the one picture that is identical to the stimulus picture. (Preschoolers choose from among four variants.) Two scores are obtained: the child's latency to respond and the total response errors. Children who have short latencies and high error scores are classified as cognitively impulsive. Sensitive to treatment effects, the MFFT is a frequently used outcome measure in intervention studies with distractible, impulsive, and non-self-controlled children. Kendall and Finch (1979), in a review of extensive research on the MFFT, conclude that latency scores have adequate test-retest reliability, but the test-retest reliability of error scores tends to be below acceptable standards, especially for impulsive children. The lack of temporal consistency is not completely unexpected, given the fact that impulsive and distractible children's performances are more variable. A revision of this test developed by Cairns and Cammock (1978) contains 20 items and is reported to have superior psychometric properties.

Means-end problem-solving is the ability to plan carefully, in sequential fashion, the step-by-step procedures or "means" necessary to reach a stated goal (Shure & Spivack, 1972). The original Children's Means-End Problem-Solving (MEPS) Test consists of six stories. An open-middle format is used, such that each story presents an initial interpersonal problem and the final outcome. The task is described as imaginative storytelling, and the child is asked to "fill in the middle of the story," including different ways the given solution could be reached. The story problems include getting even with another child who has said something nasty, being new in the neighborhood and making friends, successfully stealing a diamond from a store window, averting mother's anger for having broken her favorite flowerpot, earning money to buy mother a birthday present, and becoming the owner of a desired sportscar. A child's story completions are scored for the number of means, elaboration of specific means, perception of potential obstacles to carrying out means, and references to time in the problem-solving process.

The Children's MEPS, along with an adolescent and an adult version, is the topic of an extensive review by Butler and Meichenbaum (1981) and a review by Kendall, Pellegrini, and Urbain (1981). These reviewers conclude that the Children's MEPS has good interrater reliability, but test-retest reliability is somewhat lower than accepted standards. Considerable evidence supports the view that the Children's MEPS discriminates between populations of socially maladjusted and adjusted children even when group differences in IQ are statistically controlled (e.g., Shure & Spivack, 1972; Spivack, Platt, & Shure, 1976). Additionally, MEPS scores are sensitive to treatment effects (Larcen, reported in Allen, Chinsky, Larcen, Lochman, & Selinger, 1976).

One obstacle to evaluating the Children's MEPS is the modifications in the test made by various researchers (Allen et al., 1976; Gesten, de Apodaca, Rains, Weissberg, & Cowen, 1979; Lochman & Lampron, 1986; Lochman, Lampron, Burch, & Curry, 1985; McClure, Chinsky, & Larcen, 1978; Pellegrini, 1980; Urbain & Kendall, 1981).

These modifications have attempted to improve certain deficiencies in the MEPS. The newest generation of the open-middle problem-solving format is the Problem-Solving Measure for Conflict (PSMC; Lochman & Lampron, 1986). The PSMC scores the quality as well as the quantity of children's responses, employs more real-to-life story content, obtains separate scores for different interpersonal contexts (parents, teachers, and peers) as well as for the level of others' intent in conflicts (ambiguous or hostile provocation), and exclusively employs problems involving interpersonal conflict. Results document that nonaggressive boys produce more verbal assertive solutions in peer conflicts than do aggressive boys, and aggressive boys produce more direct action solutions with teachers. A discriminant analysis function based on PSMC scores correctly classified 78 percent of nonaggressive boys and 70 percent of aggressive boys, for an overall classification accuracy of 74 percent. Especially relevant to earlier criticism of the MEPS (Butler & Meichenbaum, 1981) are the findings of strong situational effects on problem-solving and the finding that aggressive and nonaggressive boys differ more in the type of solutions produced than in the total number of solutions.

A problem common to the MEPS and to other task performance measures that employ hypothetical-reflective methods is the difficulty of generalizing problem solving about hypothetical problems to real-life problem solving. Tests like the MEPS measure a child's problem-solving capabilities rather than actual problem-solving performance. There is a pressing need to examine the behavioral validity of these measures by relating test performance to naturalistic problem-solving performance (Butler & Meichenbaum, 1981).

SECTION II

COGNITIVE BEHAVIOR THERAPY WITH SPECIAL POPULATIONS

4
Children's School-Related Anxieties: An Overview

Fears and anxieties are a normal part of childhood and show clear developmental trends. Whereas fears of animals, personal injury, and supernatural beings are common in the preschool and early elementary years, fears related to social and academic performance take center stage from middle childhood through adolescence (Morris & Kratochwill, 1983). In a frequently cited study on the prevalence of children's fears, Lapouse and Monk (1959) found that parents of children between the ages of 6 and 12 years reported that 43 percent of their children experienced seven or more fears, with girls having more fears than boys. Children's fears are often transient in nature, and older children report having fewer fears (Morris & Kratochwill, 1983).

Because fears are a normal part of childhood, intervention is not necessary for most children's fears. In fact, fears may have a beneficial effect on children's development because fears provide children opportunities to develop coping mechanisms for dealing with future sources of stress and anxiety.

Some fears and anxieties do require intervention. Morris and Kratochwill (1983) recommend clinical intervention when a child's fear (a) is excessive, (b) has lasted a relatively long time, and (c) creates problems in living for the parents or child. Although these three criteria are not operationally defined, they provide a pragmatic set of guidelines for educators and clinicians who must decide whether or not treatment is indicated. Fears that meet these three criteria (intensity, chronicity, and interference) are referred to as clinical fears (or clinical anxiety) to distinguish them from the normal fears and anxieties of childhood.

Some clinical fears are referred to as phobias. The definition of phobia proposed by Miller, Barrett, and Hampe (1974) has received wide acceptance. A phobia is defined as a special form of fear that meets seven criteria:

1. It is out of proportion to the demands of the situation.
2. It cannot be explained or reasoned away.

3. It is beyond voluntary control.
4. It leads to avoidance of the feared situation.
5. It persists over an extended period of time.
6. It is unadaptive.
7. It is not age or stage specific (p. 90).

The terms anxiety and fear are often used interchangeably. Anxiety is used sometimes to refer to a trait ("she has an anxious personality") and sometimes to refer to a response to specific situations ("she is test anxious"). Consistent with the social learning theory of personality, anxiety is here viewed as a learned response to specific situations. Furthermore, anxiety consists of three response components, or channels, that are not highly correlated (Neitzel & Bernstein, 1981). These three channels are the cognitive, physiological, and motor systems. The cognitive channel refers to an individual's subjective, verbal experience. Fear surveys and interviews that ask children about their subjective experience of worry, anxiety, and fear assess the cognitive channel. Anxiety in the physiological channel is assessed by measures of autonomic nervous system activity, including measures of heart rate, galvanic skin response, temperature, and muscular tension. Additionally, individuals can verbally report on their physiological experiences of anxiety. For example, both the Revised Manifest Anxiety Scale (Reynolds & Richmond, 1978) and the Test Anxiety Scale for Children (Sarason, Davidson, Lighthall, Waite, & Ruebush, 1960) ask children to report on their physiological response ("When the teacher says she is going to find out how much you have learned, does your heart begin to beat faster?"). The motor, or behavioral, channel refers both to the observable behavioral consequences of physiological arousal (e.g., trembling) and to avoidance behaviors (turning away from the social initiation of a classmate).

Conceptualizing fear, anxieties, and phobias in terms of the three response channels directs attention to an individual's pattern of behavior in response to particular situations. As argued by Morris and Kratochwill (1983), defining children's fears in terms of these three response channels has important implications for assessment and treatment. When a child's fear is of clinical import, the child's individual response to the feared situation should be assessed in each system. Based on this assessment, treatment may be aimed at one or all of the different systems. Children who experience fear in different channels may respond differently to a given treatment. In the case of test anxiety, one child may worry a great deal during tests, engaging in self-preoccupied thinking. A second child may experience heightened autonomic nervous system arousal, with little subjective experience of anxiety or worry. A third child may avoid test-taking situations and the evaluative threat they represent by skipping class. Different treatments might be differentially effective with these three children.

Unfortunately, clinical researchers have not typically followed Morris and Kratochwill's (1983) recommendation. Instead, a child's anxieties and fears often are assessed in only one channel. Therefore, test anxiety is assessed in the cognitive channel with self-report measures, and social anxiety is assessed in the behavioral channel based on frequency of social interaction.

ANXIETIES, FEARS, AND PSYCHIATRIC DIAGNOSIS

According to the revised third edition of the *Diagnostic and Statistical Manual of Mental Disorders* (American Psychiatric Association, 1980), anxiety is the central symptom in three childhood psychiatric disorders: separation anxiety, avoidant disorder of childhood or adolescence, and overanxious disorder. In *separation anxiety disorder*, the predominant feature is excessive anxiety on separation from major attachment figures or from home or other familiar surroundings (American Psychiatric Association, 1987:58). The child's excessive anxiety concerning separation from attachment figures must be manifested by at least three of the following:

1. Unrealistic and persistent worry about possible harm befalling major attachment figures or fear that they will leave and not return.
2. Unrealistic and persistent worry that an untoward calamitous event will separate the child from a major attachment figure, e.g., the child will be lost, kidnapped, killed, or an accident victim.
3. Persistent reluctance or refusal to go to school in order to stay with major attachment figures or at home.
4. Persistent reluctance or refusal to go to sleep without being next to a major attachment figure or to go to sleep away from home.
5. Persistent avoidance of being alone in the home and emotional upset if unable to follow the major attachment figure around the home.
6. Repeated nightmares involving theme of separation.
7. Complaints of physical symptoms on school days, e.g., stomach aches, headaches, nausea, and vomiting.
8. Recurrent signs or complaints of excessive distress in anticipation of separation from home or major attachment figures, e.g., temper tantrums or crying, pleading with parents not to leave.
9. Recurrent signs of complaints of excessive distress when separated from home or major attachment figures (p. 61).

In *avoidant disorder of childhood or adolescence,* the central feature is a persistent and excessivc shrinking from contact with strangers of sufficient severity so as to interfere with social functioning in peer relationships, coupled with a clear desire for affection and acceptance, and relationships with family members and other familiar figures that are warm and satisfying (p. 61). School phobia is a type of avoidant disorder. Although children with avoidant disorders rarely initiate social interaction and may avoid the initiations of others, they appear to desire social relationships. Timidity and acute embarrassment prevent the child from seeking out social relationships.

Although the anxiety in avoidant disorder and overanxious disorder is somewhat focused on specific objects or situations, anxiety in overanxious disorder is relatively diffuse. The child worries about "future events such as examinations, the possibility of injury, or inclusion in peer group activities; or about meeting expectations, such as deadlines, keeping appointments, or performing chores" (p. 63). The anxiety is often expressed as concern with competence and, more specifically, with the possibility of negative performance evaluations of others, particularly persons in authority. The child may complain of feeling nervous in a variety of school situations and report somatic complaints such as dizziness, headache, nausea, shortness of breath, and gastrointestinal distress. These children tend to be described by teachers as perfectionistic. Even though the child's performance may be average or above average, the child is plagued by self-doubts and performance worries.

A child may demonstrate symptoms characteristic of all three disorders, and differential diagnosis is often problematic. Therefore, these diagnoses, although important for certain research and applied purposes, do not assist very much in designing interventions for children with clinical fears and anxieties. Describing a child's pattern of response in the cognitive, physiological, and motor channels to certain situations or objects has more clinical utility.

SCHOOL STRESS AND ANXIETY

Consistent with the focus of this book, the following two chapters focus on children's school-related anxieties and fears. In this regard, researchers have identified two major types of school stress: social and academic (Phillips, 1978). The two major self-report measures of school anxiety, the School Anxiety Scale (SAS; Phillips, 1978) and the Test Anxiety Scale for Children (TASC; Sarason et al., 1960), include items related to both social and academic stressors. Both scales have similar factor structures (Phillips, 1978). Phillips labeled these factors fear of assertiveness and self-expression, test anxiety, lack of confidence in meeting expectations of others, and physiologic reactivity associated with low tolerance of stress. Because the SAS and the TASC are multidimensional and emphasize situational factors in school anxiety, they are especially useful in efforts to assess the nature of children's school-related anxieties. Both of these tests are discussed in greater detail in the next two chapters. Chapter 5 reviews assessment and intervention procedures with socially anxious children, whereas chapter 6 focuses on text anxiety in children. Finally, a third category of school-related fears, school phobia, is also discussed in chapter 6.

5
Social Anxiety

COGNITIVE-BEHAVIORAL ASSESSMENT PROCEDURES WITH SOCIALLY ANXIOUS CHILDREN

Clinical concern for the socially withdrawn, shy child is based on research supporting the view that satisfactory peer relationships in childhood are crucial to the development of adequate social relationships in later adolescence and adulthood (Hops & Greenwood, in press). Children who interact infrequently with peers miss important opportunities to develop social skills, including social-cognitive and moral reasoning skills. Socially isolated children tend to be depressed and lonely and perform less well in school (Green, Forehand, Beck, & Vosk, 1980).

Children who engage in low rates of peer interaction are sometimes referred to as socially anxious. However, there are several competing explanations for the child's low rate of social participation that must be considered before a determination of social anxiety is warranted. For example, the child may lack the social behaviors or skills necessary to initiate or maintain social participation, or both. Consider a girl who joins in social activities but in an abrasive, disruptive manner that causes the other children to reject her. The girl ends up spending much time alone, not because she avoids social interaction but because she is purposefully excluded by her classmates. Alternatively, a "withdrawn" child may not be motivated to engage in social interaction. The child feels no threat inherent in social participation, such as the threat of embarrassment or social rejection. Rather, the child is not peer-oriented and does not value social interaction, at least not with the particular social group with which he or she infrequently interacts. Finally, a child may be eager for social interaction, skillful, and not timid, but the social group excludes the child because of some attribute (e.g., appearance, ethnicity, or handicap) the group devalues. In this case, the problem lies within the situation instead of within the child.

As these examples illustrate, social anxiety cannot be defined strictly in terms of the rate of interaction. Neither can it be defined in terms of peer acceptance. A child who receives no or few nominations from peers as "best friend" or "likes most" is termed a sociometric isolate. Sociometric isolates may be socially anxious and avoid social participation. Alternatively, a child may be ignored by his or her classmates for reasons other than the child's social anxiety and avoidant behavior. The view that the peer group contributes to the maintenance of isolate status is supported by the finding that many neglected children (children who receive no or few positive or negative nominations in a sociometric procedure) lose their neglected status when they change peer groups (Coie & Dodge, 1983).

Therefore, in order to distinguish the socially anxious child from children whose peer relationship problems are a result of causes other than anxiety, behavioral observations and sociometric procedures need to be combined with a child interview and self-report measures. Next, these specific assessment procedures are discussed.

Sociometric Assessment

Sociometric assessment of children's social competence has been the topic of several recent reviews (Asher & Hymel, 1981; Hops & Greenwood, in press; Hughes, in press-a). The most common sociometric procedure is peer nomination. In this procedure, each child in a classroom is asked to select a restricted number of classmates with respect to a given criterion. Positive criteria include "like the most," "best friend," and "like the most to play with." Negative criteria include "like the least" and "like least to play with." A child's score is the number of nominations received. Positive nomination scores are considered an index of the child's popularity, or peer acceptance. Negative nominations are an index of the child's rejection. Positive and negative scores are only moderately negatively correlated (Gottman, 1977; Hymel & Asher, 1977; Landau, Milich, & Whitten, 1984) or not at all (Hartup, Glazer, & Charlesworth, 1967). Thus, positive and negative nominations measure different dimensions of social competence. When only positive nominations are used, it is not possible to distinguish between two types of unpopular children, neglected and rejected children. Both types of children receive few positive nominations. The neglected child also receives few negative nominations, whereas the rejected child receives many negative nominations. The rejected child is at greater risk for later maladjustment than is the neglected child (Kendall & Morrison, 1984). The socially neglected child appears shy, timid, and withdrawn, but the rejected child is socially active and has a disruptive and aggressive impact on the peer group (Coie & Dodge, 1983). Evidence of behavior differences between rejected and neglected children (Coie, Dodge, & Coppotelli, 1982; Dodge, Schlundt, Schocken, & Delugach, 1983) as well as evidence that rejected status is more stable (Coie & Dodge, 1983) supports the combined use of positive and negative nominations for unbinding these two types of unpopular children. These behavioral differences also suggest that different interventions may be differentially effective with neglected and rejected children.

Several researchers have developed classification systems based on positive and negative nominations (Coie et al., 1982; Gronlund, 1959; Peery, 1979). Strong evidence of concurrent and predictive validity, as well as long-term stability, has accumulated for the system developed by Coie and his associates. According to this classification system, which refines a system proposed by Peery (1979), two new sociometric scores are derived from the like most and like least nomination scores. Raw score nominations for like most (LM) and like least (LL) are standardized within classrooms. These standard scores (Z scores) are used to generate social preference ($Z_{LM} - Z_{LL}$) and social impact ($Z_{LM} + Z_{LL}$) scores. The derived social impact and social preference scores are used to identify children for five distinct social status groups (i.e., popular, average, controversial, neglected, and rejected; see Coie et al., 1982, for classification formulas). The neglected group consists of all children who receive a social impact score of less than −1.0 and like most and like least standard scores of less than 0.

In a 5-year longitudinal study of the stability of these classifications, the neglected status was the least stable (Coie & Dodge, 1983). During the elementary and junior high school years, only 25 percent of neglected children remain neglected over a 1-year period. This figure is 27 percent for a 2-year interval, 22 percent after 3 years, and 24 percent after 4 years.

An alternative to peer nominations for identifying shy children is the peer behavioral description procedure. In this procedure, children are provided descriptions of children's social behavior and asked to name classmates who best fit each of these descriptions. Coie and Dodge (1983) asked third and fifth graders to nominate three children who fit the shy behavior description: "this person acts very shy with other kids, seems always to play or work by themselves. It's hard to get to know this person" (p. 266). A child's shy score is the number of persons writing his or her name next to the shy description. Year-to-year correlations document an increase in the stability of children's shy status as they grow older (correlation coefficient is 0.35 for grades 3 and 4, 0.45 for grades 4 and 5, 0.65 for grades 5 and 6, 0.54 for grades 6 and 7, and 0.85 for grades 8 and 9). One implication of these data is the importance of intervention in the early school years, before shy behavior becomes more stable (or before peers' perceptions of the shy child become solidified).

Rating scales offer yet another alternative to the peer nomination sociometric procedure. In the roster and rating sociometric procedure, each child in a classroom is presented with an alphabetized class roster. Next to each child's name is a 5- or 7-point Likert scale. The respondent is asked to rate his or her degree of liking for each person on the roster. The child's score is the average of all the ratings he or she receives. When used with preschool or kindergarten children, the child rates his or her degree of liking by assigning photographs of classmates to boxes represented by one of three faces: happy face (children you like a lot), neutral face (children you kind of like), and a sad face (children you do not like). Ratings are more stable than nomination scores (Asher, Singleton, Tinsley, & Hymel, 1979) and minimize the ethical concerns associated with a negative nomination question (Asher & Hymel, 1981). Although ratings and nominations are significantly correlated (Asher et al., 1979; Hughes & Hall, 1985), they measure different aspects of sociometric relationships. Ratings tend to measure peer acceptance or likability, whereas nominations measure friendship patterns (Schofield & Whitley, 1983). In assessing the shy and socially neglected child, ratings are less useful than combined positive and negative nominations or behavioral descriptions because ratings do not discriminate between rejected and neglected children. When concerns are raised about asking children to list names of children they do not like, a procedure based on ratings and positive nominations, developed by Asher and Dodge (1986), can discriminate between rejected and neglected children. According to this procedure, a rating of 1 on a 1 to 5 rating scale is treated as if it were a negative nomination. Social preference and social impact scores are then computed using the Coie et al. (1982) system. The Asher and Dodge procedure yields results very similar to the classifications yielded by the use of positive and negative nominations. Although agreement between the two methods is particularly high for rejected children, it is less accurate in classifying neglected children.

Behavior Ratings

Behavior rating scales and checklists of children's social behaviors are the topic of several recent reviews (Asher & Hymel, 1981; Cartledge & Milburn, 1986; Hops & Greenwood, in press; Hughes, in press-a). Teacher rating scales are economical, easy to administer and score, and demonstrate adequate test-retest and interrater reliability (Bolstad & Johnson, 1977; Connolly & Doyle, 1981). With respect to validity, teacher ratings of social behavior predict direct behavior observations, diagnostic classifications, and peer sociometric measures (Hughes, in press-a). Limitations of ratings include their inability to specify problem behaviors or skilled behaviors and inadequate opportunities for teachers in the upper grades to observe those social interactions crucial to peer acceptance and possible rater bias (Hughes, in press-a).

One teacher rating scale is specific to the assessment of social withdrawal (Hops et al., 1978). The Social Interaction Rating Scale (SIRS) is an 8-item scale developed as part of the PEERS (Procedures for Establishing Effective Relationship Skills) program for withdrawn children (Hops et al., 1978). A score of 28 or less (Table 5.1) successfully discriminated between children

Table 5.1. Items on the Social Interaction Rating Scale (SIRS; Hops et al., 1978)

Child's Name________________ Teacher________________
School________________ Grade________________
Date________________ Consultant________________

	not descriptive or true			moderately descriptive or true			very descriptive or true
1. Verbally responds to a child's initiation.	1	2	3	4	5	6	7
2. Engages in long conversations (more than 30 seconds).	1	2	3	4	5	6	7
3. Shares laughter with classmates.	1	2	3	4	5	6	7
4. Spontaneously contributes during a group discussion.	1	2	3	4	5	6	7
5. Volunteers for "show and tell."	1	2	3	4	5	6	7
6. Freely takes a leadership role.	1	2	3	4	5	6	7
7. Spontaneously works with a peer(s) on projects in class.	1	2	3	4	5	6	7
8. Verbally initiates to a peer(s).	1	2	3	4	5	6	7
	TOTAL SCORE:						

Source: H. Hops, D. H. Fleischman, J. Guild, S. Paine, H. Street, H. M. Walker, and C. P. Greenwood, *Program for Establishing Effective Relationship Skills (PEERS): Consultant Manual*, 1978, Eugene, Oregon: Center at Oregon for Research in the Behavioral Education of the Handicapped. Reprinted by permission.

referred for social withdrawal and their normal nonreferred classmates with a 90 percent correct classification rate. Furthermore, scale items were found to correlate significantly with observed time engaged in social behavior during recess.

More general teacher rating scales that include a withdrawal subscale score are the Social Competence Schedule (Kohn, 1977) for use with preschool and primary grade children, the Child Behavior Checklist—Teacher Report Form (CBCL; Achenbach & Edelbrock, 1983), and the Walker Problem Behavior Identification Checklist (WPBIC; Walker, 1976). The WPBIC correlates with observed interaction rates (Greenwood, Walker, Todd, & Hops, 1979) and has been sensitive in a treatment program for socially withdrawn children (Weinrott, Corson, & Wilchesky, 1979). Asking teachers to rank children on frequency of peer verbal interaction is a reliable and valid procedure for identifying the least socially responsive child in preschool classrooms (Greenwood et al., 1979).

Teacher ratings and rankings of social participation will identify not only the socially anxious child but also children whose low rates of social interaction are a result of other causes, such as delayed language skills or lack of interest in social participation. Like sociometric procedures, teacher ratings are best used as a screening measure to identify children who are experiencing peer relationship problems. Additional assessment data are necessary to specify the nature of the child's problem. In this regard, self-report data are critical to the assessment of the socially anxious child.

Self-Report

Because the child is the expert on his or her subjective experience of anxiety, the child's self-report is essential to the assessment of the shy, socially anxious child. Assessment generally proceeds from broad-band, low fidelity instruments to narrow-band high fidelity ones. Self-report assessment of the socially anxious child might begin with a general measure of anxiety, followed by more specific measures. The Revised Child Manifest Anxiety Scale (RCMAS; Reynolds & Richmond, 1978), a revision of the Children's Manifest Anxiety Scale (CMAS; Castaneda, McCandless, & Palermo, 1956), is a general measure of a child's chronic state of anxiety. The RCMAS differs from the CMAS in specific item content, ordering of items, and new norms. Items for the RCMAS are reported in Table 5.2. Recently, Reynolds and Paget (1982) presented national norms and reliability data for the RCMAS. Published data on the validity of the RCMAS include evidence of content (Reynolds & Richmond, 1978) concurrent (Reynolds, 1980), construct (Reynolds & Richmond, 1978), and predictive validity (Reynolds, 1981). Factor analytic studies of the RCMAS (Reynolds and Paget, 1981) yield three anxiety factors: physiological, worry/oversensitivity, and concentration. An interesting characteristic of the scale is the provision of a lie scale. In summary, the RCMAS appears to be a reliable and valid measure of chronic, general anxiety (trait anxiety). However, the scale does not identify situations that are anxiety-provoking for a child. Therefore it is useful for diagnosis (e.g., that of overanxious disorder) but not for identifying the sources of stress and anxiety or the individual's pattern of response to anxiety.

Items on both the School Anxiety Scale (SAS; Phillips, 1978) and the Test Anxiety Scale for Children (TASC; Sarason et al., 1960) are more situationally specific. As indicated in chapter 4, the factor structure of these measures is similar. Twenty-six of the 30 items of the TASC are included in the SAS. These 26 items are identified by an asterisk in Table 5.3, which lists the 74 items of the SAS. Items 47, 48, 57, 61, 64, and 74 had the highest loadings on the factor identified as Fear of Assertiveness and Self-Expression, the factor most relevant to the assessment of social anxiety in children.

The SAS has adequate internal consistency (KR-21 coefficient values of 0.95 or higher) and test-retest reliabilities of 0.50 to 0.67 for intervals up to 2 years (Phillips, 1978). Evidence of concurrent and construct validity for the SAS is good (Phillips, 1978).

The RCMAS, SAS, and TASC are measures of children's self-reported anxieties. Two additional self-report measures that are especially relevant to the assessment of social anxiety measure children's perceptions of their peer relationships. The Loneliness Scale (Asher, Hymel, & Renshaw, 1984) assesses a child's perceived loneliness. Table 5.4 lists the 24 items that

Table 5.2. Items on the Revised Children's Manifest Anxiety Scale

1. I have trouble making up my mind.
2. I get nervous when things do not go the right way for me.
3. Others seem to do things easier than I can.
4. I like everyone I know.
5. Often I have trouble getting my breath.
6. I worry a lot of the time.
7. I am afraid of a lot of things.
8. I am always kind.
9. I get mad easily.
10. I worry about what my parents will say to me.
11. I feel that others do not like the way I do things.
12. I always have good manners.
13. It is hard for me to get to sleep at night.
14. I worry about what other people think about me.
15. I feel alone even when there are people with me.
16. I am always good.
17. Often I feel sick in my stomach.
18. My feelings get hurt easily.
19. My hands feel sweaty.
20. I am always nice to everyone.
21. I am tired a lot.
22. I worry about what is going to happen.
23. Other children are happier than I.
24. I tell the truth every single time.
25. I have bad dreams.
26. My feelings get hurt easily when I am fussed at.
27. I feel someone will tell me I do things the wrong way.
28. I never get angry.
29. I wake up scared some of the time.
30. I worry when I go to bed at night.
31. It is hard for me to keep my mind on my school work.
32. I never say things I shouldn't.
33. I wiggle in my seat a lot.
34. I am nervous.
35. A lot of people are against me.
36. I never lie.
37. I often worry about something bad happening to me.

Source: C. R. Reynolds and K. D. Paget, "Factor Analysis of the Revised Children's Manifest Anxiety Scale for Blacks, Whites, Males, and Females with a national normative sample," 1981, *Journal of Consulting and Clinical Psychology, 49*, 352–359. Copyright 1981 by the American Psychological Association. Reprinted by permission.

comprise this scale, including 8 items pertaining to the child's hobbies or interests that are not included in computing a child's score. Scores on the Loneliness Scale correlate significantly with peer nomination scores. Therefore, scores on the loneliness scale may be a useful substitute for peer sociometrics when sociometric assessment is impractical.

Socially anxious children lack self-confidence that they can successfully engage in social interactions and they tend to attribute successful social outcomes to external causes (e.g., luck) and unsuccessful outcomes to their social incompetence (Goetz & Dweck, 1980; Ames, Ames, & Garrison,

Table 5.3. Items on the School Anxiety Scale

1.* Do you worry when the teacher says that she is going to ask you questions to find out how much you know? (2)
2.* Do you sometimes dream at night that you did poorly on a test you had in school that day?
3.* Do you worry a lot *while* you are taking a test? (2)
4. Is it hard for you to do well as the teacher expects you to do in class? (3)
5.* Do you sometimes dream at night that the teacher is angry because you do not know your lessons? (4)
6. Do you often have the fear that other children might think you dumb?
7. Do you usually feel nervous when speaking to the principal?
8. Are you sometimes afraid of expressing yourself in class because you think you might make a foolish mistake? (3)
9. Are you often worried that the teacher will scold or punish you?
10. When it is your turn to get up and recite in class, do you feel your heart pounding hard?
11.* When you are at home and you are thinking about your arithmetic lesson for the next day, do you become afraid that you will get the answers wrong when the teacher calls upon you?
12.* Do you worry about being promoted, that is, passing from the ____ grade to the ____ grade at the end of the year? (2)
13.* Do you worry a lot *before* you take a test? (2)
14.* Do you think you worry more about school than other children?
15.* *After* you have taken a test, do you worry about how well you did on the test? (2)
16.* If you did very poorly when the teacher called on you, would you feel like crying, even though you would try not to cry?
17. Do you ever worry about knowing your lessons?
18.* When the teacher asks you to get up in front of the class and read aloud, are you afraid that you are going to make some bad mistake?
19. Do your knees shake when you are asked to recite in class? (4)
20. Do you sometimes have a fear of fainting in class? (4)
21.* When you are home and you are thinking about your reading lesson for the next day, do you worry that you will do poorly on the lesson?
22. Do you sometimes shake all over when you are asked to recite in class? (4)
23. When the teacher fails to notice and comment on your work, does it make you unhappy?
24.* When you are in bed at night, do you sometimes worry about how you are going to do in class the next day?
25. Does your teacher sometimes give you a lower grade than you think you deserve?
26. Do you always feel uncomfortable when you do not know what is expected of you in class?
27.* Do you sometimes dream at night that you are in school and cannot answer the teacher's questions? (4)
28. Does your voice sometimes shake when you are asked to recite in class?
29. Is it hard for you to tell someone you're scared?
30. Do you have a hard time keeping up with the other students in class? (3)
31. If anything happens that tends to make you look foolish, do you tend to think about it for a long time afterwards?
32. Do you worry that you might forget your lines when you recite a poem in front of the class?
33. Do some of your friends think you are a sissy because you make good grades?
34. Do you dread choosing up sides to play games because you are usually one of the last ones chosen? (3)
35. Do you ever worry about something bad happening to someone you know?
36.* When you are taking a hard test, do you forget some things you knew very well before you started taking the test?
37. Do you wish a lot of times that you didn't worry so much about a test? (2)
38.* When you are taking a test, does the hand you write with shake a little?
39. Have you ever been afraid of getting hurt?
40. Do the students that do poorly on the tests that the teacher gives lose the approval of the teacher?
41. If you think someone doesn't like you, does it bother you?
42. When someone is slow, does it bother you; or does it not bother you?
43. When you've done something wrong, is it hard for you to say you're sorry?
44. Do you sometimes worry about being different from many of the children in your class?
45. Do you usually feel awkward meeting new students who have just come into the class?
46.* When the teacher says that she is going to find out how much you have learned, does your heart begin to beat faster? (4)
47. Are you sometimes afraid of getting into arguments? (1)
48. Do some children in the class say things to hurt your feelings? (1)

Table 5.3. *continued*

49. Does it seem like most of the children in the class never pay any attention to you?
50.* When the teacher says that she is going to give the class a test, do you get a nervous or funny feeling?
51. Do you dislike reciting in class because you might make a mistake and others would laugh at you?
52. Do you ever worry about what is going to happen?
53. When one of our friends won't play with you, do you feel badly?
54. Is it hard for you to have as good a report card as your parents expect you to have? (3)
55. Do some children in the class seem to get angry when you do better than they do?
56. Are you afraid that other children will laugh at you when you show your work to them?
57. Are you frequently afraid you may make a fool of yourself? (1)
58.* Are you afraid of school tests?
59.* When the teacher says that she is going to give the class a test, do you become afraid that you will do poorly?
60. Do you worry a lot about your school work because you are afraid your parents might find out you are not doing as well as they expect you to do?
61. Do you ever worry about what people think of you? (1)
62. Do you feel nervous if the whole class watches you when you are making something?
63.* Do you sometimes dream at night that other boys and girls in your class can do things that you cannot do?
64. Do your classmates sometimes make fun of the way you look and talk? (1)
65. Do you feel nervous when others look at work you have done?
66.* When the teacher is teaching you about reading, do you feel that other children in the class understand her better than you?
67.* While you are on your way to school do you sometimes worry that the teacher may give the class a test?
68. Do you ever worry that you won't be able to do something that you want to do?
69. Are you often worried that you might be sick in class?
70.* While you are taking a test do you usually think you are doing poorly?
71.* When the teacher asks you to write on the blackboard in front of the class, does the hand you write with sometimes shake a little?
72. Do you feel cross and grouchy sometimes?
73. In your school work, do you often forget; or do you feel sure you can remember things? (3)
74. When you recite in class do you often wonder what others are thinking of you? (1)

Source: B. N. Phillips, *School Stress and Anxiety: Theory, Research, and Intervention* (pp. 20–23), 1978, New York: Human Sciences Press. Copyright 1978 by Human Sciences Press. Adapted by permission.
Note: Items of the school anxiety factor marked with an asterisk are in the TASC, and the six items representing each of the factorial dimensions of school anxiety are identified by the numbers in parentheses, with the factors marked as follows: 1 = Fear of Assertiveness and Self-Expression; 2 = Test Anxiety; 3 = Lack of Confidence in Meeting Expectations of Others; and 4 = Physiological Reactivity Associated with Low Tolerance of Stress.

1977). Furthermore, Goetz and Dweck (1980) found that children who attribute social rejection to internal, stable characteristics (e.g., "It's hard for me to make friends") are less likely to persist in a social exchange following an intitial rejection. Thus, assessment of the socially anxious child should include an assessment of the child's self-efficacy for social interaction and attributions for social outcomes.

The Children's Self-Efficacy for Peer Interaction Scale (CSPIS; Wheeler & Ladd, 1982) assesses a child's beliefs about his or her ability to use verbal persuasion to influence others or to participate in social activities. Each item consists of a statement describing a social situation ("You want to start a game"), followed by an incomplete statement requiring the child to evaluate his or her ability to perform a verbal persuasive skill in that situation ("Asking other kids to play is ______ for you."). For each item, children circle one of four response choices: HARD! (1), hard (2), easy (3), or

Table 5.4. Items on the Loneliness Scale (Asher, Hymel, & Renshaw, 1984)

1. It's easy for me to make new friends at school.
2. I like to read.
†3. I have nobody to talk to.
4. I'm good at working with other children.
*5. I watch TV at lot.
†6. It's hard for me to make friends.
*7. I like school.
8. I have lots of friends.
†9. I feel alone.
10. I can find a friend when I need one.
*11. I play sports a lot.
†12. It's hard to get other kids to like me.
*13. I like science.
†14. I don't have anyone to play with.
*15. I like music.
16. I get along with other kids.
†17. I feel left out of things.
†18. There's nobody I can go to when I need help.
*19. I like to paint and draw.
†20. I don't get along with other children.
†21. I'm lonely.
22. I am well-liked by the kids in my class.
*23. I like playing board games a lot.
†24. I don't have any friends.

*Hobby or interest item.
†Items for which response order was reversed in scoring.
Source: S. R. Asher, S. Hymel, and P. R. Renshaw, "Loneliness in Children," 1984, *Child Development, 55*, 1457. Copyright 1984 by the Society for Research in Child Development. Adapted by permission.

EASY! (4). Table 5.5 includes items on the CSPIS. The CSPIS is an internally consistent and reliable measure with an alpha coefficient of 0.85 for the total scale and test-retest coefficients over a 2-week period of 0.90 for boys and 0.80 for girls. Evidence of the scale's concurrent validity is supported by several findings. The strongest correlations between scores and factors on the Piers-Harris Self-Concept Scale (Piers & Harris, 1964) were with the anxiety factor, with a correlation of −0.41 for the total sample of children in the third to fifth grades. Therefore, children who lack confidence in their social abilities report more anxiety. CSPIS scores also correlated significantly with peer ratings of social influence, "play with" nominations, and teacher ratings of social efficacy.

A final self-report measure helpful in the assessment of the socially anxious child is the Peer Preference Test (Evers-Pasquale, 1978), a measure of the reward value of peers to children. Children who are socially anxious desire social interaction, but their shyness and anxiety prevent them from active social participation. The Peer Preference Test can help distinguish between the shy child and the child whose social withdrawal is a result of a lack of interest in social participation. The importance of considering the reward value of peers to withdrawn children is illustrated in a study by

Table 5.5. The Children's Self-Efficacy Scale (Wheeler and Ladd, 1982)

Instructions:
For each question, circle how difficult it is for you to do what is asked.

* * * * * *

1. Some kids want to play a game. Asking them if you can play is _____ for you.	HARD! hard easy EASY!
2. Some kids are arguing about how to play a game. Telling them the rules is _____ for you.	HARD! hard easy EASY!
3. Some kids are teasing your friend. Telling them to stop is _____ for you.	HARD! hard easy EASY!
4. You want to start a game. Asking other kids to play the game is _____ for you.	HARD! hard easy EASY!
5. A kid tries to take your turn during a game. Telling the kid it's your turn is _____ for you.	HARD! hard easy EASY!
6. Some kids are going to lunch. Asking if you can sit with them is _____ for you.	HARD! hard easy EASY!
7. A kid cuts in front of you in line. Telling the kid not to cut in is _____ for you.	HARD! hard easy EASY!
8. A kid wants to do something that will get you into trouble Asking the kid to do something else is _____ for you.	HARD! hard easy EASY!
9. Some kids are making fun of someone in your classroom. Telling them to stop is _____ for you.	HARD! hard easy EASY!
10. Some kids need more people to be on their teams. Asking to be on a team is _____ for you.	HARD! hard easy EASY!
11. You have to carry some things home after school. Asking another kid to help you is _____ for you.	HARD! hard easy EASY!
12. A kid always wants to be first when you play a game. Telling the kid you are going first is _____ for you.	HARD! hard easy EASY!
13. Your class is going on a trip and everyone needs a partner. Asking someone to be your partner is _____ for you.	HARD! hard easy EASY!
14. A kid does not like your friend. Telling the kid to be nice to your friend is _____ for you.	HARD! hard easy EASY!
15. Some kids are deciding what game to play. Telling them about a game you like is _____ for you.	HARD! hard easy EASY!
16. You are having fun playing a game but the other kids want to stop. Asking them to keep playing is _____ for you.	HARD! hard easy EASY!
17. You are working on a project. Asking another kid to help is _____ for you.	HARD! hard easy EASY!
18. Some kids are using your play area. Asking them to move is _____ for you.	HARD! hard easy EASY!
19. Some kids are deciding what to do after school. Telling them what you want to do is _____ for you.	HARD! hard easy EASY!
20. A group of kids wants to play a game that you don't like Asking them to play a game you like is _____ for you.	HARD! hard easy EASY!
21. Some kids are planning a party. Asking them to invite your friend is _____ for you.	HARD! hard easy EASY!
22. A kid is yelling at you. Telling the kid to stop is _____ for you.	HARD! hard easy EASY!

Source: V. A. Wheeler and G. W. Ladd, "Assessment of Children's Self-Efficacy for Social Interactions with Peers," 1982, *Developmental Psychology, 18,* 798.

Evers-Pasquale and Sherman (1975). They found that withdrawn preschool children's scores on the Peer Preference Test predicted the efficacy of a filmed modeling intervention designed to increase the frequency of social interaction. Children were classified as peer-oriented or non-peer-oriented on the basis of the Peer Preference Test. After viewing the modeling film, peer-oriented subjects increased their rates of social interaction significantly more than did non-peer-oriented subjects. The authors replicated these findings in a second study (Evers-Pasquale, 1978).

Interview

The child interview is especially critical in assessing social anxiety, because it is the presence of the subjective experience of anxiety, or apprehension, that defines socially anxious children and differentiates them from children whose social withdrawal or low levels of peer acceptance are the result of other factors. The interview is ideally suited for discovering the child's cognitions and affective experience related to social interaction. The interviewer can learn the situations in which the child feels most anxious, the child's pattern of physiological, cognitive, and motor responses to these situations, the child's interest in social participation, and any past negative experiences that might account for the child's social anxiety.

Hughes and Hall (1987) suggest the psychologist present the child a series of social problem situations by means of stories representing different contexts. The child is asked a number of questions about each story. These questions are designed to obtain information on cognitive and affective variables that may mediate the child's ability to comprehend social situations, to generate and evaluate social solutions, and to apply social solutions. For example, children who have difficulty joining in may be told a story about a child who is watching a group of familiar children playing with a frisbee before school. The story child is described as watching the game from the sidelines, standing alone. The interviewer asks the child a series of questions, such as the following.

READ

I. What is the story about:
   A. What does the child want?
   B. Why does the child want that?
   C. What is the child thinking and feeling?
   D. What are the other children thinking?

GENERATE

II. What could the child do to get what he or she wants?
   A. What might happen next if the child did that?
   B. What else could the child do?
      1. What might happen if the child did that?
      2. What would be the best thing to do?
      3. What would be the best thing to do if the child wanted to play with other children?

APPLY

III. Is that what you would do?
  A. How good are you at doing that?
  B. Show me how you would do that.

The interviewer can also ask the child questions about his or her responses on the self-report measures in order to obtain a more complete understanding of the child's experience. For example, following administration of the Children's Self-Efficacy for Peer Interaction Scale (Wheeler & Ladd, 1982) the interviewer might say: "OK. You said asking kids if you can play a game is hard for you. Would it be easier or harder if you knew the kids pretty well—if they were in your class? Would it be easier or harder if the game was one you played pretty well? A lot easier (harder) or just a little easier (or harder)?" Continuing with this line of questioning, the interviewer can discover the situations that are most problematic for the child as well as the child's thoughts about social interactions that influence his or her behavior.

Another interview approach appropriate for older children involves asking the child to report his or her thoughts. For example, "When you are thinking about joining in a game at recess, what do you say to yourself?" "When your class is getting ready to select partners for a class project, and you are thinking about asking someone to be your partner, what other thoughts go through your head?"

Behavioral Observations

The use of behavioral observation in assessing children's social competence is discussed in several recent reviews (Asher & Hymel, 1981; Hops & Greenwood, in press; Hughes, in press-a). Briefly, the advantages of behavioral observations include the low inference required in interpreting behavioral data, the ability of behavioral observations to specify target behaviors as well as important contextual variables, the fact that they are nonreactive, and their sensitivity to treatment effects. Limitations include inadequate opportunities to observe important social behaviors at older ages, their expense, and their lack of sensitivity to qualitative aspects of social behaviors.

The simplest observational data to collect is rate-of-interaction data. Withdrawn children are defined by rates of interaction that are significantly lower than average for the group of which the child is a member. Rate-of-interaction data provide global information and do not discriminate between the withdrawn, socially anxious child and the child whose withdrawal is a result of other factors. Therefore, it is important to consider the quality of a child's social behavior as well as the amount of social behavior. Lack of eye contact, nervous mannerisms, and whispering characterize the social interactions of the timid, shy child.

The importance of combining qualitative and quantitative data in behavioral observations is illustrated in a study by Panella and Henggeler (1986) with adolescents. They found that observation methods that measure the quality of behaviors correlate more highly with other indexes of social competence than do methods that measure the quantity of social behaviors.

Direct observation of behavior may occur in the child's natural setting (Gottman, Gonso & Rasmussen, 1975; Foster & Ritchey, 1985), in a contrived setting (Panella & Henggeler, 1986; Putallaz, 1983), or in a role-play setting (Bornstein et al., 1980). Contrived settings avoid some of the disadvantages of direct observations already discussed, providing an economical and practical alternative to direct observation in the natural environment. Because contrived settings permit greater standardization of observational procedures, differences between children are more likely to be a result of child variables versus setting differences.

An example of an observation in a contrived setting that is practical for practitioners is offered by Franco, Christoff, Crimmins, and Kelly (1983). A 14-year-old extremely shy boy was taught conversation skills using behavioral interventions. The effectiveness of training was assessed by coding the child's performance during contrived, unstructed conversations with a variety of unfamiliar persons. The observational categories included asking questions, making reinforcing comments, and eye contact. A multiple baseline design across behaviors permitted the documentation of changes in the taught skills as a result of the behavioral intervention.

Bornstein, Bellack, and Hersen (1977) used behavior observations in role plays to select four unassertive children ranging from 8 to 11 years of age for social skills training. Of 12 children initially referred for unassertiveness, 4 met the researchers' criteria of at least three kinds of deficient behaviors: poor eye contact, short speech duration, inaudible responses, and inability to make requests. Treated children improved their performance of these skills on novel role-play scenes. A limitation of their behavioral observation procedure is the lack of empirical evidence that socially competent children engage in these behaviors more frequently than do socially incompetent children. Furthermore, the researchers did not measure the impact of training on children's naturalistic behaviors or peer acceptance. Therefore, the observational system demonstrated sensitivity to treatment effects but did not demonstrate a functional relationship between these behaviors and peer acceptance or naturalistic social interactions.

COGNITIVE-BEHAVIORAL INTERVENTIONS FOR SOCIALLY ANXIOUS CHILDREN

The most successful interventions for withdrawn, neglected children are multicomponent programs. Common components of these programs are modeling, contingency management, practice opportunities, coping skills training, and coaching (instruction, practice, and feedback). These components will be described briefly and evidence of their effectiveness summarized. Evidence of the treatment efficacy of selected treatment packages will be reviewed.

Modeling

Basic Procedures

Modeling is frequently used to treat children's fears (Morris & Kratochwill, 1983). The beneficial effects of modeling may be a result of the instructional value of the modeling display, its facilitative effect on performance of existing skills, or a combination of these two effects. Both the skill training and fear reduction contributions of modeling are highlighted by Bandura (1969):

> [Through modeling] one can acquire intricate response patterns merely by observing the performance of appropriate models; emotional responses can be conditioned observationally by witnessing the affective reactions of others undergoing painful or pleasurable experiences; fearful and avoidant behavior can be extinguished vicariously through observation of modeled approach behavior toward feared objects without any adverse consequences accruing to the performer, . . . and, finally, the expression of well-learned responses can be enhanced and socially regulated through the actions of influential models (p. 118).

The modeling procedure involves one or more models (e.g., therapist, peers, and teacher) approaching a situation or object that the child observer has a history of avoiding. It is important that the model experience positive and safe consequences while engaging in the feared behavior. It is also recommended that the intensity of the model's behavior gradually increase. For example, Bandura and Menlove (1968) showed dog-phobic children a film depicting a model petting a dog through the fence. Gradually, the model engaged in increasingly more involved dog play, eventually playing with and feeding the dog inside the pen.

Bandura (1969, 1977) postulated four component processes that govern learning through observation: attentional processes, retentional processes, motor reproduction processes, and motivational processes. Bandura (1977) presented research findings supporting the importance of these processes to modeling. The effectiveness of modeling in reducing a child's fearful, or anxious, behavior depends on whether the child (1) attends to the modeling display and can note the relevant aspects of the situation and the model's response, (2) retains what has been learned from observing the model's performance, (3) can motorically reproduce the model's response, and (4) is motivated to reproduce the model's response.

Perry and Furukawa (1980) reviewed research on factors contributing to the effectiveness of modeling. Their findings are summarized in Table 5.6.

Table 5.6. Factors That Enhance Modeling

- I. Factors enhancing acquisition (learning and retention)
  - A. Characteristics of the model
    1. Similarity in sex, age, race, and attitudes
    2. Prestige
    3. Competence
    4. Warmth and nurturance
    5. Reward value
  - B. Characteristics of the observer
    1. Capacity to process and retain information
    2. Uncertainty
    3. Level of anxiety
    4. Other personality factors
  - C. Characteristics of the modeling presentation
    1. Live or symbolic model
    2. Multiple models
    3. Slider model
    4. Graduated modeling procedures
    5. Instructions
    6. Commentary on features and rules
    7. Summarization by observer
    8. Rehearsal
    9. Minimization of distracting stimuli
- II. Factors enhancing performance
  - A. Factors providing incentive for performance
    1. Vicarious reinforcement (reward to model)
    2. Vicarious extinction of fear of responding (no negative consequences to model)
    3. Direct reinforcement
    4. Imitation of children
  - B. Factors affecting quality of performance
    1. Rehearsal
    2. Participant modeling
  - C. Transfer and generalization of performance
    1. Similarity of training setting to everyday environment
    2. Repeated practice affecting response hierarchy
    3. Incentives for performance in natural setting
    4. Learning principles governing a class of behaviors
    5. Provision of variation in training situations

Source: M. A. Perry and M. J. Furukawa, "Modeling Methods," 1980. In F. H. Kanfer and A. P. Goldstein (Eds.), *Helping People Change* (2nd ed.). New York: Pergamon Press. Copyright 1980 by Pergamon Press. Reprinted by permission.

With respect to the characteristics of the model, high prestige child models are expected to be the most effective models in treating children's fears (Kornhaber & Schroeder, 1974). Regarding observer characteristics, the child-observer should not be highly anxious during the modeling presentation, because high anxiety interferes with attention to modeling cues and retention of what has been learned from the modeling situation. Therefore, initial modeling presentations should depict relatively nonthreatening situations, and the fear intensity should gradually increase so that the child does not become highly anxious during observation of the model. Relaxation training could be used with highly anxious children to help them relax enough to focus on the modeling situation and the model's response. Additional observer characteristics that enhance modeling include a high need for social approval and high dependency.

Several characteristics of the modeling presentation enhance modeling effects. Live models are better than filmed models, and multiple models and situations are better than one model. Because modeling films usually include multiple models, there is a trade-off between a single, live model and multiple filmed models. Filmed models have the obvious practical advantage of being reused repeatedly. In considering the relative merits of live versus filmed models, Bandura (1969) concluded that "the diminished efficacy of symbolic modeling can be offset by a broader sampling of models and aversive (feared) stimulus objects" (p. 180).

Modeling is also more effective when a narration (first or third person) accompanies the modeling presentation and when the observer is required to verbally or behaviorally rehearse the model's behavior (Ross, 1981). Models who display some fear and hesitancy at first but who gradually overcome their fear and behave in a fearless, confident manner are termed coping models. Mastery models display only confident behavior. Coping models are more effective than mastery models (Gottman, Gonso, & Schuler, 1976; Jakibchuk & Smeriglio, 1976; Melamed & Siegel, 1975). Meichenbaum (1971) suggests that the greater efficacy of coping models is a result of observers identifying with the coping models, whom they perceive as more similar to themselves. Alternatively, the coping model provides a cognitive model of coping self-talk, and this aspect of the modeling may account for its greater efficacy.

A type of modeling referred to as participant modeling (or contact desensitization) involves the observer as an active participant rather than a passive participant who merely observes the modeling sequence. In participant modeling the fearful or anxious child first observes a model demonstrate the feared response. The therapist (who may or may not also be the model) then encourages the child to engage in the behavior, offering such physical support as hand holding or guiding the child's movements. As in live and symbolic modeling, a gradual increase in the intensity of the approach behavior is recommended. Several factors probably contribute to the effectiveness of participant modeling in reducing children's fears. The practice opportunities help the child retain the modeled behaviors. Also, the child gains confidence from actually engaging in the feared response. Because the child experiences safe and positive consequences, the child's outcome expectancies too change as a result of participant modeling. Participant modeling is similar to coaching in several ways. Both include modeling, practice opportunities, and performance feedback. Participant modeling, unlike coaching, involves physical support and a graded sequence of feared behaviors.

Morris and Kratochwill (1983) review supportive evidence of the treatment efficacy of symbolic, live, model, and participant modeling in the treatment of children's fears. Most of the research on modeling has been conducted on children's fears of animals and dental and hospitalization fears. Therefore, the research findings may not generalize to the treatment of social anxiety. In the treatment of children's social withdrawal, symbolic (filmed) models have been most prevalent, and this research is reviewed next.

Supportive Evidence

In an often cited study, O'Connor (1969) showed a 23-minute film depicting increasing social interaction among children to isolated and withdrawn preschool children. Isolated children were selected on the basis of two criteria: nomination by teachers as one of the five most withdrawn children in their classrooms and low rates of social interactions. Isolated children were randomly assigned to the symbolic modeling condition or to an irrelevant film condition. Following exposure to the film, children in the symbolic modeling condition showed a dramatic increase in social interaction, whereas the control group showed no change. In a replication study, O'Connor (1972) improved his methodology by including follow-up assessments and comparing four conditions: symbolic modeling alone, modeling with external reinforcement, external reinforcement alone, and the same control condition as before (irrelevant film). Treatment effects on naturalistic social interaction were assessed at posttreatment and 3 and 6 weeks following treatment. All treatment conditions produced an increase in social interaction when compared with the control group; however, external reinforcement alone produced only temporary gains. Furthermore, external reinforcement did not add to the effectiveness of the modeling film. Similar findings of the superiority of modeling were reported by Keller and Carlson (1974), Evers-Pasquale and Sherman (1975), and Evers and Schwartz (1973). Because all of these studies involved preschool children, the findings cannot be generalized to treating social withdrawal in older children.

Accepting the demonstrated effectiveness of filmed models in increasing social interaction in preschool children, what characteristics of the modeling sequence account for its effectiveness? The narration that accompanied the O'Connor film (1969, 1972) describes desirable social responses and points out the positive outcomes of social interaction. Therefore, films provide an instructional component (Conger & Keane, 1981). The importance of the sound track of modeling films is demonstrated in another study on the effects of symbolic modeling on withdrawn behavior in preschool children (Jakibchuk & Smeriglio, 1976). As in the foregoing studies, children were selected for treatment on the basis of teacher nomination as withdrawn and behavioral assessment of minimal social interaction. Two experimental groups were compared with a no treatment group and an irrelevant film control group. In the self-speech (coping) film condition, the child models guided themselves with coping self-statements. In the narration film condition, child models performed the same behaviors, but the narration was in the third rather than the first person. Both experimental groups increased in social interaction measures. However, the coping self-talk condition was superior to the narration condition at 3-week follow-up assessment, at which time only children in the self-speech condition did not differ significantly from a nonisolate baseline on all measures.

Coaching

Whereas modeling is used primarily with preschool children, coaching is used primarily with older children. Coaching is itself a multicomponent intervention consisting of instructions, structured practice opportunities, and feedback. As Ladd and Mize (1983) note, the instructions in coaching can be either verbally stated rules and behavior, modeling sequences, or both. Coaching is used with a range of socially incompetent children. Coaching studies which selected children on the basis of low levels of interaction plus low peer acceptance are reviewed in this section. Coaching interventions with aggressive and rejected children are reviewed in chapter 9.

Whitehead, Hersen, and Bellack (1980) coached four socially isolated children in conversational skills. Children ranging in age from 8 to 10 years were selected for training on the basis of the following three criteria: (a) status as an isolate based on a sociometric procedure that differentiates between rejected and isolated (neglected) children, (b) teacher ratings of problem behaviors in groups, and (c) behavioral assessment of low levels of social interaction in the classroom. Conversational skills training was applied sequentially and cumulatively to three target behaviors over a 3-week period in a multiple baseline design across behaviors. The three skills taught were asking open-ended questions, making informative statements, and requesting a shared activity. Treatment involved role plays in which social situations were described and the child and model enacted the target conversational skill. The role-play procedure involved instructing the child in the target skill, an adult model demonstrating the skill, child behavioral rehearsal, and feedback to the child on his or her skill performance. The cycle of modeling, behavioral rehearsal, and feedback continued until the child's performance of the target skill was satisfactory. Following treatment in a specific skill, children's performance of that skill on novel role plays improved. Failure of the researchers to find meaningful improvement on the sociometric or teacher ratings casts doubt on the degree to which the skills generalized to naturalistic social interactions. Although treated children decreased the amount of time spent alone immediately following treatment, this change was not evident at 8-week follow-up.

In a well-designed study, Ladd (1981) coached low-accepted third-grade children in three social skills: asking questions, leading, and offering support to peers. Selection of children for treatment was based on low peer acceptance scores and low rates of target behaviors in the classroom. The coaching procedures were similar to those of Oden and Asher (1977). Specifically, children were trained in dyads for eight 45- to 50-minute sessions conducted on alternating school days. In each session, the same steps were followed in sequence for each skill concept:

> (1) the coach proposed that the concept (e.g., participation) was important in helping to make a game fun or enjoyable to play with another person; (2) the coach probed the child's understanding by requesting specific behavioral examples of the concept in reference to the game the child had previously played; (3) the coach repeated or rephrased the child's examples, suggested shorter phrases, or provided an example if the child did not respond; (4) the child was asked to provide specific behavioral examples of the opposite types of behavior; (5) the coach asked the child to evaluate whether each of the behavioral examples (including the opposite types) would be likely to result in making the game fun or enjoyable for both the child and the other person" (Oden & Asher, p. 499).

Following step 5, the therapist asked the children to try out the skill in a brief game situation and then provided feedback contingent on the children's attempts to enact the skill during play. In the seventh and eighth training sessions, children engaged in self-directed rehearsal and self-evaluation of the trained social skills. Children were instructed to verbally rehearse each skill concept. Next, children were instructed to practice each skill in a subsequent play session with two nonisolate classmates who were not involved in training. After the play session, the therapist asked the children to evaluate their performance of the taught skill, perceptions of peers' responses, reasons for undesirable outcomes, and ways to improve performance.

Coached children improved on behavioral assessment of skill performance in the classroom and in peer acceptance, compared with children in an attention control condition. Furthermore, the gains were maintained at 4-week follow-up.

Subjects in the Ladd (1981) study were selected on the basis of low levels of peer acceptance and infrequent use of positive social skills. Therefore, subjects probably included both rejected/aggressive and neglected/shy children. The mixed nature of the sample makes it impossible to determine whether neglected, shy children were helped. It is reasonable to expect that shy children benefited from the coaching program, because the program included components likely to increase children's self-efficacy for social interactions and modify their attributions for social failure. Shy and neglected children lack confidence in their social competence (Wheeler & Ladd, 1982) and tend to attribute social failure to their own incompetence (Goetz & Dweck, 1980). The self-guided rehearsal component of the Ladd program increased the probability the child would be successful in his or her social initiatives, thus increasing the child's self-efficacy. The self-evaluation component encourages children to take responsibility for the social reception they receive from peers, thus affecting children's attributions for social success and failure.

Although the results of the Ladd (1981) study are encouraging, the relatively short follow-up period does not permit documentation of the durability of gains. In this regard, Bierman and Furman (1984) demonstrated that without involving the child's peers in cooperative learning tasks with the treated child, initial gains in peer acceptance following coaching in social skills are not maintained.

Bierman and Furman (1984) used a coaching procedure to teach conversational skills to low-accepted fifth- and sixth-grade children who were observed to be deficient in conversational skills. Therefore, the selection criteria were similar to those of Ladd (1981). Children were assigned to one of four treatment conditions: (a) individual skill training (coaching) only, (b) positive peer involvement (group experience) only; (c) group experience with coaching; or (d) no treatment. All treatments consisted of 10 half-hour sessions over a 6-week period.

Children in the coaching conditions (individual or group) were trained in three conversational skills: self-expression, questioning, and leadership. Children in the positive peer involvement conditions were given opportunities to interact with peers under a superordinate goal (making a videotape together). A superordinate goal requires the cooperation of all members for goal attainment. Children in the combined coaching and peer involvement condition received skill training (coaching) within the context of making a film about friends.

As predicted, coaching (whether individual or group) produced strong and sustained improvements in children's conversational skill performance and rate of social interaction. Positive peer involvement (with or without coaching) produced significant but temporary improvement in children's peer acceptance, rate of social interaction, and self-efficacy for social interaction. The investigators concluded that peer involvement and coaching have strong, positive, and differential effects on the social competence of low-accepted children. Furthermore, these effects are additive, because only children receiving combined treatment showed general and sustained improvement in peer acceptance, rate of social interaction, and frequency of conversational skills. Although children who received individual coaching changed their behavior, their peers did not increase their liking for them. Children in the peer involvement only condition experienced an immediate but short-lived increase in peer acceptance. Without skills to maintain peer relations, the effects of a positive group experience were short-lived.

The results of Bierman and Furman (1984) and Ladd (1981) are encouraging. However, their use of selection criteria that fail to separate rejected and neglected children necessitates caution in generalizing these results to neglected and socially anxious children. Nevertheless, neglected, socially anxious children do have low self-efficacy, interact infrequently, experience low levels of peer acceptance, and are deficient in conversational skills (Jones, Hobb, & Hockenbury, 1982). Because these programs document improvement on measures of self-efficacy, social interaction, peer acceptance, and conversational skills, they are likely to benefit the socially anxious child.

Contingency management

Several studies (Allen, Hart, Buell, Harris, & Wolf, 1964; Hart, Reynolds, Baer, Brawley, & Harris, 1968) demonstrate that contingent adult social reinforcement (praise and positive interaction) increases the frequency of social interaction for withdrawn preschool children. However, gains are not retained when contingent social attention is withdrawn (Evers & Schwartz, 1973; O'Connor, 1972). Also, contingent attention does not increase the effectiveness of modeling in increasing withdrawn preschool children's social interaction (O'Connor, 1972). Furthermore, there is no evidence to support the use of contingent attention alone with socially withdrawn older children. With younger children, contingent attention might be a useful way to initially increase social interaction; however, unless it is combined with modeling or skill training, the improvement is temporary.

Structured Practice Opportunities

Interventions that provide withdrawn children with positive peer experiences attempt to alter the child's social environment and are therefore more ecologically oriented. Furman, Rahe, and Hartup (1979) found that providing withdrawn preschoolers with opportunities to play in pairs with younger children increased their social interaction and prosocial behaviors with their same-age classmates. Because no follow-up assessment was conducted, the durability of these gains cannot be determined from their study. Moreover, the treated children were not extremely withdrawn, as the selection criterion was engaging in peer interaction less than 33 percent of the observational period. The study is important because it shifts the treatment focus from the child to the social environment. In this regard, Scarlett (1980) found that preschool isolates engage in more peer interaction when in smaller and more structured groups. Hops et al. (1978) reported that peer pairing in the context of cooperative learning tasks increased withdrawn children's rates of peer interaction.

As the Bierman and Furman (1984) study suggests, a combination of structured positive peer interactions and coaching in social skills may result in sustained improvements for withdrawn children.

Self-Control

Self-control refers to a set of loosely related interventions that share an emphasis on the individual's self-regulatory capabilities. "Although appearing to encompass a defined therapy approach, self-control actually encompasses numerous intervention methods with the recognition of the contribution of cognitive processes to behavior change and the view that individuals can regulate their own behavior as its common base" (Morris & Kratochwill, 1983:78). In self-control therapies, the therapist teaches individuals how to use their own cognitions to change their behavior.

According to Meichenbaum and Genest (1980:403), self-control training involves the therapist helping the child: (1) to become aware of the negative thinking styles that impede performance and lead to emotional upset and inadequate performance; (2) to generate, in collaboration with the trainer, a set of incompatible, specific self-statements, rules, strategies, and so on, which the trainee can then employ; and (3) to learn specific adaptive cognitive and behavioral skills. Although self-control has been applied successfully to children's fears of the dark (Kanfer et al., 1975; Graziano, Mooney, Huber, & Ignasiak, 1979) and medical fears (Melamed & Siegel, 1975; Peterson & Shigetomi, 1981), self-control proper has not been applied to the treatment of children's shyness and social withdrawal. However, there is indirect support for including a self-control component in interventions for socially anxious children. As just noted herein, Jakibchuk and Smeriglio (1976) demonstrated that a modeling film in which the child model demonstrated coping self-talk was superior to a modeling film with the same content, but narrated in the third person. Children in the Jakibchuk and Smeriglio (1976) study were isolate preschool children. They viewed a series of videotapes depicting children displaying progressively more active social participation. The model in the self-speech condition verbalized initial doubts and coping self-talk before joining in:

> My name is Danny and I go to nursery school. I'm sitting here all by myself looking at a book. . . . Those children over there are playing together. . . . I would like to play with them, but I'm afraid. I don't know what to do or say. . . . This is hard. But I'll try. . . . I'm close to them. . . . I did it. Good for me. . . . I like playing with Johnny and Bobby. I'm really glad I decided to play with them. I'm having lots of fun (p. 839).

The superiority of the self-speech (coping model) condition was maintained at 3-week follow-up.

Rational emotive therapy (RET; Ellis, 1962, 1973) is a self-control intervention that teaches the individual to recognize maladaptive cognitions that lead to emotional distress (e.g., anger and anxiety) and maladaptive responding. When a child's social withdrawal is maintained by negative thoughts and beliefs, RET might be a useful component of an intervention plan.

Grieger and Boyd (1983) examined childhood anxieties in terms of children's irrational beliefs. They suggest that typical irrational ideas that underline social withdrawal include:

> I must do well and be lovable in all respects or I will be rejected. Others not liking me makes me nothing. If I do not do well and/or if I am not lovable, then I will be worthless. I must therefore avoid trying and getting noticed at all costs. So long as I can be left alone and nothing is demanded of me, my worthlessness will not be obvious, and I won't feel worthless (p. 224).

Although there is some indirect evidence supportive of self-control training in the treatment of social withdrawal, caution should be exercised in applying self-control training (i.e., self-instructional training or RET) to this population until its use is supported by empirical evidence of treatment efficacy.

TREATMENT IMPLICATIONS: WORKING WITH SOCIALLY ANXIOUS CHILDREN

The most effective approach to treating social withdrawal is different at different ages. Preschool children respond to viewing films depicting self-verbalizing coping child models engaged in progressively more active peer interaction. Such modeling treatments should be combined with structured positive peer interaction (Hops et al., 1978) to ensure adequate opportunities for the child to practice new skills under favorable conditions.

Primary grade children require more complex interventions. For example, Ladd's successful program combined coaching, peer interaction opportunities, and self-evaluation. In another successful multicomponent program with withdrawn third graders, Gottman, Gonso, and Schuler (1976) combined self-verbalizing coping models, coaching, and instruction in social-cognitive skills. The 10-minute modeling film attempted to teach the child how to initiate interaction. The coaching component attempted to teach specific social behaviors that differentiate between popular and unpopular third- and fourth-grade children. Games requiring perspective-taking skills were used in the third stage of treatment to teach referential communication skills. At 9-week follow-up assessment, results indicated that socially isolated children in the treatment group gained in peer acceptance. Although treated children did not increase their rate of peer interaction, they did redistribute their interaction to peers.

With older elementary school children and adolescents, coaching in social skills needs to be combined with opportunities for positive peer involvement, as in the Bierman and Furman (1984) study. Individual coaching alone has not been very successful with this age group (LaGreca & Santogrossi, 1980), presumably because reputational factors play a more important role in contributing to the older child's isolated or neglected status.

Christoff et al. (1985) combined group coaching in conversational skills and problem-solving training in a treatment program for shy adolescents. Eight 40-minute training sessions were conducted at a junior high school over a 7-week period. Results indicated training was effective in improving the frequency of social interaction based on in vivo behavioral observations and an increase in self-efficacy for initiating and continuing specific social interactions. Subjects also improved on paper-and-pencil measures of problem-solving skills and on a role-play measure of conversational skills. Follow-up assessments 5 months after treatment indicated that treatment effects were durable.

TREATMENT IMPLICATIONS: WORKING WITH TEACHERS

Studies employing contingent attention use teachers as intervention agents (Allen et al., 1964; Hart et al., 1968). The school psychologist collaborates with the teacher in the behavioral assessment of the child's problem and consults with the teacher on implementation of the contingency program. Although contingent attention programs result in an immediate increase in preschool children's frequency of social interaction, these gains are not maintained after withdrawal of contingent attention, and they do not generalize to other settings.

To increase generalization, contingent attention may be combined with a skill training approach. Tarplay and Sandargas (1981) combined contingent teacher attention with modeling and class discussions concerning the positive aspects of social participation in a preschool classroom. Additionally, the teacher increased her participation with other children. Because the target child was observed to "cling" to the teacher, having the teacher participate with the other children brought the target child into closer physical proximity to the other children in class. This procedure is similar to in vivo desensitization, because the teacher provided encouragement and guidance to the child as he engaged in social participation. The teacher also served as a model for joining in and playing with the children. The treatment produced strong, immediate, and positive effects on the child's frequency of peer interaction. Anecdotal reports from other teachers indicated that the positive results generalized across settings. Unfortunately, the researchers did not obtain data on the durability of treatment gains after the intervention was withdrawn.

White and Poteat (1983) investigated the effectiveness of teacher consultation and teacher-directed activities in increasing the frequency of interaction of three withdrawn kindergarten children. Each of the eight intervention sessions, each one lasting 30 to 45 minutes, involved the entire kindergarten class, and the withdrawn children were not singled out for special training. Before the first intervention session, the school psychologist and teacher met for three consultation sessions, focusing on the importance of social skills and techniques for improving social skills. Oden and Asher's (1977) coaching procedure was employed and children were taught four social skill strategies: (a) participation in a game or activity, (b) cooperating, taking turns, and sharing, (c) communication, talking, and listening to others, and (d) validating or supporting, giving attention or help, being friendly, nice, and fun. The coaching procedure involved instruction in the skill concept, teacher-directed discussion relating the skill concept to the objective of making games fun, opportunities to practice the skill in a game, and self-evaluation of skill performance. The school psychologist led the first session, the teacher led the second session, with the psychologist present, and the teacher alone led the last five sessions. Treatment resulted in increased rates of social interaction for two of the three children, and improved teacher ratings. Importantly, the teacher reported that the majority of classroom students improved in social skills and several students were less aggressive.

Several methodological shortcomings (no control group, teacher-ratings may be biased) limit confidence in the White and Poteat findings. However, the results suggest the premise that a teacher-led classroom-wide intervention may improve the social interaction of withdrawn children with positive social gains for other children too. Furthermore, the results of this study are consistent with research demonstrating that classroom-based social skills training programs improve behavioral adjustment and social problem-solving skills (Allen et al., 1976; Elardo & Caldwell, 1979; Gesten et al., 1979; McClure et al., 1978). Classroom-wide social problem-solving programs are reviewed in chapter 10.

6
Test Anxiety and School Phobia

THE NATURE OF TEST ANXIETY

Sarason (1975:27–28) defines test anxiety as:

> a type of self-preoccupation characterized by self-awareness, self-doubt, and self-depreciation. These cognitive activities exert impacts on both overt behavior and physiological reactivity. . . . These covert behaviors and activities are assumed to be products of the individual's history and to function as mediators between experience and behavior.

This self-preoccupation occupies the person's attention and interferes with performance by reducing attention to task-relevant cues and interfering with encoding and transforming data. Saying things to the self like "I am stupid" or "Maybe I won't pass" during a test interferes with attention to the task and problem solving. "Worry is immistakably an attentionally demanding and emotionally arousing cognitive activity" (Sarason, 1975:28). Incidence figures for test anxiety range from 10 to 30 percent of all students (McReynolds, Morris, & Kratochwill, in press).

Other researchers have also emphasized the role of cognition in test anxiety. For example, Wine (1971) provided evidence that high test-anxious (HTA) individuals engage in more task-irrelevant self-talk than do low test-anxious (LTA) individuals. Hollandsworth, Glazeski, Kirkland, Jones, and Van Norman (1979) suggested HTA individuals engage in more thoughts that impair performance (task-debilitating cognitions) and fewer thoughts that improve performance (task-facilitating cognitions).

Although research with adults has demonstrated that HTA individuals report more task-debilitating (off-task, irrelevant) cognitions and fewer task-facilitating cognitions during testing than do LTA adults (e.g., Arkin, Kolditz, & Kolditz, 1983), children show a different pattern. Like adults, HTA children engage in more task-debilitating thoughts and negative self-evaluations; surprisingly, HTA children also report more task-facilitating (coping) self-statements (Zatz & Chassin, 1983; 1985).

A large body of evidence supports the view that test anxiety impairs performance (Sarson, 1980). This performance decrement is strongest on tasks in which performance is perceived by the individual as indicative of one's abilities or related to important achievement-oriented outcomes (Sarason, 1980). When test anxiety is divided into worry and emotionality components (Deffenbacher, 1980), the worry component appears responsible for the decrement in performance (Gjesme, 1983), supporting the self-preoccupation explanation of the effects of test anxiety.

A person × environment conceptualization of test anxiety has been recommended (Zatz & Chassin, 1985; Phillips, 1978; Sarason, 1980). Research demonstrating a negative relationship between test anxiety and performance only under a condition of high evaluative threat (Zatz & Chassin, 1985; Dusek, Kermis, & Mergler, 1975) supports this interactional conceptualization.

COGNITIVE-BEHAVIORAL APPROACHES TO ASSESSING TEST ANXIETY

Test Anxiety Scale for Children

The Test Anxiety Scale for Children (TASC; Sarason et al., 1960) is the most extensively researched and widely used measure of children's test anxiety (Dusek, 1980). The TASC is a group-administered paper-and-pencil test consisting of 30 items to which the child responds "yes" or "no." The TASC items are included in Table 5.3, marked with an asterisk. Twelve of the items specifically mention the word test (e.g., "Do you worry a lot while you are taking a test?"). Others ask about worry over classroom performance ("When the teacher is teaching you about arithmetic, do you feel that other children in the class understand her better than you?"). Some items ask about physiological experiences of anxiety ("When you are taking a test, does the hand you write with shake a little?"). The TASC is reliable and valid (Phillips, 1978; Dusek, 1980). Children's scores on the TASC show high stability over the elementary school years (Phillips, Martin, & Meyers, 1972), and girls typically score higher than boys (Zatz & Chassin, 1985).

As related in chapter 3, the TASC and the School Anxiety Scale (SAS, Phillips, 1978) have similar factor structures and correlate 0.82 (corrected $r = 0.61$) with each other (Phillips, 1978). Although the SAS may measure these four factors more adequately, there is no evidence that it is a better measure of the test anxiety factor. Also, the TASC is much shorter than the SAS (30 versus 74 items) and has been researched extensively as a measure of test anxiety. Thus, the TASC is recommended as a measure of test anxiety.

The four factors of the TASC are stable across grades and sex (Feld & Lewis, 1967). These factors have been labeled test anxiety, somatic signs of anxiety, comparative poor self-evaluation, and remote school concern (Feld & Lewis, 1967, 1969).

Despite the multidimensional nature of the TASC, children are identified as high test anxious based on their responses to all 30 items. For purposes of classifying children, children scoring between 10 and 15 are considered moderately test anxious, and children scoring over 15 are classified as high test anxious. As already noted, girls tend to score higher than boys (Zatz & Chassin, 1985).

Because the TASC has no lie scale, researchers frequently administer the Lie Scale for Children (Sarason et al., 1960) along with the TASC to identify children who may underreport their test anxiety on the TASC. This practice is supported by evidence that children with high lie scores underreport their test anxiety (Eaton, 1980).

Validity data on the TASC are extensive. For example, high test anxious children report more nervousness and more self-derogatory and off-task self-statements in test situations (Zatz & Chassin, 1983, 1985), experience more performance decrement in high evaluative situations (Zatz & Chassin, 1985; Dusek, 1980), and achieve less in school, when IQ is partialled out (Phillips, 1978).

In summary, the TASC is a reliable and valid measure of children's test anxiety.

Behavioral Observation

Behavioral observations are rarely used in assessing test anxiety. Morris, Brown, and Halbert (1977) demonstrated that behavioral observations may be useful in identifying high test-anxious preschool children for whom self-report measures are less valid. Behavioral indicators of worry and emotionally were observed in preschool children before and after their exposure to an anxious 6-year-old model. Behavioral indicators of the worry component were frowning, shaking the head, looking at the examiner for feedback, looking at task-irrelevant stimuli, and spontaneous comments concerning self-preoccupation or evaluation of one's performance. Behavioral indicators of emotionality included fingernail biting, hand trembling, excessive shifting in chair, hair pulling, playing with hands, chewing lips, and verbal responses expressing physical discomfort. Children who observed an anxious 6-year-old model in an evaluative situation increased their frequency of behavioral indicators of emotionality and worry. Conversely, children who observed a nonanxious child model in an evaluative situation decreased their frequency of behavioral indicators of emotionality and worry.

Another approach to assessing test anxiety is to administer a cognitively demanding task to children under game-like and achievement-orienting (ego-involved) instructions. Children who demonstrate relatively large performance decrements under the achievement-orienting instructions are classified as test anxious.

Report of Cognitive Activity

Given the well-documented finding that the cognitive activity of HTA children differs from that of LTA children, it is surprising that children's reports of their own cognitive activity has not been used more frequently in assessing test anxiety. Zatz and Chassin (1983) developed a self-report measure of children's cognitions during test taking, The Children's Cognitive Assessment Questionnaire (CCAQ). The revised CCAQ (1985) includes 50 items, each prefaced by the words "I thought . . ." Children indicate on a 4-point scale how frequently they think a specific thought while taking a test. The measure includes five subscales: positive and negative evaluation, on-task, off-task, and coping statements. Table 6.1 includes the items on each of the subscales. The CCAQ has adequate internal consistency and test-retest reliability (1983, 1985).

Zatz and Chassin examined the relationship between CCAQ scores, test anxieties, and task performance in both analogue testing (1983) and naturalistic (1985) classroom testing situations. The predicted relationships between cognitions and test anxiety and between cognitions and task performance were found. The HTA children report more off-task thoughts, more coping statements, more negative evaluations, and fewer positive evaluations than do LTA children. It was predicted that HTA children would show performance decrements on classroom tests only in high-threat classrooms. To test this hypothesis, classes were divided into high and low perceived threat categories, based on a median split on two subscales of the Classroom Environment Scale (Trickett & Moos, 1973). As predicted, test anxiety and perceived classroom threat exerted interactive effects on test performance such that HTA children performed more poorly than did either low or moderate test-anxious children only in high-threat classrooms. In high evaluative threat classrooms, there was a negative correlation between math performance and both off-task thoughts and negative self-evaluation. Similarly, there were significant positive correlations between positive self-evaluations and math test performance. Furthermore, in high-threat classrooms all of these correlations held when children's math achievement scores were partialled out (1985). In summary, in high perceived threat classrooms, off-task thoughts, negative self-evaluations, and coping statements were all associated with poorer math performance.

The CCAQ is useful in specifying maladaptive cognitions characteristic of HTA children. These cognitions could be the target of cognitive behavior modification programs. Of special significance is the finding that HTA children did not engage in fewer coping statements than did LTA children. Furthermore, coping self-statements were not related to performance. "Thus, these data do not support a role for training in on-task or coping statements in the treatment of test anxious children" (p. 399). The data do

Table 6.1. Items on the Children's Cognitive Assessment Questionnaire

On-Task Thoughts
1. Guess if you have to.
2. Work as quickly as possible.
3. Follow the instructions.
4. Work as carefully as possible.
5. Skip the hard ones and come back to them later.
6. Read each question carefully.
7. Answer the easy ones first.
8. One step at a time.
9. Answer every question.
10. Check your answers over.

Off-Task Thoughts
1. My mind keeps wandering.
2. I am hungry.
3. I wonder what the examiner is going to find out about me.
4. I wish I were home.
5. I wish I were playing with my friends.
6. I am nervous and worried.
7. I keep on daydreaming.
8. I wish this were over.
9. Pretty soon I'll get to do something else.
10. I can't seem to sit still.

Positive Self-Evaluations
1. I'm bright enough to do this.
2. I catch on quickly to tests like this.
3. I'm pleased with how I'm doing.
4. I'm doing better on this than the others.
5. My grade will be higher than the other kids.
6. I understand how to do this.
7. I do well on tests like this.
8. My answers to this are correct.
9. I'm fast enough to finish this.
10. This test is easy for me to do.

Negative Self-Evaluations
1. I have a bad memory for things like this.
2. Tests like this are harder for me than the others.
3. I don't do well on tests like this.
4. I'm doing worse than the others on this.
5. I'm doing poorly on this.
6. The others probably think I'm too dumb to do this.
7. My answers to this aren't good enough.
8. I'm too dumb to do this.
9. I must be making many mistakes.
10. I can't do this — I give up.

Coping Self-Statements
1. Try to calm down.
2. Forget about how the others are doing.
3. Try to relax.
4. Stop daydreaming.
5. Don't think so poorly of yourself.
6. There's no need to get upset about this.
7. Just do the best that you can.
8. Worrying won't help anything.
9. Get back to working on the test.
10. Stop worrying about how you'll do.

Source: Laurie Chassin, 1985. Unpublished test. Department of Psychology, Arizona State University, Tempe, AZ. Reprinted by permission.

support the view that interventions should focus on decreasing disrupting, debilitating cognition rather than on increasing task-facilitating cognitions.

COGNITIVE-BEHAVIORAL INTERVENTIONS WITH TEST-ANXIOUS CHILDREN

Desensitization

The single most extensively researched treatment for test anxiety in children is desensitization. Although desensitization proper is based on Wolpe's (1958) theory of reciprocal inhibition, both relaxation training and desensitization procedures have been conceptualized within a self-control framework (Allen, Elias, & Zlotlow, 1980). According to this view, the individual learns to use relaxation as a coping response in evaluative situations.

A detailed discussion of desensitization procedures with children is included by Morris and Kratochwill (1983). Essentially, there are three stages to systematic desensitization. In the first stage, which typically lasts three to four sessions, the child is taught deep muscle relaxation by alternately tightening and relaxing different muscles. The child is instructed to practice relaxation at home 10 to 15 minutes each day, often while listening to audiotaped relaxation instructions. The child is taught to notice the different body sensations that go along with feeling tense and relaxed. In the second stage, the therapist helps the child develop an anxiety hierarchy. The child writes situations related to the fear or anxiety on index cards, which have been assigned values ranging from 0 to 100, indicating the degree of anxiety the child experiences in that situation. An example test anxiety hierarchy used with secondary students is presented in Table 6.2 (Deffenbacher & Kemper, 1974). Standardized test anxiety hierarchies like the one in Table 6.2 are used in group desensitization treatment. Because children's experiences with test-taking situations are similar, standardized test anxiety hierarchies may be appropriate for group treatment. After the child has learned self-relaxation on command and the test anxiety hierarchy is complete, the third stage, desensitization proper, begins. First, the child relaxes himself or herself. Then the therapist asks the child to vividly imagine the first (least threatening) situation on the hierarchy while remaining relaxed. If the child feels the least bit of anxiety or tension while imaging a scene, he or she is told to signal immediately with the right finger. The therapist instructs the child to imagine a lower scene on the hierarchy until relaxed again. Each scene is presented three or four times for increasing periods of time (up to 10 seconds). Each session lasts about 15 to 20 minutes, during which time three or four scenes on the hierarchy are presented in ascending order. Treatment is complete when the child can remain relaxed when visualizing the most threatening situation on the hierarchy.

Table 6.2. Test Anxiety Hierarchy Example

You are attending a regular class session.
You hear about someone else who has a test.
You are studying at home. You are reading a normal assignment.
You are in class. The teacher announces a major exam in 2 weeks.
You are at home studying. You are beginning to review and study for a test that is 1 week away.
You are at home studying, and you are studying for the important test. It is now Tuesday and 3 days before the test on Friday.
It is Thursday night, the night before the exam on Friday. You are talking with another student about the exam tomorrow.
It is the night before the exam, and you are home studying for it.
It is the day of the exam, and you have 1 hour left to study.
It is the day of the exam. You have been studying. You are now walking on your way to the test.
You are standing outside the test room talking with other students about the upcoming test.
You are sitting in the testing room waiting for the test to be passed out.
You are leaving the exam room, and you are talking with other students about the test. Many of their answers do not agree with yours.
You are sitting in the classroom waiting for the graded test to be passed back by the teacher.
It is right before the test, and you hear a student ask a possible test question that you cannot answer.
You are taking the important test. While trying to think of an answer, you notice everyone around you writing rapidly.
While taking the test, you come to a question you are unable to answer. You draw a blank.
You are in the important exam. The teacher announces 30 minutes remaining, but you have an hour's work left.
You are in the important exam. The teacher announces 15 minutes remaining, but you have an hour's work left.

Source: J. L. Deffenbacher and C. C. Kemper, "Systematic Desensitization of Test Anxiety in Junior High Students," 1974, *The School Counselor, 22,* 219. Copyright 1974 by the American Association for Counseling and Development. Reprinted by permission.

Several research studies document the effectiveness of both individual and group desensitization in reducing children's self-reported anxiety and improving task performance (Morris & Kratochwill, 1983). Methodological shortcomings that limit confidence in these findings include failure to include follow-up assessment (Barabasz, 1973; Kondas, 1967; Miller, 1972) and inadequate assessment of treatment outcomes (Deffenbacher & Kemper, 1974; Kondas, 1967). Furthermore, treatment frequently does not result in improvement on measures of children's academic achievement (Laxer, Quarter, Kooman, & Walker, 1969).

In summary, desensitization may help decrease test anxiety. Controversy exists concerning the reason for its effectiveness. In support of the self-control explanation for its effectiveness are results of several studies demonstrating that relaxation training alone and desensitization are equally effective in the treatment of test anxiety among college students (Allen et al., 1980).

Modeling

HTA college subjects benefit from exposure to coping models (Sarason, 1975). Raskind and Nagle (1980) investigated the effectiveness of coping models on HTA fifth-graders' performance on individual intelligence tests. High and low test-anxious children were randomly assigned to one of three treatment groups. The control group saw a film unrelated to test-taking. Children in the observation condition saw a film depicting an anxious boy and girl taking a simulated Wechsler Intelligence Scale for Children-Revised (WISC-R) with a supportive examiner. Children in the coping condition saw the same film, except the supportive examiner discussed the children's anxieties and provided coping techniques for doing well on the test. All child models expressed anxiety initially but gradually verbalized confidence in their performance, according to Meichenbaum's (1971) mastery modeling procedure. The only outcome measure was children's WISC-R scores. Results did not support the modeling treatment.

Too few studies on the effects of modeling on test anxiety have been conducted to permit an evaluation of this procedure. However, the findings of Zatz and Chassin (1985) suggest that procedures intended to teach children to increase their coping self-talk may not be effective with HTA children.

Attention Training

Dusek and colleagues (Dusek, Kermis, & Mergler, 1975; Dusek, Mergler, & Kermis, 1976) have provided evidence supportive of the attentional deficit interpretation of the deleterious effect of test anxiety on performance. In evaluative situations, HTA children between 8 and 12 years of age attend more to irrelevant task stimuli than do LTA children. Furthermore, when HTA children are trained to increase their attention to relevant cues and decrease their attention to irrelevant task cues, the performance differences between high and low test-anxious children are eliminated (Dusek et al., 1975, 1976; Ribordy, Tracy, & Bernotas, 1981). Little and Jackson (1974) compared attention training alone (an auditory cue reminded the child to attend), relaxation training alone, and attention training plus relaxation training in minimizing performance decrements in test-anxious eighth-grade children. They found the combined treatment to be more effective than either procedure alone. Finally, Ribordy et al. (1981) found that attention training enabled HTA children in grades 4 to 6 to perform as well as LTA children on a perceptual task requiring nonattention to irrelevant task cues. The HTA children in a placebo and a no training control group made significantly more errors on the perceptual task than did LTA children. Given the brief duration of treatment (1 hour in the Ribordy et al. study), these results are promising. However, additional research studies that include follow-up assessment and that measure treatment effects on children's performance on classroom examinations are necessary before any conclusions can be reached on the effectiveness of attention training.

Coping Skills Training

Coping skills training (also referred to as self-instructional training, anxiety management, and stress inoculation) is a self-control approach that combines instruction, relaxation, training in problem-solving and self-instruction, and modeling. Therefore, coping skills training is a "package" cognitive behavioral treatment.

Meichenbaum (1977) delineated the common treatment components that underlie the several different coping skills programs:

> The components include: (1) teaching the client the role of cognitions in contributing to the presenting problem, through both didactic presentation (often in the form of Socratic dialogue) and guided self-discovery; (2) training in the discrimination and systematic observation of self-statements and images, and in self-monitoring of maladaptive behaviors; (3) training in the fundamentals of problem-solving (e.g., problem definition, anticipation of consequences, evaluating feedback); (4) modeling of the self-statements and images associated with both overt and cognitive skills; (5) modeling, rehearsal, and encouragement of positive self-evaluation and of coping and attentional focusing skills; (6) the use of various behavior therapy procedures, such as relaxation training, coping imagery training, and behavioral rehearsal; (7) in vivo behavioral assignments that become increasingly demanding (p. 147).

The success of coping skills training with HTA college students has been reported in many studies (Allen et al., 1980). However, few studies have investigated the efficacy of cognitive skills training with children and young adolescents.

Stevens and Pihl (1983) compared the efficacy of two coping skills training programs with 42 seventh-grade students who had been found to react adversely to test situations. Both coping skills programs were similar in several ways. Training occurred in dyads for 10 45-minute daily sessions over 2 weeks. Both programs included rehearsal, modeling, and role-playing, and both emphasized the role of self-control in dealing with stress. However, the structured program included training in self-instruction techniques and a problem-solving sequence. The cognitive program was more flexible, and students were encouraged to discuss various coping strategies and to develop their own strategy. Both training groups experienced gains on measures of nonverbal intelligence, coping ability, and teacher-rated coping ability. A nonsignificant trend toward better performance on an academic task under high evaluative threat for the treated groups was noted, especially for children with a history of school failure.

Genshaft (1982) provided self-instructional training to seventh-grade girls whose math achievement was at least 1 year below their reading achievement and who were identified by their math teacher as experiencing some degree of math anxiety. Three experimental groups were employed in the study: a no-treatment control group, a tutoring group, and a tutoring plus self-instructional training group. Training sessions occurred twice a week for 8 weeks. In self-instructional training, the girls were taught to monitor their negative self-evaluations and to focus their attention on the task. The desired type of self-instruction was to follow these general guide lines:

> First, ask yourself, "What am I supposed to do in this problem?" Then answer the above question, "I am supposed to solve this problem on. . . ." Talk to yourself through each step of the problem. For example, "First, I need to change this percent to a decimal fraction. Then, I need to set up the problem so I can multiply. Next, I. . . ." Praise yourself when you are finished, "Good job! I knew I could do it!" (p. 33).

The combined SIT-plus-tutoring group was the only group to improve on a standardized test of math achievement and on a measure of attitude toward math.

Several studies have compared the relative effectiveness of systematic desensitization and cognitive behavior modification (CBM) with test anxious undergraduates (e.g., Holroyd, 1976; Kaplan, McCordick, & Twitchell, 1979; Meichenbaum, 1972). Both treatments produce positive effects, with the results favoring cognitive behavior modification. One study (Leal, Baxter, Martin, & Marx, 1981) compared the effectiveness of these two treatments with 30 test anxious tenth-grade students. Subjects in the CBM group were instructed in the role of thoughts and self-statements in test anxiety. They learned to recognize maladaptive self statements and to replace them with alternative, adaptive ones. Subjects in the desensitization group received a standard desensitization treatment involving relaxation training, and a test anxiety hierarchy. Both groups met for six 1 hour weekly sessions. Dependent measures were a performance measure (Raven's Standard Progressive Matrices; Raven, 1965) and two self-report measures of anxiety. Results clearly support the superiority of CBM on the self-report measures. Due to unusual statistical properties of the data, no clear cut conclusion could be reached on the relative effectiveness of the two treatments on the performance measure. However, both treatments produced gains on the performance measure of test anxiety.

SCHOOL PHOBIA

Classification of School Phobia

The school phobic child experiences such heightened anxiety in the school setting that he or she avoids attending school. Somatic complaints often are present, and the child may report gastrointestinal upset, dizziness, or a headache on school mornings and while at school. The school phobic child may experience high test anxiety or social anxiety or both. Incidence figures for school phobia range from 3.2 to 17 per 100 (McReynolds et al., in press). It is most frequent around 5 to 7 years of age, when children are adjusting to separation from their parents. Prevalence increases again about the time of the transition from elementary school to middle school or junior high. Finally, around age 14 a slight increase in prevalence occurs, when the school phobia is often associated with depression (McReynolds et al., in press).

Kennedy (1965) distinguished between two types of school phobias based on data of 50 cases from the Human Development Clinic of Florida State University. Kennedy (1965) proposed that a differential diagnosis between two types of school phobia could be made on the basis of any 7 of 10 differential symptoms. Kennedy's 10 differential symptoms are listed in Table 6.3. A child who demonstrates 7 of the 10 symptoms in the left-hand column is classified as having type 1 school phobia. Kennedy (1965) reported that all 50 type 1 cases responded to the brief therapy approach with complete remission of the school phobic symptoms.

The rapid treatment program is the recommended approach for type 1 school phobias. This treatment involves coordination with school personnel, early referral for treatment, avoidance of emphasis on somatic complaints, forced school attendance, having the father take the child to school, allowing the mother to stand in the hall (if necessary), providing the parents with a concrete plan for what to do on school mornings, and removing secondary gains for school refusal. The treatment also includes a child interview. Interestingly the interview approach used by Kennedy (1965) bears a striking resemblance to coping skills training:

> The content of the interviews should be stories which stress the advantage of going on in the face of fear; how student pilots need to get back into the air quickly after an accident, and how important it is to get right back on the horse after a fall. In addition, the therapist can describe real or imaginary events in his own childhood when he was frightened for a while but everything turned out all right; all to stress to the child the transitory nature of the phobia (pp. 288–289).

Children with type 2 school phobias are not as responsive to the rapid treatment program, and it is these recurrent cases with an incipient onset that pose the greater challenge for the therapist.

Table 6.3. Ten Differential School Phobia Symptoms

Type 1	Type 2
1. The present illness is the first episode.	1. Second, third, or fourth episode.
2. Monday onset, following an illness the previous Thursday or Friday.	2. Monday onset following minor illness not a prevalent antecedent.
3. An acute onset.	3. Incipient onset.
4. Lower grades most prevalent.	4. Upper grades most prevalent.
5. Expressed concern about death.	5. Death theme not present.
6. Mother's physical health in question: actually ill or child thinks so.	6. Health of mother not an issue.
7. Good communication between parents.	7. Poor communication between parents.
8. Mother and father well adjusted in most areas.	8. Mother shows neurotic behavior; father, a character disorder.
9. Father competitive with mother in household management.	9. Father shows little interest in household or children.
10. Parents achieve understanding.	10. Parents very difficult to work with.

Source: Kennedy, W. A. (1965). "School Phobia: Rapid Treatment of Fifty Cases." *Journal of Abnormal Psychology, 70*, pp. 285–289. Reprinted by permission.

Behavioral Treatment

Behavioral treatment of the child with a type 2 school phobia is discussed by Morris and Kratochwill (1983) and Ross (1981). Desensitization (Taylor, 1972; Miller, 1972; Lazarus, 1960), in vivo desensitization (Garvey & Hergrenes, 1966; Lazarus, Davison, & Polefka, 1965), and shaping and contingency management programs (Vaal, 1973; Ayllon, Smith, & Rogers, 1979) have achieved some success with children with school phobias. Additionally, family therapy from a systems model has been successful in treating the school-phobic child (Hsia, 1984). Because evidence of the effectiveness of these approaches comes from case studies, it is difficult to compare treatment efficacy. Also, case studies that provide considerable detail about treatment procedures indicate that the actual treatment typically involves several procedures. These procedures include modeling, relaxation training, gradual exposure to school situations, contingency management, and changing family interactional patterns. For example, Lazarus et al. (1965) combined the use of positive reinforcement, in vivo desensitization, emotive imagery, and medication to reduce the school phobia of a 9-year-old boy. The treatment steps in the Lazarus et al. study are listed in Table 6.4.

Cognitive-Behavioral Treatment

Compared with the many studies on behavioral treatments of school phobia, there are few studies on the efficacy of cognitive-behavioral approaches with school phobia. O'Farrell, Hedlund, and Cutter (1981) used self-control training and desensitization in treating a school-phobic boy who

Table 6.4. Steps in Treatment of School-Phobic Boy

1. On a Sunday afternoon, accompanied by the therapists, he walked from his house to the school. The therapists were able to allay Paul's anxiety by means of distraction and humor, so that his initial exposure was relatively pleasant.
2. On the next 2 days at 8:30 A.M., accompanied by one of the therapists, he walked from his house into the schoolyard. Again, Paul's feelings of anxiety were reduced by means of coaxing, encouragement, relaxation, and the use of "emotive imagery" (i.e., the deliberate picturing of subjectively pleasant images such as Christmas and a visit to Disneyland, while relating them to the school situation). Approximately 15 minutes were spent roaming around the school grounds, after which Paul returned home.
3. After school was over for the day, the therapist was able to persuade the boy to enter the classroom and sit down at his desk. Part of the normal school routine was then playfully enacted.
4. On the following three mornings, the therapist accompanied the boy into the classroom with the other children. They chatted with the teacher and left immediately after the opening exercises.
5. A week after beginning this program, Paul spent the entire morning in class. The therapist sat in the classroom and smiled approvingly at Paul whenever he interacted with his classmates or the teacher. After eating his lunch he participated in an active ball game and returned to his house with the therapist at 12:30. (Since parent-teacher conferences were held during that entire week, afternoon classes were discontinued.)
6. Two days later when Paul and the therapist arrived at school, the boy lined up with the other children and allowed the therapist to wait for him inside the classroom. This was the first time that Paul had not insisted on having the therapist in constant view.
7. Thereafter, the therapist sat in the school library adjoining the classroom.
8. It was then agreed that the therapist would leave at 2:30 P.M. while Paul remained for the last hour of school.
9. On the following day, Paul remained alone at school from 1:45 P.M. until 2:45 P.M. (Earlier that day, the therapist had unsuccessfully attempted to leave the boy alone from 10 until noon.)
10. Instead of fetching the boy at his home, the therapist arranged to meet him at the school gate at 8:30 A.M. Paul also agreed to remain alone at school from 10:45 A.M. until noon, provided that the therapist returned to eat lunch with him. At 1:45 P.M. the therapist left again with the promise that if the boy remained until school ended (3:30 P.M.), he would visit Paul that evening and play the guitar for him.
11. Occasional setbacks made it necessary to instruct the lad's mother not to allow the boy into the house during school hours. In addition, the teacher was asked to provide special jobs for the boy to increase his active participation and make school more attractive.
12. The family doctor was asked to prescribe a mild tranquilizer for the boy to take on awakening to reduce his anticipatory anxieties.
13. After meeting the boy in the mornings, the therapist gradually left him alone at school for progressively longer periods of time. After 6 days of this procedure, the therapist was able to leave at 10 A.M.
14. The boy was assured that the therapist would be in the faculty room until 10 A.M., if needed. Thus, he came to school knowing the therapist was present, but not actually seeing him.
15. With Paul's consent the therapist arrived at school shortly after the boy entered the classroom at 8:40 A.M.
16. School attendance independent of the therapist's presence was achieved by specific rewards (a comic book and variously colored tokens that would eventually procure a baseball glove) contingent upon his entering school and remaining there alone.
17. Because the therapist's presence seemed to have at least as much reward value as the comic books and tokens, it was necessary to enlist the mother's cooperation to effect the therapist's final withdrawal.
18. Approximately 3 weeks later, Paul had accumulated enough tokens to procure his baseball glove. he then agreed with his parents that rewards of this kind were no longer necessary.

Source: Lazarus, A. A., Davison, G. C., & Polefka, D. A. (1965). "Classical and Operant Factors in the Treatment of School Phobia." *Journal of Abnormal Psychology, 70*: 225–229. Reprinted by permission.

had not attended school for more than 5 months. The boy was seen with his parents for the initial session and than alone for eight therapy sessions. Both parents and the boy were seen for a final session. Treatment proceeded according to the following outline.

Session 1. After a history of the problem was obtained, the parties agreed that 4 weeks would be invested in teaching Richard coping skills for his nonschool-related fears before school-related fears would be addressed. Richard would not attend school during the first 4 weeks. Richard agreed to keep a daily diary of upsetting events, rating the degree of upset he experienced.

Session 2. A personal fear hierarchy was constructed. The therapist discussed with Richard his specific behavioral manifestations of tension and anxiety and his antecedent thoughts. Richard practiced relaxation and was assigned relaxation practice as homework. Self-monitoring of fearful situations continued.

Session 3. Richard practiced relaxation and relaxation was discussed as a coping response.

Session 4. In this session, during the self-monitoring review, Richard's thoughts when he felt most anxious were considered. The therapist introduced thought stopping as a self-control response to excessive anxiety.

Sessions 5–9. Richard was assigned the task of gradually returning to school. The therapist instructed Richard to use relaxation and thought stopping to cope with anxiety-provoking situations related to school attendance. Desensitization was used with scenes from the anxiety hierarchy. Richard was attending school each day.

Session 10. The therapist reviewed with Richard and his parents the progress made and made arrangements for a "booster session" if the need arose.

During the 18 months following treatment, Richard attended school 96 percent of the days, as compared with 36 percent for the year before treatment. Parent and child reports indicated positive treatment gains were maintained 12 months after treatment. Additional positive change in attitude and social behavior, especially increased assertiveness, was reported.

This case illustrates the incorporation of a cognitive component (coping skills training) into desensitization. The positive treatment results are encouraging, especially considering the severity of the boy's fears and his age. Nevertheless, additional and well-controlled studies on the efficacy of this procedure are certainly needed before any definitive conclusions on its efficacy can be reached.

7 Depression

DEFINITIONAL AND CONCEPTUAL ISSUES

Whereas attention deficit disorder took center stage in research on childhood disorders during the decade 1975 to 1985, depression may now be the focal childhood disorder. The several factors accounting for a surge in research attention to childhood depression are: (a) a consensus that depression exists in childhood; (b) research demonstrating similarities between depression in childhood and that in adulthood; (c) advances in assessment of childhood depression; (d) research linking depression to suicide; (e) the increased rate of suicide among adolescents; (f) the relatively high prevalence of depressive symptoms among children and adolescents; and (g) research with adults that demonstrates the efficacy of cognitive-behavioral treatments with depressed adults. Each of these factors is briefly reviewed and a cognitive model of childhood depression is presented.

Depression Exists in Childhood

Depression is viewed not as a symptom (e.g., I am feeling depressed today), but as a symptom cluster, or syndrome. In addition to depressed affect, the syndrome may include symptoms such as lowered self-esteem, apathy, low energy level, social withdrawal, sleeping and eating disturbances, an overly pessimistic view of the future, and suicidal ideation or attempts (Finch & Saylor, 1984; Reynolds, 1985). The existence of a depressive syndrome in childhood was questioned by theorists who believed children lacked the requisite cognitive, affective, or intrapsychic mechanisms to experience depression. Until recently, the prevailing view was that the child's superego was not strong enough for the self-reproach and pathological guilt that is central to depression. It is important to note that most of the persons writing about childhood depression before the late 1970s were psychiatrists with psychoanalytic orientations. A second view of childhood depression was that because depressive symptoms in childhood are both frequent and transitory, these symptoms were best viewed as part of normal development rather than as constituting a clinical syndrome (Lefkowitz & Burton, 1978).

The view that childhood depression exists as a diagnosable clinical syndrome was endorsed by participants at an important national conference on childhood depression (Schulterbrandt & Raskin, 1977). Since that time, research on the diagnosis of childhood depression and on assessment of depressive symptoms has been reported frequently in psychological journals pertaining to childhood disorders.

Similarities between Depression in Childhood and in Adulthood

Some theorists in the late 1960s and early 1970s posited that depressed children express their depression in ways different from those of adults (Cytryn & McKnew, 1972). These authors argued that children "mask" their depression behind a wide range of internalizing and externalizing symptoms such as delinquency, aggression, psychosomatic illness, and hyperactivity. This "masked depression" conceptualization of childhood depression proved impossible to subject to empirical verification, because almost any child behavior symptoms could be viewed as an expression of depression. Therefore, it had no explanatory or predictive benefits. Kovacs and Beck (1977) concluded the concept of masked depression was so overly inclusive and redundant as to be worthless as a diagnostic criterion. Cytryn, McKnew, and Bunney (1980) modified their earlier conceptualization of masked depression, stating that acting out behaviors may accompany depression in children but do not constitute part of a depression syndrome.

According to the revised third edition of the American Psychiatric Association's *Diagnostic and Statistical Manual of Mental Disorders* (DSM-III; American Psychiatric Association, 1987), depression in childhood and adolescence is diagnosed under the major heading of mood disorders. Depression was omitted from the category of disorders usually first evident in infancy, childhood, or adolescence based on research demonstrating similarities between the symptoms of depression in childhood and those in adulthood (e.g., Cytryn et al., 1980). Depressed children, like depressed adults, have low self-esteem, problems in attention and concentration, poor peer relationships, and are socially withdrawn (Strauss, Forehand, Frame, & Smith, 1984). Additionally, depressed children manifest the same cognitive distortions and attributional style as depressed adults (e.g., Leitenberg, Yost, & Carroll-Wilson, 1986; Seligman et al., 1984) and respond similarly to antidepressant medication (Reynolds, 1985).

According to the DSM-III-R, depressive syndromes fall under the general classification of mood disorders and include major depression, bipolar disorders, and dysthymia. These syndromes are differentiated by specific clusters of symptoms, age of onset, and duration of disturbance (Reynolds, 1984). Of primary interest to school psychologists are major depression and dysthymia. The diagnostic criteria for these two disorders are basically the same for children and adults, with a few minor modifications. Diagnostic criteria for major depressive episode include a loss of interest or pleasure in all or almost all usual activities and the presence of at least five of the following symptoms nearly every day for at least 2 weeks.

1. depressed mood (or can be irritable mood in children and adolescents) most of the day, nearly every day, as indicated either by subjective account or observation by others)
2. markedly diminished interest or pleasure in all, or almost all, activities most of the day, nearly every day (as indicated either by subjective account or observation by others' of apathy most of the time)
3. significant weight loss or weight gain when not dieting (e.g., more than 5% of body weight in a month), or decrease or increase in appetite nearly every day (in children, consider failure to make expected weight gains)
4. insomnia or hypersomnia nearly every day
5. psychomotor agitation or retardation nearly every day (observable by others, not merely subjective feelings of restlessness or being slowed down)
6. fatigue or loss of energy nearly every day
7. feelings of worthlessness or excessive or inappropriate guilt (which may be delusional) nearly every day (not merely self-reproach or guilt about being sick)
8. diminished ability to think or concentrate, or indecisiveness, nearly every day (either by subjective account or as observed by others)
9. recurrent thoughts of death (not just fear of dying), recurrent suicidal ideation without a specific plan, or a suicide attempt or a specific plan for committing suicide (American Psychiatric Association, 1987:222).

Diagnostic criteria for dysthymia include depressed mood (or can be irritable mood in children and adolescents) for most of the day or most days and the presence of at least two of the following symptoms:

1. poor appetite or overeating
2. insomnia or hypersomnia
3. low energy or fatigue
4. low self-esteem
5. poor concentration, or difficulty making decisions
6. feelings of hopelessness (American Psychiatric Association, 1987:232).

The symptoms are not as severe as in a major depressive episode, and the depressive syndrome may be relatively persistent or separated by a period of normal mood lasting up to several weeks at a time. The depressive syndrome must have a 2-year history (or 1 year for children and adolescents).

Despite the similarity in depressive symptoms in childhood and adulthood, the expression of these symptoms will differ at different ages. Herzog and Rathbun (1982) outlined the different forms each depressive symptom may take at a given developmental period. For example, somatic complaints might take the form of encopresis in a 3- to 5-year-old child, abdominal pain in a 6- to 8-year-old, and anorexia nervosa in a 13- to 18-year-old. Clearly, it is important to consider developmental differences in applying adult diagnostic criteria to children and adolescents.

Advances in Assessment of Depression

The lack of consensus regarding both the existence of depression in children as well as diagnostic criteria impeded the development of measures of depression in children and adolescents. Since the early 1980s, several measures of childhood and adolescent depression have been the topic of empirical investigation. The availability of a criterion group of depressed children is critical to the development of measures of depression. Children and adolescents can reliably be diagnosed as depressed according to DSM-III criteria (Lobovits & Handal, 1985; Kazdin, Colbus, & Rodgers, 1986). Children and adolescents diagnosed as depressed according to DSM-III criteria comprise the depressed group in studies investigating the criterion-related validity of measures of depression. Several of these recently developed measures of depression in childhood and adolescence are discussed later in this chapter.

Link between Depression and Suicide

A consistent relationship has been found between depression and suicide in children and adolescents (Cohen-Sandler, Berman, & King, 1982; Holinger & Offer, 1981; Pfeffer, Solomon, Plutchik, Mizruchi, & Weiner, 1982). For example, Bettes and Walker (1986) examined the frequency of suicide thoughts, suicidal acts, and the symptoms of 23 major behavioral problems among adolescent first admissions to a variety of in- and outpatient psychiatric facilities. Whereas depression was the most common symptom among adolescents manifesting suicidal thoughts and/or acts, anger was the most common symptom among nonsuicidal children. The relationship between depression and suicidal thoughts and gestures was stronger in girls than in boys. Over one third of the girls who were rated as showing depression also manifested suicidal ideation and/or gestures, and almost one fourth of the girls showing depression made suicidal gestures. Bettes and

Walker (1986) concluded that depression should be viewed as a suicidal risk factor in children.

The link between depression and suicidal thoughts and gestures gains additional significance when data on the rate of adolescent suicide are considered. The rate of adolescent suicide has tripled in the past 20 years and is the third leading cause of death among adolescents in the United States (Holinger & Offer, 1981).

Prevalence of Depression

Reynolds (1984) reviewed studies reporting prevalence rates ranging from 19 to 59 percent among clinic populations of children and adolescents. This variability is probably a result of differences in diagnostic criteria, age groups, and referral populations. Lobovits and Handal (1985) investigated the prevalence of depression among 8- to 12-year-olds referred to an outpatient psychological clinic. Using DSM-III criteria, 34 percent of children were diagnosed as depressed, based on a child clinical interview, as compared with 22 percent diagnosed as depressed based on parent interviews. Of particular concern to school psychologists is the prevalence of depression among public school students. Reynolds (1986) reports the results of several epidemiologic studies of depression that he and his colleagues conducted involving over 8,000 children and adolescents in public and private schools. Using the Beck Depression Inventory (BDI; Beck et al., 1961) with adolescents and employing the recommended cutoff scores for adults, Reynolds found that 7 percent of high school students are severely depressed, 9 percent moderately depressed, and 18 percent mildly depressed. The mildly depressed category is considered to reflect a subclinical level of depression. Thus, 16 percent of high school students score in the clinically depressed range of the BDI. Using a downward extension of the BDI, the Children's Depression Inventory (Kovacs, 1983; 1980/1981), Reynolds reported that 13 percent of children in grades 4 to 6 score above the recommended cutoff score of 19. Reynolds concluded that at any one time, 14 percent of children in grades 4 to 6 and 16 percent of adolescents manifest clinical levels of depression. Similar results using self-report measures have been reported by other researchers (Smucker, Craighead, Craighead, & Green, 1986). Certainly, these findings suggest a significant number of children and adolescents manifest clinically relevant levels of depressive symptomatology.

Efficacy of Cognitive Therapy with Depressed Adults

The singular most important development in the psychological treatment of depressed adults is cognitive therapy patterned on Beck's (1967) cognitive therapy and Ellis's (1962) rational-emotive therapy. Cognitive therapies for depression attempt to change a person's thinking patterns that produce depressive symptoms. Depressed persons have a systematically negative bias in their thinking that causes them to have a negative view of themselves, the world, and the future. The depressed individual distorts reality by engaging in distorted thinking. Both Beck and Ellis believe these cognitive distortions, or errors, produce the motivational and affective symptoms of depression. The cognitive model of depression is summarized later in this chapter.

Evidence of the efficacy of cognitive therapy and its modifications with depressed adults is reviewed by Rush, Beck, Kovacs, and Hollon (1977) and Coyne and Gotlib (1983). The success of cognitive therapy with adults has stimulated interest in using a modified form of cognitive therapy with children and adolescents (e.g., Butler, Miezitis, Friedman, & Cole, 1980; Reynolds & Coats, 1986).

A COGNITIVE MODEL OF CHILDHOOD DEPRESSION

Depressed adults are characterized by a negative view of themselves (i.e., low self-esteem), the world, and the future. This negative triad is maintained by cognitive processes that permit the individual to systematically distort reality such that their negative bias is confirmed (Beck, 1976). For example, depressed individuals make causal explanations for success and failure that help them maintain a negative view of themselves and of their chance of future success (Sweeney, Anderson, & Bailey, 1986). Specifically, depressed individuals, compared with nondepressed individuals, tend to attribute successful outcomes to external, specific, and unstable causes. Yet, they tend to attribute failures to internal, stable, and global causes. Therefore, when depressed individuals succeed, they attribute success to variable factors outside their control (e.g., luck, task ease). Because they do not credit themselves with success, they do not experience a boost to their self-esteem when they are successful. Furthermore, the success experience does not lead them to be more self-confident when confronted with the same situation a second time. When depressed individuals fail, they blame themselves for the failure (e.g., I am just not any good at that). Because they attribute failure to their own ability (or lack thereof), they expect to fail again when confronted with the same situation. Their attributional style maintains their low self-esteem and sense of hopelessness. There is substantial evidence that depressed children demonstrate the same depressogenic attributional style as depressed adults (Kaslow, Rehm, & Siegel, 1984; Seligman et al., 1984; Fielstein et al., 1985).

Depressed individuals distort experience in other ways that confirm their negative view of themselves, the world, and the future. A central theme of Beck's cognitive model of depression (1967) is that depressed individuals characteristically make specific dysphoria-provoking cognitive errors in response to ambiguous or negative life experiences. Beck, Rush, Shaw, and Emery (1979) described seven of these cognitive errors, summarized by Leitenberg, Yost, and Carroll-Wilson (1986):

> overgeneralization (believing that if a negative outcome occurred in one case, it will occur in any case that is even slightly similar); selective abstraction (attending exclusively to negative features of a situation in the belief that only the negative features matter); assuming excessive responsibility or personal causality (seeing oneself as responsible for all bad things, failures, and so on); presuming temporal causality or predicting without sufficient evidence (believing that if something bad happened in the past then it's always going to be true); making self-references (believing oneself, especially one's bad performances, to be the center of everyone's attention); catastrophizing (always thinking of the worst on the premise that it's most likely to happen to one); and thinking dichotomously (seeing everything as one extreme or another, black or white, good or bad (p. 528).

Although a substantial body of literature supports the view that depressed adults are prone to these cognitive errors (Coyne & Gotlib, 1983), only recently have researchers investigated the role of cognitive distortions in childhood depression. Leitenberg and his colleagues (Leitenberg et al., 1986) found that children in fourth to sixth and in eighth grade reporting symptoms of depression, low self-esteem, and evaluation anxiety make more of Beck's cognitive errors than do children not reporting these symptoms.

Depressed individuals also show self-control deficits that enable them to maintain their depressive state. Rehm's (1977) self-control model of depression is derived from Kanfer's self-control model (Kanfer & Karoly, 1972) and incorporates aspects of the models of Beck (1967), Lewinsohn (1974), and Seligman (1975). Depressed individuals are hypothesized to have deficits in one or more of the three stages of self-control: self-monitoring, self-evaluation, and self-reinforcement. The self-control deficits that characterize depressed individuals are as follows: (1) selective monitoring or attending to negative events and reduced attention to positive events; (2) selective monitoring of immediate as opposed to delayed consequences of behavior; (3) setting of overly stringent self-evaluation criteria; (4) failing to make accurate internal attributions of causality; (5) insufficient self-reinforcement; and (6) excessive punishment.

Depressed individuals' self-reinforcement practices also differ from those of nondepressed individuals in ways that maintain their depressive state. Children classified as depressed on a self-report measure of depression, the Children's Depression Inventory (Kovacs, 1983), set more stringent standards for a poor score, prefer punishing over rewarding consequences for performance, expect to perform more poorly, and evaluate their performance more negatively than do nondepressed children (Kaslow et al., 1984).

These findings support the view that depressed children demonstrate the same self-control deficits found in depressed adults.

Self-control deficits are assumed to be a result of a lifetime of learning, with early parent-child interactions playing a crucial role in the ontogenesis of depressogenic self-control processes. Supporting evidence of the importance of parent-child interactions is provided by studies reporting a high incidence of depression in children of mothers hospitalized for depression (e.g., Eisenbruch, 1983). Recently Cole and Rehm (1986) provided additional evidence to support the role of parental reinforcement practices in childhood depression. Parents of depressed children were found to set higher standards for reinforcement and to reward less frequently than were parents of nondepressed children.

COGNITIVE BEHAVIORAL APPROACHES TO THE ASSESSMENT OF DEPRESSION

Assessment of depression in children and adolescents should include multiple sources of information (e.g., parent, child, and therapist ratings) and both impact and specifying assessment measures. Impact assessment measures are used for screening and identification as well as for assessing the outcome of intervention. Specifying assessment measures are used to identify specific cognitive and behavioral targets (e.g., deficit self-reinforcement practices, faulty attributional processes, and cognitive distortions). Reynolds (1986) proposed a three-stage school-based assessment model for screening and identifying depression. This model, which incorporates self-report measures and clinical interviews, is excellent for assessment at the impact assessment level. In the folowing section this model is described briefly and assessment measures recommended by Reynolds at each stage of the model are reviewed. Additionally, a parent report measure of depression is reviewed. Finally, measures of specific cognitive and behavioral deficits that characterize depressive individuals are reviewed.

Reynolds' School-Based Assessment Model

Reynolds (1986) presents a multistage model that can be used by school psychologists to identify children and adolescents manifesting clinically relevant levels of depression in grades 3 and above. Reynolds and his colleagues tested the model with over 8,000 children and adolescents during the years 1980 to 1985. The model consists of three primary assessment stages: (1) school-wide tests with self-report measures of depression; (2) retests 3 to 6 weeks following school-wide assessment of those children who, on the basis of the large group screening at stage 1, manifest clinically relevant levels of depression; and (3) individual clinical interviews with children who meet cutoff scores for depression at both stage 1 and stage 2 evaluations. The rationale for the stage 2 retest is to distinguish between those children and adolescents experiencing transient mood fluctuations and those experiencing clinical levels of depression. In this regard, DSM-III criteria require that the depressive symptoms be manifest for at least 2 weeks (for major depression) or for 1 year for (dysthymic disorder). Support for retesting also comes from research demonstrating that between 18 and 20 percent of students score above cutoff scores on the first administration of self-report measures. On retesting, between 25 and 30 percent of these students no longer score in the depressed range. This reduction is due, in part, to the consistent but unexplained finding that individuals obtain lower scores on self-report depression inventories on the second administration (Reynolds, 1986).

The model identifies approximately 12 to 15 percent of a school population as manifesting clinical levels of depression based on stage 1 and stage 2 assessments. This is still a relatively large percentage of the school population that advances to the third assessment stage, the clinical interview. The third stage assessment is the most costly and labor-intensive. However, only those individuals who manifest clinically relevant levels of depression receive the benefit of this 20- to 40-minute interview. Only 20 to 40 percent of the adoescents interviewed at stage 3 are identified as not depressed. Therefore, the model demonstrates good cost efficiency. Overall, use of the complete model results in the identification of approximately 7 to 12 percent of the student population as manifesting clinical levels of depression. Reynolds cautions that the model is intended not to provide a formal diagnosis of depression but to identify children and adolescents who require some intervention.

Reynolds recommends either the Children's Depression Inventory (Kovacs, 1983, 1980/1981) or the Child Depression Scale (Reynolds, in press) for stage 1 and stage 2 assessment of children. For adolescents, he recommends the Adolescent Depression Scale (RADS; Reynolds, 1987a, 1987b) or the Beck Depression Inventory (BDI; Beck et al., 1961). The Children's Depression Rating Scale (Poznanski et al., 1984) is recommended for the child clinical interview at stage 3, and the Hamilton Depression Rating Scale (Hamilton, 1960, 1967) is recommended for stage 3 assessment of adolescents. These measures will be described and evidence of their psychometric properties summarized.

The Children's Depression Inventory

The Children's Depression Inventory (CDI; Kovacs, 1983, 1980/1981) is the most widely cited self-report childhood depression measure (Saylor, Finch, Spirito, & Bennett, 1984). The CDI is a 27-item downward extension of the popular Beck Depression Inventory (Beck et al., 1961). Each item is designed to assess one symptom of depression, and the total score is considered an index of the severity of depressive symptoms. Each item asks children to choose one of three alternatives that best describes them for the last 2-week period. Items sample the domain of overt symptoms of childhood depression including sadness, anhedonia, suicide ideation, and sleep and eating disturbances. It differs from the BDI in the addition of six items pertaining to school and age-related symptoms. The three alternatives are assigned weights of 0, 1, or 2 in the direction of increasing depressive symptoms. The range of scores is 0 to 54.

Numerous research investigations using the CDI are reviewed by Finch and Saylor (1984), Reynolds (1984, 1985, 1986), and Saylor, Finch, Spirito, and Bennett (1984). The following summary is based on these reviews as well as more recent investigations (Lobovits & Handal, 1985; Kazdin, Colbus, & Rodgers, 1986; Saylor, Finch, Baskin, Furey, & Kelly, 1984; Smucker et al., 1986).

Test-retest reliability of the CDI is good, ranging from 0.38 to 0.83 for periods of 1 to 4 weeks, with most studies reporting reliabilities in the upper end of this range. Scores are fairly stable over periods up to 6 months (Seligman et al., 1984). The CDI is internally consistent, with alpha coefficients ranging from 0.71 to 0.94.

Although the CDI does a good job of discriminating emotionally disturbed from nonemotionally disturbed children, it is not very good at discriminating depressed children and nondepressed emotionally disturbed children. In this regard, CDI scores correspond with a broad range of symptoms and pathologic patterns, including low self-esteem, anger, anxiety, and aggression (Saylor, Finch, Baskin, Furey, and Kelly, 1984). Thus, the CDI is sensitive to emotional distress but not to the depressed syndrome as compared with other emotional disorders (Saylor, Finch, Baskin, Furey, & Kelly, 1984).

Correlations between CDI scores and therapist ratings of depression have been inconsistent, perhaps because of differences in the sample, ages, and diagnostic criteria of depression. In a well-designed study, Lobovits and Handal (1985) administered the CDI to clinic-referred children who were or were not diagnosed as depressed, according to DSM-III criteria. Using the recommended cutoff score of 19 (Kovacs, 1980/1981), the CDI correctly classified 84 percent of children, with no false-positive results. However, use of this cutoff score correctly classified only 47 percent of the depressed children. The cutoff score resulting in the highest classification accuracy was 12. This cutoff score produced an 88 percent overall classification accuracy, with 76 percent of the depressed children classified as depressed on the CDI. Although 12 appears the optimal cutoff score for emotionally disturbed populations (Kazdin, Colbus & Rodgers, 1986), a cutoff score of 19 is a more appropriate screening measure for use in the schools because of the large percentage of children scoring above 12 in a normal population. Smucker and his colleagues reported norms of the CDI based on 1,252 school children aged 8 to 16 years. The mean score was 9 (standard deviation 7), and a cutoff score on the CDI of 19 identified the upper 10 percent of the distribution. Reynolds reported that 13 percent of a population of normal school children score at or above 19 on the CDI.

Child Depression Scale

The Child Depression Scale (CDS; Reynolds, in press) is a 30-item paper-and-pencil self-report measure with psychometric properties very similar to those of the CDI (Reynolds, in press; Reynolds et al., 1985; Bartell & Reynolds, 1986) The CDS and the CDI correlate highly with each other ($r = 0.70$) as well as with measures of anxiety and self-esteem.

Beck Depression Inventory

Beck Depression Inventory (BDI; Beck et al., 1961) is a 21-item self-report measure of symptom severity that has been researched extensively with adults. It is the most frequently used measure of depression in adults (Reynolds, 1985). Each item has four alternatives varying in symptom severity. A respondent selects the one alternative that best describes him or her over the last 2 weeks. Although intended for adults, the BDI is frequently used with adolescents. Research on its use with adolescents indicates it has good test-retest reliability and internal consistency (Strober, Green, & Carlson, 1981; Teri, 1982; Reynolds & Coats, 1982). The BDI scores correlate with therapists' global ratings of depression and discriminate between depressed and nondepressed psychiatrically hospitalized adolescents (Strober et al., 1981).

Reynolds Adolescent Depression Scale

The Reynolds Adolescent Depression Scale (RADS; Reynolds, 1987a, 1987b) is a self-report measure developed specifically for use with adolescents. Extensive normative and psychometric data on the RADS are reported in the RADS manual (Reynolds, 1987a). The RADS is reliable and internally consistent, and the RADS scores correlate highly (r is between 0.71 and 0.89) with BDI scores and clinical interviews.

In summary, the CDI and CDS for children and the BDI and RADS for adolescents are reliable and internally consistent self-report measures of the severity of depressive symptoms. The major limitation of these scales is that scores are specific not to depression but to emotional distress in general.

Interview Assessment

Among several interview formats for assessing depression in children and adolescents, two are recommended by Reynolds on the basis of their relatively brief administration time of 20 to 40 minutes. Both of these interview schedules are specific to depression, whereas other diagnostic interview schedules, such as the K-SADS (Puig-Antich & Chambers, 1978), are designed to yield differential diagnoses.

The Children's Depression Rating Scale (CDRS; Poznanski et al., 1984) is intended for children between 6 and 12 years of age. A downward extension of the Hamilton Depression Rating Scale, the CDRS is completed by the interviewer after a 30- to 40-minute child interview. Rather than yielding a diagnosis, the CDRS yields a measure of the severity of depressive symptoms, with recommended cutoff scores for classifying depressed children. The CDRS scores discriminate between depressed and nondepressed psychiatric inpatients and correlate significantly with therapists' global ratings of depression. Test-retest reliability for a 2-week period was 0.86 in a psychiatric sample (Poznanski et al., 1984).

Parent Ratings

The screening and identification model proposed by Reynolds can be supplemented with parent rating scales, parent interviews, or both. For example, parents of children and adolescents who score above cutoff scores at stages 1 and 2 could be asked to complete the Child Behavior Checklist (CBCL; Achenbach & Edelbrock, 1983). Children who appear depressed on the basis of self-report measures and the CBCL could be interviewed by the psychologist.

Parent rating scales and interviews also can be used with child self-report measures and child interviews in assessing depression in children referred to the psychologist. The CBCL is the most respected and best validated behavior rating scale for children between ages 4 and 16. Parallel forms exist for parent, teacher, and child raters. Subscales representing narrow-band syndromes were derived from separate factor analyses for each age group and sex. The 17-item depression subscale is one of nine narrow-band behavior problem scales and one of five scales composing the broad bandwidth internalizing factor. Children's scores on the internalizing scales of the teacher report form correlate with their scores on the CDI (Kaslow et al., 1984). However, parents' ratings of depression do not correlate significantly with children's responses on the CDI or interview measures of depression (Kazdin, French, Unis, & Esveldt-Dawson, 1983).

SPECIFYING ASSESSMENT MEASURES

Specifying measures of depression based on cognitive models of depression attempt to define the cognitive distortions and biases that permit the individual to filter experiences in such a way as to confirm the negative view of the self, the world, and the future. The KASTAN (Kaslow, Tanenbaum, & Seligman, 1978), Attributional Style Questionnaire (Fielstein et al., 1985), Cognitive Errors Test (Leitenberg et al., 1986), and Hopelessness Scale (Kazdin, Rodgers & Colbus, 1986) are three such specifying assessment measures. In addition to these measures, which are specific to depression, measures of interpersonal problem solving may be relevant to assessing depressed children. Measures of problem solving are reviewed in chapter 10.

KASTAN

The KASTAN consists of 48 items. Each item includes a situation (e.g., You get good grades) and two possible attributions to explain why the situation occurred (e.g., I am a hard worker *versus* School work is simple).

> Children are instructed to choose the alternative that describes best why the event in question happened to them. Half of the situations represent "good" outcomes; half represent "bad" outcomes. There are six subscales, with 8 items on each: (1) Good-Internal/External, (2) Good-Stable/Unstable, (3) Good-Specific/Global, (4) Bad-Internal/External, (5) Bad-Stable/Unstable, (6) Bad-Specific/Global. Two composite scores were derived: a "good" composite score (the sum of subscales 1, 2, and 3 above), and a "bad" composite score (the sum of subscales 4, 5, and 6 above). The overall summary score for the KASTAN is the "good" composite score minus the "bad" composite score. The lower the score, the more depressogenic the attributional style (Kaslow, Rehm, & Siegel, 1984:610–611).

KASTAN scores correlate with self-reported depression (Palmer, Pfefferbaum, & Stowe, 1986; Kaslow et al., 1984; Saylor, Finch, Baskin, Furey, & Kelly, 1984). Psychometric properties of the KASTAN are not yet published. The KASTAN is a promising measure of depressive attributional style; however, until evidence of its psychometric properties is published, it cannot be considered a reliable and valid measure of depressogenic attributional style.

Attributional Style Questionnaire

Developed by Fielstein and his colleagues (1985), the Attributional Style Questionnaire consists of 12 vignettes, each describing either a social, athletic, or academic event and an outcome of that event (success or failure).

Children select one of four possible causal attributions for the success or failure: skill/lack of skill; effort/lack of effort; good luck/bad luck; and task ease/difficulty. Example vignettes depicting athletic success and social failure follow (the labels in parentheses are not included on the instrument):

(Athletic Success)
You and some friends are playing soccer. You get the ball, dribble past someone on the other team, and score a goal. Which of the following reasons best explains why this happened?
(a) I'm good at soccer (skill).
(b) I tried my best (effort).
(c) I got lucky (luck).
(d) It was an easy game (task ease).

(Social Failure)
You have two friends whom you like to walk to school with. One day you see them walking to school together and they didn't come to get you. Which of the following reasons best explains why this happened?
(a) People never like me as much as they like their other friends (lack of skill).
(b) They were not in a friendly mood that day (bad luck).
(c) It's hard to be friendly with more than one person at the same time (task difficulty).
(d) I didn't let them know how much I wanted to walk with them (lack of effort).

Respondents receive scores for each type of attribution, for success scenes and failure scenes, and for each content area (social, athletic, and academic). Test-retest reliability of attributional choices was determined by computing the mean percentage of agreement between response choices over two test administrations. Over a 4-week interval for a sample of 99 fourth- fifth- and sixth-grade children, the mean percentage of agreements ranged from 62 to 96 percent for success scenes and from 52 to 85 percent for failure scenes. Children with high and low self-esteem differed in their attributions for success and failure. Children with high self-esteem chose skill more often than did children with low self-esteem to explain successful outcomes in each content area. Children with low self-esteem made more causal attributions to effort and task ease for successful outcomes in social situations but not in athletic or academic situations. Finally, children with low self-esteem, compared with children with high self-esteem, were more likely to attribute success to good luck in all three areas. In every situation, children with low self-esteem used lack of skill to explain failure more often than did children with high self-esteem. Children with low self-esteem, compared with children with high self-esteem, generally attribute their success to unstable factors such as good luck and effort and their failure to the internal and more stable category of lack of ability. The authors argue that their results support the need to distinguish between two types of internal attributions (ability and effort), as differing results were obtained for effort and ability attributions. Although these group results were obtained with children with high and low self-esteem, given the strong correlation between self-esteem and depression, the same pattern of results is expected with depressed and nondepressed children. In this regard, Seligman et al. (1984), using a different attributional measure, found similar attributional differences between depressed and nondepressed children.

Hopelessness Scale

Hopelessness, or negative expectations toward the future, is central to cognitive theories of depression (Beck, 1976). Hopelessness constitutes part of the negative triad that maintains depressive symptoms in adults (Beck, 1976). Kazdin and his colleagues (Kazdin, French, Unis, Esveldt-Dawson, & Sherick, 1983; Kazdin, Rodgers & Colbus, 1986) developed a measure of hopelessness for children. The rationale for the hopelessness scale is that hopelessness and negative self-esteem are associated with a sense of futility and social withdrawal. Additionally, hopelessness may be associated with suicidal ideation and behaviors in children as it is in adults.

The Hopelessness Scale for Children is patterned on an adult measure of hopelessness (Beck, Weissman, Lester, & Trexler, 1974) and it consists of 17 statements which children endorse as true or false. Example items (with the response scored for hopelessness in parentheses) are "I want to grow up because I think things will be better" (F) and "I don't think I will have any real fun when I grow up" (T). Higher scores reflect greater hopelessness. The use of the scale in 262 inpatient psychiatric children between the ages of 6 and 13 demonstrated its good internal consistency. Test-retest reliability over a 6-week interval was 0.52. Although the short-term stability is low, the transient nature of depressive symptoms in nondepressed populations must be taken into account in evaluating the scale's stability. Regarding the scale's validity, hopelessness was positively correlated with self-reported depression and with an interview assessment of depression and negatively correlated with self-esteem and self-reported social skills. Hopelessness scores did not correlate significantly with parent ratings of social competence or child behavior problems. Therefore, scores correlate with other self-report measures but not with behavior ratings from other sources. Additionally, hopelessness scores were not associated with the diagnosis of depression or with the severity of dysfunction in general. These results may be due to the restricted range of the sample (inpatient psychiatric children). The Hopelessness Scale is a promising instrument; however, it needs to be examined with a broader range of children to determine whether it is sensitive to emotional disturbance in general and, more specifically, to depression.

Cognitive Errors Test

Cognitive errors are central to Beck's theory of depression in adults (Beck, 1967). Leitenberg et al. (1986) developed a self-report questionnaire designed to measure cognitive errors in children. The Children's Negative Cognitive Error Questionnaire (CNCEQ) was modeled on an adult cognitive error questionnaire (Lefebvre, 1981). The CNCEQ consists of 24 items, each of which is composed of a brief description of a hypothetical situation or event, followed by a statement that reflects one of four cognitive errors (catastrophizing, overgeneralizing, personalizing, and selective abstraction). The categorization of items was based on a consensus of 10 clinical psychology graduate students as to which error the item represents. Children rate the similarity of each statement to their own thoughts when they imagine being in that situation or experiencing that event. Items depict situations and events in three content areas: social, athletic, and academic. Children rate each item on a 5-point scale from "not at all like I would think" (1) to "almost exactly like I would think" (5). A total cognitive distortion score is computed by adding the ratings on all 24 items. Subscale scores are obtained for each content area. Examples of two items follow (information in parentheses is not included in the item):

> Your cousin calls you to ask if you would like to go on a long bike ride. You think, "I probably won't be able to keep up and people will make fun of me." (catastrophyzing in the athletic area)
> You call one of the kids in your class to talk about your math homework. He/she says, "I can't talk to you now, my father needs to use the phone." You think, "He/she didn't want to talk to me." (personalizing in the social area)

Test-retest reliability over a 4-week interval was investigated in a sample of 143 children in grades 5 to 8. The test-retest correlation for the total score was 0.65 and for error types ranged from 0.44 to 0.58. The scale is internally consistent (alpha coefficient = 0.89). Normative data on the CNCEQ were obtained from 637 children in fourth, sixth, and eighth grades in public schools in Rochester, New York. More cognitive errors were made in the social content than in the athletic or academic areas, presumably because of more ambiguous criteria for success in social contexts. Younger children obtained higher total scores than did older students. The relationship of cognitive errors to depressive symptoms was investigated in three different samples of school children. Cognitive error scores were associated with self-reported depression, low self-esteem, and evaluation anxiety.

The CNCEQ is sensitive to internalizing symptoms (depression, low self-esteem, and anxiety). The question of whether it is sensitive to general psychopathology or, more specifically, to depressive symptoms has not been addressed in research to date. Research with aggressive children has documented systematic cognitive errors made by aggressive children in interpreting social cues (Dodge, Murphy, and Buchsbaum, 1984). The type of cognitive errors made by different groups of disturbed children may differ of course, and future research needs to address which cognitive errors are associated with which clinical syndromes. Additionally, future research needs to demonstrate that cognitive error scores are associated with children's thoughts and actions in real-life situations.

COGNITIVE-BEHAVIORAL INTERVENTIONS

In comparison with the recent surge in research on assessment of depression in children and adolescents, little has appeared on psychological treatment of depression in children and adolescents. In a comprehensive review of the literature, Reynolds (1985) was able to find only four such intervention studies. One case study (Petti, Bornstein, Delamater, & Conners, 1980) combined pharmacologic and multimodal therapy in the treatment of a hospitalized adolescent. Because the design did not permit a determination of the contributions of the different treatment elements or their interactions, it does not contribute very much to our understanding of the effectiveness of psychological treatment. It is not at all clear that subjects in one of the studies reviewed by Reynolds (Frame, Matson, Sonis, Fialkov, & Kazdin, 1982) were depressed, as no measure of depression was used at pretest. The two remaining studies (Butler et al., 1980; Reynolds & Coats, 1986) are especially interesting because they demonstrate the feasibility and efficacy of school-based cognitive-behavioral programs with depressed children. These two studies plus a more recent study (Stark, Reynolds, & Kaslow, 1987) are described later in this chapter.

Several authors (Kashani & Cantwell, 1983; Kaslow & Rehm, 1983) have argued that the treatment of depression in children and adolescents should focus on specific depressive symptoms, such as social withdrawal, low self-esteem, helplessness, and low activity level. Next, two intervention studies that focus on specific symptoms of depression are reviewed.

Social Skills Training

Depressed children are not as well accepted by their peers as are nondepressed children (Faust, Baum, & Forehand, 1985). Also, depressed children tend to be socially withdrawn (Strauss et al., 1984). Interventions that focus on improving depressed children's and adolescents' social skills may improve depressive symptoms.

In a single subject case study of a coaching intervention with a shy adolescent boy (Franco, Christoff, Crimmins, & Kelly, 1983:569–570), the diagnosis of extreme shyness was based on a comprehensive assessment of the subject's social interactional problem:

> The subject was a 14-year-old male referred to our outpatient clinic by his parents who were concerned about their son's longstanding shyness and deficient relationships with peers. [His parents] reported that he still had no friends of his own age and primarily associated with children 5 to 8 years younger than himself after school. At other times, the adolescent confined himself to his bedroom for long periods of time and conversed minimally with others. When he did talk with neighbors or relatives, his interactions were reported to be brief, accompanied by little affect and the avoidance of eye contact.

In addition to information obtained from the parent interview, assessment data included interviews with school personnel regarding the teenager's social interactions, direct observations, and an interview with the teenager, who reported he was unhappy because he did not have friends. He reported that he had no fearful cognitions or physiologic arousal associated with social interaction. "The subject appeared to be a somewhat depressed young person with minimal conversational skills, no friends, and a longstanding socially isolated lifestyle" (Franco et al., 1983:570).

A multiple baseline design across behaviors was used to assess the effects of conversational skills. Conversational skills were assessed by having the adolescent initiate and maintain a conversation with an unfamiliar partner after each treatment session. The frequencies of each targeted conversational skill were rated during these unstructured conversations. Generalization of training effects was assessed by teacher, parent, and self-reports of social behaviors. Also, unfamiliar, popular peers rated the teenager's conversational performance based on videotapes made during baseline and at posttreatment. These ratings included skill performance as well as how much the peer judges themselves would enjoy talking to the subject. Targeted skills were selected based on previous research evidence that they were related to positive ratings of conversational competence and loneliness in teenagers. Trained skills included asking questions, making reinforcing/acknowledging comments, eye contact, and affective warmth.

Training consisted of 30 sessions lasting 20 to 30 minutes over a period of 15 weeks. The coaching procedure included five steps:

1. Rationale for skilled behavior.
2. Modeling of skill.
3. Verbal or behavioral rehearsal.
4. Feedback.
5. Homework assignment to practice the skill with others.

Training resulted in marked and durable improvements in each skill. Peer judges' ratings validated improvement in conversational skills and provided support for the social validity of the selected skills. Teacher and parent ratings indicated marked and lasting improvement in academic performance, social adjustment, participation in extracurricular activities, conversational skill, and the ability to make friends.

Attribution Retraining

Studies have demonstrated that depressed children, compared with nondepressed children, attribute success to external, unstable, and specific factors and failure to internal, stable, and global factors (Seligman et al., 1984; Fielstein et al., 1985). Thus, the attributional style of depressed youth was similar to that of helpless children in research conducted by Dweck and her colleagues (Diener & Dweck, 1978; Dweck, 1975; Dweck & Reppucci, 1973). Helpless children, compared with mastery children, give up after failure and attribute failure to their lack of ability. After failure, their performance deteriorates sharply. Helpless children are also less likely to attribute success to their ability, expect to do poorly in the future, and believe other children would do better than they had done. Thus, depressed and helpless children have an attributional style that maintains their negative views of themselves and of the future. In an attribution retraining study, Dweck (1975) compared the effects of two training procedures on helpless children's reactions to failure on an experimental task. One group was given success experiences only. The second group was given attribution retraining, which taught them to attribute failure to a lack of effort (an internal, unstable cause) versus a lack of ability (an internal, stable cause). After training, the performance of children in the success only treatment continued to deteriorate after failure. However, children in the attribution retraining group maintained or improved their performance. The conclusion that the performance change was mediated by a change in attributional style was supported by the finding that children in the attribution retraining condition increased the extent to which they attributed their failure to a lack of effort. Although training demonstrated the efficacy of attribution training in changing helpless students' achievement behavior on an experimental task, it cannot be assumed that the effects of training would generalize to the classroom. As Dweck noted, explicit generalization would probably be required to assure such generalization. Especially noteworthy is the failure of the success only condition to alter students' task persistence. The frequent recommendation to teachers to provide helpless children with more reinforcement and to ensure success may not be beneficial to helpless, depressed children. If they filter success experiences in such a way that they take no credit for the success, the success will not bolster their self-confidence or change their future expectancies for success. If they continue to filter failure experiences in such a way that they believe they are incompetent, they will continue to give up in the face of failure, regardless of how many successes they have. Success and failure experiences affect self-esteem and future performance expectancies through the mediating process of attributions. Therefore, the individual's maladaptive attributions must be modified to improve persistence after failure. This point is made succinctly by Dweck (1975:684):

> An instructional program for children who have difficulty dealing with failure would do well not to skirt the issue by trying to ensure success or by glossing over failure. Instead, it should include procedures for dealing with this problem directly. This is not to suggest that failure should be included in great amounts or that failure per se is desirable, but rather, that errors should be capitalized upon as vehicles for teaching the child how to handle failure.

Dweck's (1975) results suggest attribution retraining may be a beneficial component of interventions with depressed children with low self-esteem. However, a definitive conclusion on the efficacy of attribution retraining with depressed children awaits further investigation.

School-Based Intervention Programs

Butler et al. (1980) evaluated the effects of two school-based intervention programs on depressive symptoms in fifth- and sixth-grade children. Each program consisted of ten 1-hour sessions held weekly with groups of seven children. Children were identified as depressed based on teacher referral and a depression battery that included self-report measures of depression, self-esteem, cognitive distortions, and locus of control. The role-play program resembles the interpersonal problem-solving programs described by Spivack and Shure (1974) and others (Gesten et al., 1979; Weissberg et al., 1981a). Role-plays were used to present problems relevant to the depressed child such as acceptance and rejection by peers, success and failure, guilt, and loneliness. "The overriding objectives of the role play (program) were: (a) to sensitize the child to personal thoughts and feelings, and those of others; (b) to teach skills that facilitate social interaction; and (c) to teach a problem-solving approach to threatening or stressful situations by learning to generate as many potential solutions as possible" (Butler et al., 1980, p. 113).

The cognitive restructuring program was based on Beck's (1976) model of cognitive therapy for depression and on rational-emotive therapy (Ellis, 1962; Knaus, 1974). "The objectives were: (a) to teach recognition of irrational, self-deprecating automatic thoughts, and adoption of more logical and viable alternatives; (b) to enhance listening skills; and (c) to teach recognition of the relationship between thoughts and feelings" (Butler et al., 1980, p. 113).

Individuals were assigned to one treatment group or to an attention control or waiting list control group. The attention control group involved the group investigation model of teaching (Joyce & Weil, 1972), a cooperative learning strategy that maximizes group interdependence. Both the role-play and the cognitive restructuring groups improved on self-esteem and self-reported depression, and the role-play group also improved on measures of cognitive distortions and locus of control. Based on teacher reports of classroom behavior, the role-play program resulted in greater improvement than that in the other conditions.

This study by Butler (1980) and her colleagues demonstrates the feasibility and efficacy of a school-based interpersonal problem-solving intervention using role plays in improving self-reported symptoms of depression and classroom behavior of depressed youngsters. At the preadolescent age, the problem-solving approach is probably better than a rational-emotive therapy approach, as preadolescents may lack the cognitive sophistication to benefit from rational-emotive therapy, which requires considerable facility in abstract thinking and deductive reasoning.

Reynolds and Coats (1986) also evaluated the effects of two school-based intervention programs in decreasing depressive symptoms, although their subjects were adolescents. Both treatments, relaxation training and a cognitive-behavioral intervention, consisted of 10 hour-long small group sessions during a 5-week period. A waiting list control condition was also utilized. Reynolds's (1986) school-based screening model was used to identify depressed high school students. Of a high school population of 800, 30 students met all criteria for inclusion in the study, which included parental permission and student willingness to participate. As is typical in the treatment of depressive adults, the attribution rate was somewhat high, with 24 of the subjects completing posttreatment assessment and 21 completing follow-up assessment. However, the attrition rates were proportionate across groups.

The cognitive-behavioral program, based on Rehm's (1977) self-control model of depression, consisted of three phases that emphasized the training of self-control skills, including self-monitoring, self-evaluation, and self-reinforcement. Subjects were taught how to develop a self-change plan they could use when applying the self-control skills. Instructional methods included didactic presentation of self-control principles, group discussion, and homework. A brief outline of the concepts and skills emphasized in therapy sessions follows:

Session 1. Relationship between self-observation and mood; tendency to overattend to unpleasant events.

Session 2. Relation between positive activities and mood.

Session 3. Tendency to attend to immediate versus long-term effects of behavior.

Session 4. Causal attributions for positive and negative events.

Session 5. Problem-solving steps in developing a self-change plan.

Session 6. Setting realistic and obtainable goals.
Session 7. Self-reinforcement and self-punishment; cognitive distortions.
Session 8. Covert self-reward.
Sessions 9 and 10. Review of program and remediation of self-control deficits.

Subjects in the relaxation training program were taught the relationship between stress, muscle tension, and depression. Subjects were taught specific relaxation skills, and relaxation was introduced as a coping response for dealing with stress-provoking situations.

Both cognitive-behavioral therapy and relaxation therapy produced greater improvement in self-reported depression and clinical interviews for depression, and improvement was maintained 5 weeks after treatment. At posttreatment, 11 of the 14 subjects in the two active therapy conditions scored in the nondepressed range on the Beck Depression Inventory (Beck et al., 1961). No subject in the waiting list control group scored within the nondepressed range at posttreatment. At follow-up, all subjects in the active therapy groups scored in the nondepressed range, whereas only four of the nine waiting list subjects had scores in this range. Relaxation training also produced a reduction in anxiety, and cognitive-behavioral treatment resulted in improved academic self-concept. Thus, both cognitive-behavioral therapy and relaxation training were effective in the treatment of moderately depressed adolescents, with both treatments showing roughly equivalent results.

The finding that both therapies were effective may be explained by the fact that both therapies emphasized self-control. Although self-control principles per se were not taught in the relaxation program, subjects learned to use relaxation as a self-employed coping response to anxiety-producing situations. They also learned to self-monitor anxiety-producing events and the effectivenes of relaxation in reducing their anxiety. Therefore, both programs may counter the helpless attitude that is central to depression.

Stark, Reynolds, and Kaslow (1987) compared the relative effectiveness of two school-based cognitive-behavioral treatments with 29 moderately to severely depressed children ages 9 to 12 years. Children scoring above 13 on the Children's Depression Inventory (Kovacs, 1983) on two successive administrations were randomly assigned to one of three experimental conditions: self control, behavioral problem-solving, or wait list control. Both active treatments involved 12 45-to-50 minute small group sessions lasting over 5 weeks. The two treatments shared several common elements, including instruction in the relationship between mood and the frequency of engaging in pleasant activities, self-monitoring of pleasant activities, and reinforcement for completing the pleasant activities log sheets.

The self control training based on Rehm's (1977) self control theory of depression emphasized the following self-control skills: setting more realistic standards for performance, setting realistic subgoals, self-reinforcing more, self-punishing less, and attributing success to internal, stable factors and failure to external factors (bad luck, task difficulty) or to effort. These skills were taught via didactic presentation, exercises in therapy sessions, and behavioral homework assignments.

The behavioral problem-solving training emphasized social relationships, interpersonal problem solving, and the expression of feelings. The group discussion format permitted the formation of closer ties among group members than occurred in the more structured self control training. Group members' own situations and hypothetical social problems were the subject of group problem solving discussions.

Dependent measures were administered pretreatment, posttreatment, and 8 weeks following the last treatment session. These measures included two self report measures of depression, self-esteem, and anxiety, a semi-structured child interview for depression, and parent ratings of depression, anxiety, and internalizing symptoms. Both active treatments produced positive results on the self-report measures and on the child interview. The improvement continued from posttreatment to followup, suggesting the children began to participate in more pleasant activities during therapy and continued with these activities after treatment was completed. These improvements were clinically as well as statistically significant.

There were few between group differences for the active treatments. These differences indicate a slight superiority for the self control training on the self-report data and superiority for the behavioral problem solving training on parent ratings of social withdrawal and internalizing symptoms. The few between group differences are probably a result of the shared elements between the two treatments. Both treatments emphasized increasing pleasant activities and self-monitoring, two treatment elements which have been found highly successful with adults (Rehm et al., 1981). The greater gains on parent ratings for the behavioral problem solving treatment is probably a result of its greater emphasis on social behavior and increasing activity.

In summary, the combined results of these three school-based intervention programs with depressed children and adolescents are very encouraging. Because these programs actually combine several treatment components, it is not possible at this time to state which components are effective. Elementary school children benefit from social skills training that incorporates behavioral problem solving and from self-control training. Depressed adolescents benefit from social skills training, relaxation training, and self-control training. A common element of all these interventions is the emphasis on the individual's control over his or her depression. Thus, all these interventions challenge the depressed individual's sense of helplessness and hopelessness. Because a self-control treatment and a behavioral problem solving treatment produced slightly different outcomes, a combined emphasis on self control and behavioral problem solving may be the optimal treatment package. Hopefully, future researchers will follow the example set by Reynolds and Coats (1986) and Stark et al. (1987) of comparing the outcomes of different treatments on multiple dependent measures. Additionally, the long term benefit of treatments needs to be documented in future research investigations.

8
Impulsive and Hyperactive Children

Lisa A. Moore and Jan N. Hughes
Texas A&M University

CONCEPTUAL AND DEFINITIONAL ISSUES

Hyperactive children often perplex as well as try the patience of their caretakers. These children display excessive impulsivity, apparent distractibility, problems with attention deployment, and difficulties in the general regulation of their behavior. Other symptoms commonly associated with hyperactivity include an inability to listen, difficulty in concentrating on and completing assignments, poor academic performance, and, at times, excessive motoric activity. These symptoms are most often apparent when the hyperactive child engages in activities that require self-monitoring and self-regulation, such as seat-work at school, and symptoms are less often observed when adults work one-on-one with the child or impose a rigorous structure (Barkley, 1981; Kendall & Braswell, 1985; Ross & Ross, 1982; Weiss & Hechtman, 1986).

Terminology

Historically, many alternative labels have been given to this disorder, causing confusion as to its etiology (Routh, 1983; Weiss & Hechtman, 1986). For example, "minimal brain damage" implies actual structural damage to the central nervous system; "minimal brain dysfunction" reflects the view that while observable localized damage is not evident, neurochemical or neuropsychological malfunctions may exist; and "maturational lag" or "developmental hyperactivity" suggest the idea of delayed development, with afflicted children eventually outgrowing their problems. Similarly educationally oriented professionals view hyperactivity as an academic impediment, thus constituting a learning disability. Douglas (1983), Halparin, Gittlemen, Klein, and Rudel (1984), Komm (1982), Rosenthal and Allen (1978), and Ross and Ross (1982) thoroughly discuss this terminological obfuscation.

The terminology dispute has continued. In 1980 the name of this disorder was changed to DSM-III (American Psychiatric Association, 1980) to "attention disorder disorder" (ADD) with or without hyperactivity, acknowledging the attentional deficiency as a more fundamental disability relative to the other symptoms of the disorder. The following operational criteria for diagnosis of ADD with hyperactivity were included in DSM-III: (1) qualitatively and quantitatively excessive general hyperactivity or motor restlessness for the child's age, (2) difficulty in sustaining attention, (3) impulsive behavior, (4) duration of the symptoms above for at least 6 months, (5) onset before 7 years of age, and (6) the factors mentioned above must not be attributable to psychosis or severe mental retardation.

In the 1987 edition of the DSM-III-Revised (American Psychiatric Association, 1987), hyperactivity was replaced in the name of the disorder, nor referred to as attention-deficit hyperactivity disorder (ADHD). Table 8.1 lists the diagnostic criteria for ADHD.

Barkley (1981) finds the DSM-III criteria much too vague and liberal for

Table 8.1. Diagnostic Criteria for Attention-Deficit Hyperactivity Disorder

A. A disturbance of at least six months during which at least eight of the following are present:

1. often fidgets with hands or feet or squirms in seat (in adolescents, may be limited to subjective feelings of restlessness)
2. has difficulty remaining seated when required to do so
3. is easily distracted by extraneous stimuli
4. has difficulty awaiting turn in games or group situations
5. often blurts out answers to questions before they have been completed
6. has difficulty following through on instructions from others (not due to oppositional behavior or failure of comprehension), e.g., fails to finish chores
7. has difficulty sustaining attention in tasks or play activities
8. often shifts from one uncompleted activity to another
9. has difficulty playing quietly
10. often talks excessively
11. often interrupts or intrudes on others, e.g., butts into other children's games
12. often does not seem to listen to what is being said to him or her
13. often loses things necessary for tasks or activities at school or at home (e.g., toys, pencils, books, assignments)
14. often engages in physically dangerous activities without considering possible consequences (not for the purpose of thrill-seeking), e.g., runs into street without looking.,

Note: The above items are listed in descending order of discriminating power based on data from a national field trial of the DSM-III-R criteria for Disruptive Behavior Disorders.

B. Onset before the age of seven.

C. Does not meet the criteria for a Pervasive Developmental disorder.

Source: American Psychiatric Association, *Diagnostic and Statistical Manual of Mental Disorders*, Third Edition, Revised (1987).

Table 8.2. Diagnostic Criteria for Attention Deficit Disorder (Barkley, 1981)

1. Parental and/or teacher complaints of inattentiveness, impulsivity, and restlessness.
2. Age of onset of problems by 6 years as reported by parents.
3. Deviation from age norms on a standardized parent or teacher rating scale of hyperactive behavior of at least 2 standard deviations above the mean (98% or higher). For retarded children, the child's score is compared against chronologic age norms consistent with the retarded child's mental age.
4. Problem behaviors occurring in 50% of 16 situations discussed with the parent or 12 situations discussed with the teacher (see the Home and School Situations Questionnaires in Chapter 3).
5. Duration of symptoms of at least 12 months.
6. Exclusion of deafness, blindness, or other gross sensory or motor impairment, or severe emotional disturbance (e.g., childhood psychosis).

Source: R. Barkley (1981). "*Hyperactive Children: A Handbook for Diagnosis and Treatment* (p. 6). New York: Guilford Press. Reprinted by permission.

diagnostic and subject-selection purposes. The diagnostic criteria he has found useful in clinical practice are listed in Table 8.2. Although attention-deficit hyperactivity disorder is the appropriate diagnostic terminology, it is not always obvious whether children labeled hyperactive before the advent of DSM-III fit the diagnostic criteria for ADD or ADHD. Therefore, we will adhere to the precedent set by Barkley (1981) and use these terms interchangeably.

Attention deficit disorder is said to be the most prevalent behavior problem of school-age children (Kolb & Whishaw, 1984; Reynolds & Gutkin, 1982; Safer & Allen, 1976) and the most common problem cited in referrals to child guidance clinics (Barkley, 1981; O'Leary, 1980; Safer, 1971). Estimates of the percentage of children exhibiting hyperactive symptoms range from 5 to 12 percent of school-age children (Delamater, Lahey & Drake, 1981; O'Leary, 1980). More conservative sources indicate that 1 to 6 percent of the school-age population is a more accurate estimate (Conners, 1980; Ross & Ross, 1982). Attention deficit disorder is more prevalent in males than females, with sex ratios ranging from 5:1 to 9:1. DeHass (1986), however, indicates that as many as 2 percent of all school-age girls may be hyperactive. The fact that hyperactive girls present fewer behavioral disruptions, relative to hyperactive boys, may account in part for the differential identification rate.

Developmental Aspects

Many investigators note developmental characteristics associated with ADD (Barkley, 1981; O'Leary, 1980; Ross & Ross, 1982; Waddell, 1984; Weiss & Hechtman, 1986). They relate that in infancy, children with ADD rarely smile, drastic mood swings are evident, difficult and unpredictable behaviors are common, and sleep patterns are typically erratic. During the preschool years, ADD children are short-tempered, strong willed, and excessively demanding, and display brief attention spans. In addition, preschool-aged hyperactive children may be restless and appear clumsy or accident prone. Obviously, these behaviors occur regularly in normal preschool children as well as in those evidencing attentional deficits; therefore, it is imperative that the diagnostician possess a good working knowledge of normal developmental progression. Kendall and Braswell (1985) note that symptoms in isolation are generally within the bounds of normality. Clusters of symptoms, however, are considered diagnostic.

During middle childhood, hyperactive children exhibit apparent distractibility, problems focusing attention, poor scholastic performance, mood fluctuations, poor peer relations, and in some cases, excessive motility (Ross & Ross, 1982). Adolescence is characterized by poor self-image, continued poor academic performance, lack of acceptance by parents, teachers, and peers, and increased aggression. Moreover, although excessive activity levels often diminish, attentional deficiencies remain (Ross & Ross, 1982; Weiss, Minder, Werry, Douglas, and Nemeth, 1971). Adults with a history of ADD tend to exhibit personality problems and may be predisposed to alcoholism (Weiss & Hechtman, 1986). Barkley (1981) believes that hyperactive children who fail to evidence symptomatic behavior until they are of school age are rare. In these instances, the hyperactivity is often attributable to the frustration associated with emerging learning disabilities, environmental stressors, or neurological damage.

Peer Relationships

Conners (1980) states that children with ADD are often perceived by others as socially inept. In fact, difficulty in peer relationships is considered by some researchers (DeHass, 1986) to be a major correlate of hyperactivity. Beinfeld and Peters (1986) suggest that impulsive children's maladaptive social behavior may be attributable to production deficits (low motivation) and control deficits (impulsive responding) rather than deficits in social reasoning. Whatever its impetus, Conners (1980) notes that this social ineptitude often leads to poor peer relations and, ultimately, to social rejection and isolation. Conners adds that the resulting diminished self-concept may be a catalyst for future maladjustment. Similarly, Greenberg and Erickson (1982) report that academic failure and social rejection lead to weak self-esteem in ADD children, with the adoption of diversionary, but self-defeating actions such as clowning, aggressiveness, negativism, or helplessness. In these ways, ADD children further alienate their peers, parents, and teachers, which only seems to compound their problems. In addition, these investigators note that ADD children have a difficult time processing and responding appropriately to long messages and instructions. It would seem that this particular manifestation of the cognitive deficit might reinforce an image of noncompliance or marked recalcitrance.

Cognitive Deficiencies

Numerous authors attest to the notion that hyperactive children have cognitive deficiencies that are manifested in impulsive, inattentive behavior (Meichenbaum & Goodman, 1971; Douglas, 1972, 1974, 1976; Douglas & Peters, 1979; Kendall & Braswell, 1982, 1985). Douglas and Peters (1979:67) state that these atypical behaviors are directly related to deficiencies in the cognitive mechanisms responsible for "sustained attention and effort, inhibitory control and the modulation of arousal levels to meet tasks at hand." Thus, the cognitive deficits lead to an inability to "stop, look and listen" (Douglas, 1976) which affects not only academic performance, but also social interactions. Douglas and subsequent researchers have shown that these cognitive deficiencies not only can be diagnosed but also can be remediated. These authors teach strategies for deploying and maintaining attention to task and for implementing inhibitory control. These interventions require that children utilize verbal mediators, exemplifying a generic cognitive strategy for solving problems and controlling behavior. It is this particular literature, which includes prototypical diagnostic and interventive techniques for dealing with impulsivity, that will now be reviewed.

COGNITIVE-BEHAVIORAL ASSESSMENT OF IMPULSIVITY AND HYPERACTIVITY

In view of the frequent occurrence of hyperactivity/impulsivity symptoms and considering the impact this syndrome has on afflicted children and their families, early diagnosis and intervention are imperative. Unfortunately, the diagnostic approach most often used by clinicians is based on adult discomfort with the child's behavior (Barkley, 1981). This approach capriciously labels as abnormal any behaviors exhibited by the child that parents or other significant adult caretakers view as atypical or distressing. Barkley delineates the many problems associated with such a diagnostic orientation. Primary among these problems is that caretakers often base their complaints about child behavior problems on their own subjective, at times erroneous, norms and expectations for appropriate child behavior. In addition, parents are not as accurate, objective, and reliable in their observations as might be preferred by clinicians. Temporary stressors within the family may distort or interfere with a parent's assessment of a child's problem. Finally, but along the same line, adult caretakers may tend to overestimate the frequency of a problem behavior, thereby distorting its severity. Thus it would seem obvious that no single adult's opinion, that of parent or otherwise, should be sufficient to establish a diagnosis of deviant behavior in a child (Barkley, 1981). DSM-III points out that "because the symptoms of attention deficit disorder are typically variable, they may not be observed directly by the clinician . . . typically the symptoms of this disorder in a given child may vary with situation and time" and "it is the rare child who displays signs of the disorder in all settings or even in the same setting at all times." The problem immediately arises as to which reports, settings, times, or measures should be given priority in arriving at a diagnosis. It seems advantageous in making a diagnosis or in selecting subjects for research to tap as many sources of information concerning the child's behavior as possible. Therefore, a brief discussion of assessment techniques useful in gathering information from numerous sources (i.e., directly from the child, parents, teachers, and classmates) follows.

Interviewing

Kendall and Braswell (1985) indicate that the clinical interview is the most widely used assessment technique. Because interviewing skills are all important in successful diagnostic endeavors, it is assumed that the reader has previously acquired a firm foundation in the basic principles of clinical interviewing. Therefore, the present work will not reiterate these basic principles, but rather will delineate areas of inquiry that are of particular importance in interviewing parents and teachers of impulsive children.

Barkley (1981) has numerous suggestions for professionals interviewing the parents of hyperactive/impulsive children. Barkley feels parental interviews are typically unreliable; however, the interviewer can enhance the reliability of the parental interview by adopting a highly structured interview format. Barkley stresses the importance of maintaining a behavioral orientation in seeking information concerning parental perceptions of the child's present difficulties. More specifically, the interviewer should inquire about recent examples of problematic behavior, its antecedents and consequences. At this point, it is often useful to inquire about the extent of the parents' willingness to change the way in which they respond to their child's inappropriate behavior, because parental resistance to personal change will be detrimental to any intervention attempts.

Barkley suggests that in addition to standard inquiries concerning the child's past and present physical health, the interviewer who suspects attention deficit disorder (ADD) should ask questions that explore the possibility of neurological damage or dysfunction in the child. In addition, it is important to ask parents the specific nature of any medication the child may be taking as well as the side effects associated with the prescribed drug.

Because children with ADD often evidence atypical temperament characteristics during early developmental periods (i.e., crankiness, fussiness, difficulty in getting along with others, etc.), Barkley suggests that the interviewer inquire about the child's temperament during infancy and early childhood. In addition, the interviewer should inquire about past and present disciplinary problems at school, because children with ADD often have a history of truancy, suspension, tardiness, and the like. As noted previously, children with ADD typically appear socially inept. Barkley suggests that the interviewer ask specific questions germane to this issue such as the number of close friends the child has at home and at school, as well as inquire about the way in which the child handles interpersonal conflicts. It is always important to explore in detail with parents the positive attributes their child possesses. Finally, Barkley indicates that parents of ADD children report marital discord more often than do parents of normal children. Because marital stress is likely to have a negative impact on both the child's behavior and parental receptivity to intervention demands, the clinician is wise to identify and address these issues promptly.

Ollendick (1984) suggests that because inappropriate, impulsive behavior most often is evident in academic settings where behavioral expectations are more strict, interviews with teachers are of paramount importance. Teachers generally have access to more accurate normative data than do parents and therefore are better equipped to evaluate behaviors as appropriate or inappropriate, and to indicate domains (academic, social, or behavioral) in which the child is deficient. In addition, it is often informative to compare historical data presented by the parents and the teacher, and to explore any discrepancies. As with parents, it is important to discuss the child's strengths and positive attributes with the teacher.

Observational Techniques

The most direct method by which the clinician can obtain information about a child's behavior is direct observation. Lloyd and Loper (1986) describe observational methods for assessing attention-to-task and metacognitive capabilities. In assessing attention-to-task capabilities, these authors suggest that the initial screening of children who are suspected as having attentional deficiencies be conducted informally by classroom teachers. Lloyd and Loper believe that these subjective teacher judgments are generally accurate. In the next stage, the school psychologist measures attention-to-task capability directly by systematic observation in the environments in which these behaviors are most disruptive.

Lloyd and Loper (1986) state that the observational techniques should adhere to certain guidelines as follows:

1. Observations should be conducted by trained psychological professionals.
2. Observational techniques must incorporate behavioral definitions of on- and off-task behavior.
3. Observations must be carried out on a structured schedule.
4. The data yielded by observational procedures must lend themselves to comparisons with normative standards, in order to determine the need for intervention.

Figure 8.1 shows an example of a protocol useful in recording the off-task behavior of several students at one time. A momentary time-sampling procedure may be used whereby the observer looks at a particular child at predetermined intervals and notes whether the child is on or off task. The authors state that 2-second observation intervals, progressing sequentially across all children being observed, generally approximate continuous observation. Lloyd and Loper suggest that observations be conducted for 12 to 15 minutes per day for several days. Their clinical experience indicates that children who attend to tasks less than 60 percent of the time are candidates for intervention.

Lloyd and Loper (1986) also discuss observational methods useful in assessing metacognitive capabilities. Assessment efforts should first focus on the child's awareness of important task-related information. A suggested vehicle for this evaluation is the Informed Strategies for Learning (ISL) assessment measures (Paris, Cross, & Lipson, 1984). The ISL is a 20-item multiple choice questionnaire that assesses cognitive awareness with items such as "The best way to focus on the important points of a story is to: (a) underline the main ideas; (b) read the story three to four times; (c) ask someone to explain it" (p. 1244). Lloyd and Loper (1986) suggest an informal use of this instrument with items presented initially without the alternative responses, in order to evaluate the child's ability to spontaneously describe effective cognitive strategies. The alternative form of the instrument should be administered later, complete with the response alternatives, to assess the child's ability to recognize viable cognitive strategies.

Once the child's awareness of cognitive strategies has been assessed, Lloyd and Loper (1986) suggest direct observation of the child's actual task performance to determine whether difficulties arise at the planning, strategy application, task monitoring, error correction, or evaluative stage of problem solving. The most direct methods for determining which problem-solving stages create difficulty for the child are observation of task performance and interviews. Lloyd and Loper relate some useful techniques that facilitate assessments of this nature, requiring the child to verbalize the steps he goes through in problem solving, inquiring about techniques used

FIGURE 8.1. A Sample Observation Protocol for Assessing Attention to Task of Four Students in One Classroom (Lloyd and Loper, 1986)

____

____

____________________ (date) ____________________ (observer)

Students: 1 = ________________ 2 = ________________

3 = ________________ 4 = ________________

At the moment of observation:

+ = on-task (the student was looking at assigned materials and had pencil in writing or erasing position)

0 = off-task (student was out of seat, looking around, talking with another student, handling a non-academic object, etc.)

1	2	3	4	1	2	3	4	1	2	3	4	1	2	3	4

1	2	3	4	1	2	3	4	1	2	3	4	1	2	3	4

1	2	3	4	1	2	3	4	1	2	3	4	1	2	3	4

1	2	3	4	1	2	3	4	1	2	3	4	1	2	3	4

1	2	3	4	1	2	3	4	1	2	3	4	1	2	3	4

1	2	3	4	1	2	3	4	1	2	3	4	1	2	3	4

1	2	3	4	1	2	3	4	1	2	3	4	1	2	3	4

Source: From "Measurement and evaluation of task-related learning behaviors: Attention to task and metacognition" by J. W. Lloyd and A. B. Loper, *School Psychology Review, 1986, 15,* p. 338. Copyright by National Association of School Psychologists, Washington, D.C. Reprinted by permission.

for studying at school and home, and consulting the child's classroom teacher. Intervention useful in treating metacognitive difficulties will be discussed later.

Behavioral Rating Scales

Teacher ratings are purported to be more reliable and sensitive to hyperactive behaviors than are those of parents (Barkley, 1981). At the same time, Achenbach and Edelbrock (1978) argue that parental reports are the best indexes of child behavior because parents have observed their child in a wider variety of settings and over a longer period of time than has the child's teacher. Given the reported variability of hyperactive behaviors across situations, Ollendick (1984) advocates that both parent and teacher ratings be used as complementary sources of information concerning the child's behavioral typography.

One way to avoid problems inherent in subjective parent or teacher appraisals of deviant behavior is to quantify their responses and to compile normative data on those responses, generally using questionnaires with multiple choice or numerically scaled answers. It is interesting that more rating scales have been developed to assess hyperactive behavior than for any other manifestation of child psychopathology (Barkley, 1981).

The Self-Control Rating Scale (SCRS) was designed to quantify parent and teacher perceptions of self-control in elementary school children (Kendall & Wilcox, 1979). The theoretical premise behind the SCRS is that self-controlled children have the cognitive skills to generate and evaluate numerous potential responses. In addition, self-controlled individuals have the behavioral skills needed to inhibit inappropriate responding and to instigate appropriate actions.

The SCRS consists of 33 items: 10 items pertaining to issues of self-control, 13 items inquiring about impulsive characteristics, and the remaining 10 items involving both content areas, with the rater being asked to select the adjective that best describes the child. Each response is indicated on a 7-point continuum and summed, with increased total scores indicating increased self-control deficiencies. The mean SCRS score is approximately 100 (Kendall & Braswell, 1985).

Kendall & Zupan (1981) have shown that SCRS scores correlate with observed classroom and testing session behavior, and distinguish normal from the nonself-controlled children. In addition, SCRS scores are sensitive to the effects of cognitive-behavioral interventions (Kendall & Wilcox, 1980; Kendall et al., 1981; Kendall & Braswell, 1982). Finally, SCRS mean scores were shown to vary across diagnostic categories, with lowest scores earned by children whose problems do not involve self-control deficiencies and highest scores obtained by hyperactive and conduct-disordered children (Robin, Fischel & Brown, 1984). These investigators also indicate that because parent SCRS scores approximate teacher ratings, the scale may be used by both classes of raters.

The most commonly used standardized rating scales of hyperactive behavior were developed by C. K. Conners (Barkley, 1981; Brown, 1985; Schachar, Sandberg & Rutter, 1986). Conners (1969, 1970, 1973) provides three separate forms, the Conners Parent Rating Scale (CPRS), the Conners Teacher Rating Scale (CTRS), and the Conners Abbreviated Parent Teacher Questionnaire (CAPTQ). The parent and teacher forms subsequently were revised (Goyette, Conners, and Ulrich, 1978). The revised CPRS contains 48 items that together comprise five factors, one of which is the Impulsive-Hyperactive factor (Ollendick, 1984). Although 10 items comprise the hyperactivity index, only four questions load on that factor. Each item is answered "not at all," "just a little," "pretty much," or "very much," with 0, 1, 2, or 3 points assigned for each item. A mean score of 1.5 on the hyperactivity index is generally accepted as indicative of hyperactivity, although researchers sometimes require a more stringent 2 standard deviations above the mean for diagnosis (Barkley, 1981).

The CTRS is identical in scoring procedure employed and in format to the CPRS, except that it contains 28 items which comprise three factors, one of which is the hyperactivity index (Ollendick, 1984). The CAPTQ contains 10 items common to the CTRS and the CPRS and is designed to provide a brief index of hyperactivity (Conners, 1973).

Much research attests to the adequacy of all the Conners scales with regard to test-retest reliability (Barkley, 1981; Rutter, 1983; Ollendick, 1984). Interrater reliability coefficients for teachers using the CTRS range from 0.23 to 0.76 (Conger, Conger, Wallander, Ward, & Dygdon, 1983; Glow & Glow, 1982; Goyette, et al., 1978; Taylor & Sandberg, 1984).

Important to the evaluation of the validity of the various Conners scales is the knowledge that each of the Conners scales has been shown repeatedly to discriminate between hyperactive and normal children (Goyette et al., 1978; Sprague, Christensen, & Werry, 1974; Kupietz, Bailer, & Winsberg, 1972; Conners, 1970). In addition, Brown (1985) has shown that teachers can adequately discriminate between children with ADD with and without hyperactivity using the CAPTQ. Roberts, Milich, Loney, and Caputo (1981), using a multitrait, multimethod analysis, clearly demonstrated that teachers can reliably distinguish the dimensions of aggression, hyperactivity, and inattentiveness in children. The correlations in the MTMM matrix meet Campbell and Fiske's (1959) criteria for convergent and discriminant validity. The scales have repeatedly proved to be drug sensitive, Werry & Sprague, 1974; Eisenberg & Conners, 1971; Conners, 1972; Sprague & Sleator, 1973). In addition, Copeland and Weissbrod (1978) found that ratings on the CTRS correlated significantly with observed behavioral and attitudinal differences in hyperactive and nonhyperactive males. Similarly, Schacher, et al. (1986) found a high degree of association between observed and CTRS-rated behavior. However, defiant behaviors were more reliably rated than hyperactive/inattentive behaviors. In addition, defiance towards teachers increased the probability that a child would be rated as hyperactive or inattentive.

Taylor and Sandberg (1984) report that factor-analytic studies of the CPRS and the CTRS have yielded a hyperactivity-inattentiveness factor that is distinct and independent of the conduct-disorder factor. Glow and Glow (1982) report that factor-analytic studies done on the Conners scales in Australia yielded identical factors to those found in the United States. Not all agree that the various Conners scales are the assessment instruments of choice for clinical or research purposes. Ullman, Sleator, and Sprague (1985) note serious problems with the cutoff score commonly used with the Conners scales, with the factor analytic procedures selected for data analysis, and with the integrity of the normative data collected. Ullman et al. (1985) propose that all Conners's scales be abandoned. The interested reader should consult the original source for an indepth discussion of these views.

The most comprehensive normative data available on the Conners scales are provided by Goyette et al. (1978). Presented are normative data on the CPRS and the CTRS for 540 children, including individual means and standard deviations for preschoolers through adolescents, as well as for males and females. Taylor and Sandberg (1984) provide cross-cultural normative data for boys and girls 6 to 9 years of age in South London (sample = 437), midwest USA (sample = 291), Pittsburgh, USA (sample = 570), New Zealand (sample = 418), New York, USA (sample = 92), and Australia (sample = 2,475).

Task Performance Measures

Porteus (1955) developed a series of paper-and-pencil mazes of varying difficulty that are purported to assess planning, foresight, impulsivity, and distractibility (Palkes, Stewart & Freedman, 1972). Riddle and Roberts (1974) indicate that the Porteus Maze Test possesses adequate psychometric properties. The Porteus Maze Test yields a test quotient (TQ) and a qualitative score (Q). The TQ is an index of the child's ability to solve the mazes in a specified number of trials, irrespective of the quality of solutions generated. The TQ is derived from data on the highest-level maze solved correctly and the number of trials required to solve each maze (Kendall & Braswell, 1985). Palkes, et al., (1972) indicate that the TQ is an estimate of general intellectual capacity. Douglas, Parry, Marton, and Garson (1976) state that the TQ reflects planning, judgment, and attentional capabilities. Riddle and Roberts

(1974) found the TQ to correlate highly with tests of visual abilities and spatial memory.

The Q score is based on the quality of maze execution, that is, the number of errors committed (i.e., lifting the pencil, cutting corners, etc.) while traversing the mazes (Palkes, et al., 1972). Meichenbaum and Goodman (1971) state that Q scores distinguish impulsive from nonimpulsive subjects. In addition, Q scores have been shown to distinguish criminals and delinquents from normal subjects (Kendall and Braswell, 1985).

Douglas et al. (1976) used the Porteus Maze Test to assess changes in planning, judgment, and attention-focusing abilities. Palkes et al. (1972) point out that the mazes can yield estimates of a subject's degree of distractibility as well as impulsivity. Porteus Maze scores have adequately distinguished hyperactive from normal subjects (Parry, 1973) and are sensitive to the effects of stimulant drug therapy (Conners, 1972).

Kagan (1966) developed a measure of cognitive tempo called the Matching Familiar Figures Test (MFFT). The MFFT is an index of the extent to which an individual is reflective (i.e., slow and accurate) or impulsive (i.e., fast and inaccurate) in responding to test stimuli. The MFFT consists of 12 match-to-sample items in which the child is shown a picture of a familiar object and is asked to identify the identical picture from among six variants. The MFFT yields a latency and an error score. Improvements on these scores are believed to reflect treatment-related gains in self-control and self-management (Kendall & Braswell, 1985). Messer (1976) and Salkind (1979) have compiled normative data that allow comparisons of subjects by age and by sex. Alternate forms of the MFFT are also available.

Most importantly, task performance measures, such as the Porteus Mazes and the MFFT, afford the examiner the opportunity to observe the child's behavior in response to standardized materials. These tasks allow the clinician to evaluate the child's ability to plan, initiate action, and inhibit inappropriate behavior as well as to deal with frustration and novel situations. However, the researcher interested in using instruments of this nature as outcome measures is referred to Reynolds and Stark (1986) for a discussion of the inadequacy of these measures for that purpose.

Peer Ratings

Because poor peer relationships often characterize the hyperactive child, a comprehensive assessment should include peer ratings, or peer sociometrics. Because peer nomination and rating scale approaches are discussed in detail in chapter 5, they are not reviewed here.

COGNITIVE-BEHAVIORAL INTERVENTIONS WITH IMPULSIVE AND HYPERACTIVE CHILDREN

Intervention Components

A plethora of research is emerging concerning the use of cognitive-behavioral interventions with impulsive and/or hyperactive children. Several attempts have been made to classify and organize this growing body of information (Kendall & Braswell, 1985; Kendall & Wilcox, 1980). Cognitive-behavioral interventions generally seem to focus primarily on teaching the child generic cognitive strategies both for solving academic and cognitive problems and for successfully negotiating interpersonal exchanges. Because the number of possible problem situations and solutions is infinite, cognitive interventions that focus not on imparting discrete solutions to particular problems, but on training the cognitive processes associated with the child's specific skill deficiencies seem most advantageous. These cognitive interventions most often contain a self-directive component whereby children are taught to regulate their own behavior.

One salient feature of these interventions that facilitates segregation of the various techniques into categories is the nature of the cognitive strategy being taught. These strategies seem to fall into one of two categories. In some cases, the cognitive strategy appears somewhat simplistic and consists mainly of self-directive cues to cognitively "slow down" or in some way increase the response latency interval. This response-delay training often involves the therapist in teaching the child to repeat particular self-instructive phrases at appropriate times. The self-directive verbal commands consist of statements such as "stop, look and think," "I must slow down," or "First, I have to stop and think." These cues are taught through modeling, direct instruction, or both.

The second category of cognitive strategies useful in treating impulsive children is problem solving. Problem-solving interventions necessitate a more elaborate, comprehensive approach. Problem-solving programs often contain numerous components that may be used in varying combinations as dictated by referral problems and treatment goals. These comprehensive programs most often contain a self-instructive component, training in the problem-solving process, behavioral management contingencies, a modeling component, and role-play of realistic problem situations.

Self-Directive Response Delay Training

In an initial attempt to modify impulsivity in children, Kagan, Pearson, and Welch (1966) explored the effects of response delay training on impulsive children's performance on the MFFT (Kagan, 1966). Response delay training was provided to 40 impulsive children who had scored below the median on MFFT latency scores and above the median on MFFT error scores during pretest screening. A group of 20 impulsive children with comparable MFFT scores served as an attention-control group. The children in the treatment group were instructed to delay responding to the training tasks for a fixed interval of time (10 to 15 seconds). In addition, the children were told to study the stimulus during the delay period and to think about the appropriate answer. After the delay interval, the examiner signaled the child to proceed with his or her response. The attention-control group engaged in the experimental tasks without benefit of delay training. The children were trained on a design-matching task similar to the MFFT, an inductive reasoning task, and a haptic-visual matching task.

Posttreatment assessments included alternate MFFT items and an inductive reasoning test, which required the child to put pictures in order to complete a story. Statistical analyses revealed that the response-delay training resulted in significantly improved MFFT response times (i.e., increased response latency interval), but had no significant effect of MFFT error scores. In addition, treatment failed to affect the children's inductive reasoning capabilities. The researchers discuss the differential treatment effect as an expected outcome, because training focused on inhibiting impulsive responding rather than on improving visual scanning strategies. However, if response delay training lengthens response latency with no concomitant improvement in accuracy, the treatment has not demonstrated social validity.

Palkes, Stewart, and Kahana (1968) investigated the effects of self-directive verbal commands on the Porteus Maze (Porteus, 1955) performance of 20 boys between the ages of 8 and 10 years. These children were reported to be of average intelligence and were under medical care for hyperactivity at the time of testing. Pharmacologic regimens for all children were discontinued during the study. A comparable group of hyperactive/impulsive children served as controls. Children in the treatment and control groups received individual 1-hour sessions on two successive days. During these sessions, the children were pretested on Porteus Maze items, presented with various training tasks (i.e., MFFT items and Embedded Figures Test items), and posttested on an alternative Porteus Maze series.

Treatment group subjects were trained to verbalize a set of self-directive commands before responding to the experimental task. These self-directive commands included statements such as "I must listen to directions" and "I must look and think before I answer." These verbalizations were also printed on cards that served as visual prompts during training. The control group was exposed to the training materials with no self-instructional training. Although the groups did not differ initially on the Porteus Test Quotient (TQ, an index of global intellectual capabilities) or on the Porteus Mazes Qualitative (Q) score (an index of errors in style and quality of execution), pre- and posttest analyses indicated significant improvement in the treatment group's mean TQ and Q score relative to those of the controls. The researchers conclude that self-directive verbalizations resulted in more carefully controlled performances on cognitive tasks.

Palkes, et al. (1972) attempted to replicate the research efforts of Palkes, et al. (1968) as well as to delineate the impact of overt self-directive commands on the effectiveness of the self-instructive intervention. Thirty 7- to 13-year-old boys under psychiatric care for hyperactivity were randomly assigned to a verbal training, silent reading, or attention-control group. The verbal training group was trained exactly as was the Palkes et al. (1968) treatment group. The silent reading group was trained to use the printed prompt cards as cues but were instructed to avoid overtly verbalizing the commands. The pretest/posttest assessment measures as well as the training tasks were identical to those used by Palkes et al. (1968). Data analyses revealed the verbal training group improved significantly, relative to the other groups, on the Porteus Maze Q index; however, no group differences on the Porteus Maze TQ were apparent. Unfortunately, these treatment gains were not maintained at a 2-week follow-up.

The foregoing research studies suffer from several methodologic and theoretical shortcomings. Cognitive impulsivity interventions often hold as their primary goal treatment-related performance change on psychometric instruments (i.e., MFFT and Porteus Maze Test). However, numerous investigators (Bentler & McClain, 1976; Kagan & Messer, 1975; O'Keefe, 1975; Williams & Lahey, 1977) believe these instruments lack construct validity and are therefore poor indexes of more global referral concerns. In addition, when posttest improvement on psychometric measures functions as an intermediate criterion for effective intervention, change in the ultimate criterion (the actual target behavior) is rarely evaluated; therefore, the assessment of treatment efficacy is inadequate. It is suggested that the validity of psychometric measures as predictors of target behaviors be established before their utilization as selection and/or outcome measures.

It should also be considered that although these cognitive interventions may succeed in increasing children's response latency interval, they at times fail to impact the accuracy of the children's performance. Similarly, whereas improvements are noted on certain experimental tasks, these investigations fail to provide evidence that improved cognitive functioning would generalize to more socially valid domains, such as academic performance and interpersonal relationships. In addition, the results cited by Palkes et al. (1972) in which treatment gains had deteriorated at 2-week follow-up cast some doubt on the intervention's value in effecting long-term treatment gains. Similarly, it is difficult to determine why response-delay training resulted in improved performance on global measures of intellectual capabilities (i.e., Palkes et al., 1968) and why these findings were not replicated (Palkes et al., 1972).

To circumvent previous criticisms associated with failure to incorporate socially valid training tasks and outcome measures, Burns (1972) explored the effects of self-directive commands on the arithmetic performance and activity levels of 45 elementary-age children referred by their teachers for hyperactive behavior. Pre- and posttest measures included the arithmetic computational section of a standardized achievement test. The children were randomly assigned to a 20-trial verbal training group, a 40-trial verbal training group, or an attention-control group. Following pretest evaluations, the children in the treatment groups were given two 30-minute training sessions (administered on successive days) on the use of verbal commands (the exact nature of these commands was not specified). The treatment groups were then given the specified number of training trials using verbal commands to facilitate arithmetic problem solving. Immediately after the second training session all groups were given a standardized mathematical achievement test. Pre- and postintervention activity levels were also compared. The experimenters noted an absence of treatment effects on the arithmetic and activity level dependent measures. It is impossible to adequately evaluate these outcomes because the exact nature of the intervention is left to the reader's imagination. However, these authors did incorporate socially valid criteria (i.e., academic performance) in the assessment of treatment outcome.

Thus, research efforts incorporating self-directive response delay training techniques have met with mixed results. As stated previously, improvement in a very narrow cognitive domain has been achieved (i.e., increased response latency); however, improved performance accuracy has not always followed. In addition, attempts to incorporate more socially valid training tasks and outcome measures have met with poor results. One explanation for these differential results across treatment studies is that researchers have failed to formulate and consistently utilize valid criteria for subject selection. Consequently, we have inadequate evidence that subjects share common referral problems and/or cognitive deficiencies.

Problem-Solving Training

Problem-solving strategies demand a more elaborate cognitive program, often containing numerous treatment components. A discussion of the commonly used treatment components follows. Kendall and Braswell (1985) discuss intervention components in addition to problem-solving instructions that are often included in problem-solving interventions, including instructional training, behavioral contingencies, modeling, role-play interactions, and, less often, training in the identification of feelings in self and others.

Teaching Problem-Solving Skills

In teaching problem-solving skills, the therapist attempts to teach the child a generic framework of skills to assist in identifying problems and their components, selecting strategies to facilitate progression toward problem resolution, exploring plausible alternative responses and their consequences, and planning a series of steps to achieve a desired goal (Urbain & Savage, in press). More specifically, there are numerous "problem-solving thinking skills" that can be taught through direct instruction and modeling (Urbain & Savage, in press), as follows:

1. *Problem identification*: component skills involve problem sensitivity or the ability to "sense" the presence of a problem by identifying "uncomfortable" feelings; also included are skills for identifying major problem issues as well as maintaining a general problem-solving orientation or "set" versus a tendency to deny, avoid, or act impulsively in dealing with the problem.
2. *Alternative thinking*: the ability to generate multiple alternative solutions to a given interpersonal problem situation.
3. *Consequential thinking*: the ability to foresee the immediate and more long-range consequences of a particular alternative and to use this information in the decision-making process.
4. *Means-ends thinking*: the ability to elaborate or plan a series of specific actions (a means) to attain a given goal, to recognize and devise ways around potential obstacles, and to use a realistic time framework in implementing steps toward the goal.

Self-Instruction

Self-instruction consists of a series of self-directive statements that serve as cues or prompts to facilitate adherence to the problem-solving tactics discussed previously. Each self-instructive statement prompts the child to perform differential organized problem-solving behaviors that hopefully culminate in an effective solution. For example, a self-instructive statement such as "Let's see, what am I supposed to do?" prompts the child to begin asking questions about the nature of the task and to provide answers to those questions in the form of cognitive rehearsal or planning (initial steps in the problem-solving sequence).

Self-instructive statements are of five general types: (1) identification of the problem, (2) specification of the problem-solving strategy to be used, (3) attention-focusing statements, (4) self-rewarding statements, and (5) statements designed to assist the child in coping with unfruitful efforts (Kendall & Braswell, 1985). A unique feature of the self-instructive technique is the inclusion of "coping statements." It is hoped that utilization of appropriate coping statements after unsuccessful task attempts will decrease negative self-verbalizations such as "How could I be this stupid?" or "I guess I can't do anything right" which, aside from their devastating impact on self-concept, do nothing to elicit better organized subsequent attempts.

Behavioral Contingencies

Behavioral components often associated with cognitive interventions to treat impulsivity include: (1) social reinforcement from the therapist, teacher, or parent (i.e., statements such as "Nice job!" and "Good!") for using the cognitive strategy appropriately, (2) token reinforcement, whereby children earn tokens for homework assignments that involve recalling an instance in which the self-instructive strategy was spontaneously used outside of therapy. In addition, if the child's self-ratings of daily performance match the therapist's evaluation of the child's behavior, the child is awarded extra tokens, and (3) response-cost contingencies, whereby children are fined tokens for failure to use the self-instructive strategies, incorrect responding, responding too quickly, and the like.

Modeling

Cognitive-behavioral interventions rely heavily on modeling to teach problem-solving skills. In this approach, the therapist demonstrates the problem-solving process and the use of self-instructive techniques. The therapist and child often take turns solving problems during a session, giving the therapist the opportunity to give the child direct feedback on his or her performance as well as to demonstrate a productive way to think through problems. The therapist often will initially provide a "mastery model" of ideal behavior, which consists of rapid, correct responding with minimal difficulty and frustration. Later, the therapist becomes a "coping model" who, like the child, makes mistakes, but demonstrates coping strategies for dealing with these difficulties. Dweck and Reppucci (1973) note that children with a history of failure often abandon responding at the first sign their performance is less than adequate. These children quickly become discouraged and feel helpless in affecting positive outcomes. Because difficulties of this nature are inevitable, coping strategies are modeled to decrease the probability the child will simply give up on the tasks. Examples of coping statements are included in Table 8.3.

Role Playing

Role playing, the thinking through and acting out of contrived problematic interpersonal situations, is a valuable component of cognitive-behavioral interventions. Initially, the therapist and child act out appropriate problem-solving behavior in hypothetical interpersonal situations. As therapy progresses, the therapist incorporates real-life problem situations into the role-play exercises. The object of role play is to give children the opportunity

Table 8.3. Content of Self-Instructional Procedures (Kendall and Braswell, 1985)

Problem definition:	"Let's see, what am I supposed to do?"
Problem approach:	"I have to look at all the possibilities."
Focusing of attention:	"I'd better concentrate and focus in, and think only of what I'm doing right now."
Choosing an answer:	"I think it's this one . . ."
Self-reinforcement:	"Hey, not bad. I really did a good job."
or	
Coping statement:	"Oh, I made a mistake. Next time I'll try to go slower and concentrate more and maybe I'll get the right answer."

Source: P. C. Kendall & L. Braswell (1985). *Cognitive-Behavioral Therapy for Impulsive Children.* New York: Guilford Press. Reprinted by permission.

to practice and receive feedback on their efforts to utilize the problem-solving strategy.

Feeling Identification Training

Affective training, which teaches the child to recognize and label his or her own emotional reactions as well as those of others, is an important component of an interpersonal problem-solving program. Children learn to recognize the emotions associated with various facial expressions and bodily postures, the relationship between certain emotions and situations, and the impact self-talk can have on these emotional experiences. Role play is used to teach feeling identification.

PROBLEM-SOLVING INTERVENTION OUTCOME STUDIES

It seems useful at this time to review various outcome studies involving problem-solving interventions. What follows is by no means an exhaustive review of this extensive literature. Rather, several prototypical studies that illustrate the way in which various problem-solving components may be combined to formulate an effective treatment constellation were selected for review. In addition, studies that typify problems inherent in these research endeavors were selected.

Meichenbaum and Goodman (1971)

The vast majority of current research endeavors using cognitive-behavioral interventions to treat impulsivity have their genesis in the work of Meichenbaum and Goodman (1971). Meichenbaum and Goodman applied a self-instructional program with five children placed in a special education classroom because of behavioral problems, such as hyperactivity and poor self-control. In addition to the self-instructive (SI) treatment group, an attention-control group (sample = 5) and an assessment-control group (sample = 5) comprised of similar students from the same special education classroom were included. The attention-control group and the SI treatment group met with the examiners on the same schedule, providing an index of change attributable to factors such as attention, exposure to treatment materials, and the demand characteristics associated with the outcome measures used. The assessment-control group received no treatment and served as an index of change associated with maturation and educational experiences. The groups were equated in terms of gender composition and matched in terms of WISC-R IQs.

The self-instructional training program was administered individually in four 1/2-hour treatment sessions over a 2-week period. The treatment included the following series of steps:

1. The examiner performed a task talking out loud while the child observed (examiner as model).
2. The child performed the same task while the examiner instructed out loud.
3. The child performed the task again while instructing himself out loud.
4. The child performs the task while whispering instructions to herself (lip movements).
5. Finally, the child performed the task with covert self-instructions (no lip movements).

The sequence of problem-solving verbalizations were first modeled by the examiner and then imitated by the child. The self-directive verbalizations included questions about the nature and demands of the task, answers to these questions in the form of cognitive planning and rehearsal verbalizations, and self-guidance statements. The self-guidance statements were comprised of self-reinforcing verbalizations, and coping statements for dealing with errors. The problem-solving sequence was designed to circumvent comprehension, production, and mediational deficiencies. The children were trained to use the self-instructive strategy on a variety of sensory motor and problem-solving tasks of varying difficulty. Sensory motor tasks included copying geometric patterns and coloring figures. As training progressed, the cognitive tasks increased in difficulty to include problem-solving tasks, such as following sequential instructions (from the Stanford-Binet) and items from Raven's Progressive Matrices.

Several outcome measures were used to assess the efficacy of the self-instructive program. Psychometric measures such as the Porteus Maze Test, the MFFT, and WISC-R subtests such as Picture Arrangement, Block Design, and Coding, were used to assess changes in behavioral and cognitive impulsivity. Two behavioral indexes were used as well to determine the extent to which treatment gains generalized to the classroom environment. These behavioral measures included a time-sampling observation technique to assess the children's behavioral appropriateness and attentiveness in the classroom and a teacher questionnaire designed to evaluate each child's behavioral self-control, activity level, cooperativeness, and likability. The children were observed for 2 school days 1 week before and immediately after treatment. The teachers completed their questionnaires immediately before treatment and 3 weeks subsequent to the intervention at the conclusion of a follow-up assessment.

The results indicated that children receiving self-instructional training scored significantly better than did either group of control children on the Picture Arrangement and Coding subtests, prorated WISC-R IQs, the latency score on the MFFT, and error scores on the Porteus Maze Test. These treatment gains were maintained at 3-week follow-up. Unfortunately, there were no significant changes in observed behaviors in the classroom or on teachers' ratings of classroom behavior.

A second study reported by Meichenbaum and Goodman (1971) explored the impact of the self-instructional training program on attentional strategies used by impulsive children on the MFFT. In addition, the study also explored the relative contribution of the modeling component to the overall treatment effect associated with the self-guidance training program.

Fifteen impulsive kindergarteners and first graders were selected based on their MFFT scores and their inability to profit (i.e., to improve performance subsequent to the examiner's instructions) from instructions to "slow down and work carefully" on items from the MFFT the children had initially failed. The children were randomly assigned to one of three experimental groups: a modeling plus self-instruction treatment group, a modeling alone treatment group, or an attention-control group. Each child in the modeling alone treatment group (sample = 5) observed an examiner engage in an MFFT task while modeling a set of verbalizations and reflective behaviors similar to those trained in experiment 1. After viewing the model, the child was asked to perform a similar task and was praised for using the strategy the examiner modeled. Each child in the modeling plus self-instruction group observed the same modeled behavior as did the children in the modeling alone treatment condition, but was also given explicit training in the production of self-instructions similar to those the examiner used. After the child began using the self-verbalizations, their volume was gradually reduced to a covert level. In the attention-control group, children observed an examiner model a task while making general statements to "go slow and be careful"; however, no explicit strategy training was imparted. The results indicated that the self-instruction plus modeling group significantly improved both latency and error MFFT scores. The modeling alone group showed improvements on MFFT latency scores but not on error scores. The researchers conclude that a cognitive self-instructive program that teaches children to talk to themselves can modify their impulsive behavior on a variety of psychometric indexes. In addition, the researchers feel it was shown that the incorporation of a self-instructive component to a behavioral modeling program can positively affect the attentional strategies used by impulsive children, along with their concomitant behavior.

Although the results of these studies look promising, the authors' optimistic conclusions must be qualified. Their attempt to incorporate at least a few socially valid outcome measures (measures of the ultimate criteria—classroom behavior) is laudable. Nevertheless, Meichenbaum and Goodman fail to provide evidence that the benefits of self-instruction and training generalize to more meaningful behavioral domains. It is suggested that researchers seek out more behaviorally meaningful training tasks to "build in" a generalization component. Cognitive interventions that change the way children "think" about experimental tasks, yet fail to have impact on children's academic and behavioral functioning on a daily basis (the reason for referral!) are in effect meaningless. In addition, vague selection criteria and the small number of subjects make it difficult to ascertain exactly what types of children would best benefit from this particular intervention.

Douglas, Parry, Marton, and Garson (1976)

Building on the foundation laid by Meichenbaum and Goodman (1971), Douglas, Parry, Marton, and Garson (1976) developed a self-guidance intervention that they hypothesized would prove useful in training hyperactive children to use more effective, less impulsive strategies for solving cognitive and academic problems as well as for evaluating social situations and responding appropriately. The program developed by Douglas et al. (1976) was similar to that of Meichenbaum and Goodman, incorporating modeling, self-instructive verbalizations and self-reinforcement components.

Twenty-nine boys between the ages of 6 and 10 years were selected from a larger sample of boys referred to the senior author's cognitive training program by psychologists or school personnel in the surrounding metropolitan areas. The 18 boys selected for the training group (mean age 7 years 9 months) and the 11 boys chosen for the no treatment control group (mean age 8 years 5 months) received scores of 1.5 or greater on the Conners Parent/Teacher Rating Scale of Hyperactivity (Conners, 1969) and a mean latency score of 10 seconds or less on Kagan's Matching Familiar Figures Test (Kagan, 1966). The two groups of children did not differ significantly in terms of age, IQ, or Conners Parent/Teacher Ratings.

The primary goal of Douglas et al.'s (1976) training program was to teach hyperactive children more effective ways of dealing with cognitive, academic, and/or social situations, which require attention to task, organized planning, and greater inhibitory control. The program lasted 3 months in which the children were seen for 1-hour sessions, twice per week, for a total of 24 sessions. In addition, the therapist met with each child's teacher a minimum of six times and each child's parents a minimum of 12 times. During these sessions, the parents and teachers were familiarized with the training techniques and encouraged to implement the training program at home and in school.

Douglas et al. stated their training program, which included modeling as well as self-instructional and strategy training techniques, was closely patterned after the work of Meichenbaum and Goodman (1971). The children in the treatment group observed an adult model who, while engaged in a task, verbalized clear direct statements about the nature of the task and the strategies being used. The child was then asked to imitate the model's verbalizations while engaging in similar tasks. The audible level of the child's verbalizations was gradually faded to covert levels until the child, in essence, "talked to himself." To facilitate the generalization of acquired skills to academic and social situations, a wide variety of tasks and games were employed including academic problems assigned by the child's teacher. For the same reason, children varied working alone and in pairs to better simulate the classroom environment and to give them the opportunity to practice peer interaction skills.

Numerous general strategies were emphasized in training which included defining the problem and its various components, evaluating alternative solutions before responding, checking one's own work, calmly correcting errors, and reinforcing oneself for successful task completion. Through modeling and direct instruction, children learned more effective search, focusing, and attention deployment strategies, as well as how to scan stimuli and note similarities and differences, and to sort, arrange, and classify elements of a stimulus array. The instructor/model emphasized planning ahead and considering the sequence of steps that problem resolution would require. Similarly, children learned effective means of organizing ideas and work materials, as well as to note and rehearse important aspects of the problem to be remembered. In addition, children were taught strategies for working and playing with peers. The strategies focused on the importance of taking turns, analyzing an opponent's strategies, and being sensitive to the feelings of others.

The efficacy of the training program was evaluated at the conclusion of the 3-month treatment period and again 3 months later as a follow-up measure. All children were administered tests of cognitive style (the Matching Familiar Figures Test [MFFT] and the Porteus Maze Test), measures of affective reactions to frustration (the Story Completion Test), indexes of perceptual-motor capacity (the Bender Visual-Motor Gestalt Test), tests of short-term memory (the Detroit Tests of Learning Aptitude), academic achievement tests (Durrell Analysis of Reading Difficulty and the Wide Range Achievement Test), and an index of teacher-perceived classroom behavior (The Conners Parent/Teacher Rating Scale).

Analyses of pretest and posttest data indicated that the treatment group significantly improved, relative to the control group, on indexes of cognitive style (MFFT error and latency scores), measures of affective reactions to frustration (the aggression and realistic coping responses on the Story Completion Test), and perceptual-motor tasks (the time variable of the Bender-Gestalt test) and on academic indexes (the listening comprehension variable of the Durrell Analysis of Reading Difficulty). Comparisons of the pretest and posttest performance of the treatment group revealed significant improvement on all cognitive, affective and short-term memory variables as well as on two academic indexes of oral and listening comprehension and on the Conners Teacher Rating Scale of classroom behavior. Pretest/posttest comparisons of the control group's performance indicated significant improvement on the short-term memory index only.

Relative to the control group, the treatment group improved at 3-month follow-up measures of cognitive style, affective reactions to frustration, and academic indexes of oral reading capabilities and oral comprehension. Pretest/follow-up comparisons of the treatment group's performance indicated significant improvement on all dependent measures except the Porteus Maze Test. Similar comparisons of the control group's performance showed significant improvement on the Conners Teacher Rating Scale only.

Douglas et al. (1976) concluded that there was substantial evidence indicating that cognitive interventions have a positive impact on hyperactive children. Trained children showed significant improvement in cognitive, affective, and academic outcome measures at the conclusion of treatment and at 3-month follow-up.

Although Douglas et al. (1976) credited Meichenbaum and Goodman (1971) with providing the foundation of their intervention program, there are numerous instances in which Douglas et al. build and improve on the previous research effort. For example, Douglas et al. incorporated a much longer follow-up interval than did Meichenbaum and Goodman (1971), thus providing a more realistic estimate of treatment durability. In addition, unlike research cited earlier, Douglas et al. reported explicit and, at least in part, empirically derived selection criteria that not only facilitated replication of this research effort, but also provided the clinician with more insight into the potential clinical utility of the intervention for a particular child.

By far the most innovative element of Douglas et al.'s cognitive intervention is the generalization component that was skillfully built into the treatment regimen. Efforts to enhance the generalization of treatment effects to other domains include the incorporation of more socially valid training tasks and outcome measures, the use of parents and teachers as adjunct therapists, and the placement of children into working pairs or groups, which more closely simulates the classroom environment. Lastly,

Douglas et al. (1976) note that children are less likely to use the self-directive techniques spontaneously in extra-laboratory situations when the self-verbalizations were memorized by rote. These researchers circumvent this difficulty by encouraging the children to phrase strategies in their own words and by accepting this rendition of the strategy even when it deviates from the examiner's. Therefore, Douglas et al. modeled specific strategies to children in training, but reinforced efforts aimed at formulating and evaluating multiple alternative strategies.

It is encouraging that although Douglas et al.'s intervention did not program reading tasks into the intervention, reading-content outcome measures showed significant improvement. These findings indicate at least some generalization of treatment gains across tasks. However, as with Meichenbaum and Goodman (1971), the present research provides no evidence that treatment effects generalize to classroom behavior. Douglas et al. (1976), with an argument similar to that put forth by Meichenbaum and Goodman (1971), rationalize that these findings (i.e., that treatment effects failed to effect teacher ratings of classroom behavior) should be expected, because the target domains addressed are cognitive and internal rather than behavioral and explicit. As stated earlier, this argument apparently assumes that cognitive impulsivity is unrelated to manifest behavioral impulsivity. In addition, Douglas et al.'s stand on this issue seems to directly contradict the notion that treatment interventions must evidence some element of social validity, that is, they must result in meaningful change in the behavior that prompted the child's referral or they should be abandoned. It seems more plausible that teacher perceptions of classroom behavior may be resistant to change, because teachers often have an extensive history of negative contact with a particular hyperactive child and therefore possess some salient expectations that the child will engage in inappropriate classroom behavior. In addition, it seems possible that these children may acquire secondary gains (i.e., attention) from teachers and peers as a result of atypical behavior. If either of these vignettes holds true, the classroom may be a milieu where the generalization of treatment effects is not viable or is not reinforced. Certainly, these issues point out the need to determine treatment components that enhance generalization to classroom performance and that lead to changes in teacher perceptions.

Kendall and Braswell (1982)

As discussed previously, cognitive-behavioral interventions generally contain a combination of various treatment components. The research designs employed to document the efficacy of an entire regimen often preclude evaluation of the component's differential treatment contributions (i.e., designs that fail to isolate individual treatment components and/or to include an attention-control group). The purpose of the study by Kendall and Braswell (1982) was to evaluate the use of the cognitive component involved in the intervention and to attempt to enhance the generalization of treatment gains to other behavioral domains by increasing the social validity of training tasks and outcome measures over those in previous research endeavors.

Kendall and Braswell (1982) sought to compare a cognitive-behavioral intervention, consisting of self-instructional training, modeling, and behavioral contingencies, to a behavioral treatment program that involved modeling and behavioral contingencies, but not the self-instructive component. Kendall and Braswell expanded the range of outcome measures used in previous research to include classroom observations and parental ratings. Because previous research had not addressed the effects of cognitive-behavioral interventions on self-concept, Kendall and Braswell included outcome measures germane to this issue as well.

Twenty-three male and four female subjects between the ages of 8 and 12 years were randomly assigned to one of three experimental conditions: a cognitive-behavioral treatment group, a behavioral treatment group, or an attention-control group. All subjects had been referred to the program by their teacher for exhibiting nonself-controlled behavior. The children were seen for 45 minutes, twice per week, for 12 sessions.

The children in the treatment group were trained on tasks that emphasized the sequencing of events and problem-solving steps, math problems presented via a calculator, math toys, and various board games, tasks requiring that the child label the emotions of others as presented in various pictures, and role playing of problematic social situations.

The cognitive-behavioral treatment included all the various components of problem-solving interventions discussed earlier. They will only be reviewed briefly here. However, the reader interested in a more thorough discussion of the program and its intricacies is referred to Kendall and Braswell (1985). Children in the cognitive-behavioral group were taught what Kendall and Braswell view as the five steps of problem solving: problem definition, problem approach, focusing attention, selecting an answer, and reinforcing oneself. In addition, the children were taught coping responses for dealing with task failure. In the self-instructive component, the therapist modeled self-instructive verbalizations while engaging in a cognitive task. The child was encouraged to imitate the therapist's behavior and to gradually fade the volume of overt statements in a manner similar to that of Douglas et al. (1976) and Meichenbaum and Goodman (1971). Kendall and Braswell (1982) expanded this technique by having the therapist model the use of self verbalizations during naturally occurring events throughout the session. Initially, the children were instructed to use self-statements that were concrete in nature. However, there was a gradual shift to statements that were of a more conceptual nature in the hope of increasing the program's generalizability.

Behavioral response-cost contingencies also were implemented in training sessions, whereby children were fined tokens for failing to use the self-instructive steps, going too fast, or answering incorrectly. Bonus chips could be earned by retelling an instance during the past week in which the self-instructional technique was used at home or school or by accurately evaluating their own performance during that day's session. Children were allowed to "purchase" items with their chips from a reward menu. To increase the child's cognitive awareness of the feelings of others, the therapist exposed the child to activities emphasizing the recognition and labeling of emotions, as well as the generation and evaluation of alternative outcomes associated with various responses to real-life and hypothetical problematic social situations. Children were encouraged to use these strategies at home and school.

The children placed in the behavioral treatment group were exposed to the same training tasks, exercises, and behavioral contingencies; however, they were not given self-instructional training and cognitive modeling of the problem-solving process. These children were fined tokens for responding too quickly or making incorrect responses, but not for failing to use the self-instructive verbalizations. Similarly, children earned extra tokens for accurate self-evaluation, but not for recalling an incident in which self-instruction was used during the previous week.

The attention-control group received 12 sessions of approximately 45 minutes each, in which the child and examiner worked together on tasks similar to the training tasks used with the experimental groups. These sessions involved no self-instruction, modeling, or behavioral contingencies. children were rewarded for cooperation and effort.

The children were tested 1 week before program initiation, at the end of the 12-session program, at 10-week follow-up, and at 1-year follow-up. Dependent measures used to evaluate treatment efficacy included parent and teacher blind ratings of the child's level of self-control (Self-Control Rating Scale) and the degree of manifest hyperactivity (Conners Parent/Teacher Rating Scale), an index of cognitive style (the Matching Familiar Figures Test), tests of academic achievement (Wide Range Achievement Test), an index of intellectual capabilities (the Peabody Picture Vocabulary Test), a measure of self-esteem (the Piers-Harris Children's Self Concept Scale), and behavioral observations. Behavioral codes for the observation system were: verbal or physical behavior that was off-task, attention diverted off-task, out-of-seat behavior, "bugging" others verbally, or blurting out a comment and "bugging" others physically. Finally, a Session Summary Sheet completed by the therapist at the end of each session was included. The Session Summary Sheet is a 7-item, 5-point rating scale on which the therapist recorded the extent of the child's interest and attention to tasks and his or her ability to use self-instruction, to follow general instructions, and to maintain a warm, cooperative relationship with the examiner.

Statistical analyses indicated that the cognitive-behavioral group had significantly improved teacher ratings (conducted in a blind fashion) of self-control, relative to the behavioral or control groups, at posttreatment and at 10-week follow-up. In addition, only the cognitive-behavioral group achieved significant pre- to posttest improvement on teacher ratings of self-control immediately after treatment and at 10-week follow-up. There was no significant group by treatment interactions involving teacher ratings of hyperactive behavior. Within-group pre- to posttest analyses revealed significant improvement on teacher ratings of hyperactivity for both the cognitive-behavioral and the behavioral group at posttreatment and at 10-week follow-up.

Analyses of the cognitive-style data revealed no significant group by treatment interactions for latency scores on the MFFT. Changes from pre- to posttreatment were significant for the cognitive-behavioral and the behavioral groups; however, only the behavioral group maintained this improvement at 10-week follow-up. Analyses of the error scores of the MFFT again revealed no significant group by treatment interactions, but all groups improved from pre- to posttest and at 10-week follow-up. The latter findings could represent maturational influences.

Analyses of the reading achievement data revealed no significant group by treatment interaction. Within-group pre- to posttest comparisons indicated significant improvement in the cognitive-behavioral group at posttreatment and in all groups at 10-week follow-up. The spelling achievement data produced a significant group by treatment interactions, with posttreatment and follow-up scores exceeding pretreatment scores. Pre- to posttest comparisons found spelling improvement in both the cognitive-behavioral and behavioral groups at posttreatment and at 10-week follow-up. Math achievement data revealed no significant group by treatment interaction. However, pre- to posttest improvements were found in the cognitive-behavioral and behavioral groups at posttreatment and at 10-week follow-up.

There was no significant group by treatment interactions involving the children's self-concept data. Pre- to posttest within-group comparisons revealed significant improvement at posttreatment and at follow-up only in the cognitive-behavioral group.

Parent blind ratings of self-control and hyperactivity showed no significant group by treatment interaction. In addition, no significant improvements were noted within groups at posttreatment or at 10-week follow-up.

There was a significant group by treatment interaction involving therapist ratings of subject improvement. Both the cognitive-behavioral and behavioral groups were significantly improved relative to the control group.

In addition, the cognitive-behavioral group received significantly higher therapist ratings of improvement than did the behavioral group.

The cognitive-behavioral group evidenced a decrease in off-task behavior at posttreatment, which was maintained at 10-week follow-up. Both the cognitive-behavioral and behavioral groups showed a decrease at posttreatment in verbal "bugging" of others and in physical off-task behavior; however, only the cognitive-behavioral group maintained these decreases at follow-up. In addition, only the behavioral group showed decreases in out-of-seat behavior at posttreatment and at follow-up.

Unfortunately, significant group differences across outcome measures did not persist at 1-year follow-up. However, all three groups demonstrated significant pretest to 1-year follow-up improvement on the MFFT latency and error scores as well as the reading, math, and spelling achievement indexes.

On the basis of overall treatment effects noted, Kendall and Braswell (1982) conclude that the cognitive training component does make an additive contribution to the cognitive-behavioral regimen. It should be noted, however, that this particular research design does not seem to lend itself to comparisons of that nature. The effects of the cognitive intervention alone have not been isolated; therefore, these conclusions are a bit premature. In addition, although the cognitive-behavioral interventions resulted in some significant treatment effects, the strictly-behavioral intervention produced some significant treatment gains as well.

Overall, Kendall and Braswell (1982) should be commended for attempting to enhance the social validity of their intervention program by extending the range of outcome measures utilized to include parental ratings of self-control and hyperactivity as well as an index of self-esteem. In addition, Kendall and Braswell attempt to train for generalization by using Meichenbaum and Goodman's technique in which the volume of the child's self-instructive statements is gradually faded to covert levels. Similarly, these investigators sought to enhance the generic qualities of the strategies taught (and thus to increase the probability their use would generalize to other situations) by gradually altering the statements' content from concrete in nature to abstract or conceptual. In addition, the degree of dissimilarity between the training tasks and improved outcome measures serves as an indication that some generalization of treatment gains across tasks did occur. Although there is evidence that treatment effects generalized to classroom situations, it is disappointing that there is no indication that treatment had an impact on behavior in the home (i.e., parent ratings). These findings should reemphasize the importance of training parents as adjunct therapists and including training tasks whose content overlaps, at least to some extent, the behavioral domains one wishes to affect. It should also be noted that because all groups' performances on the MFFT improved from pre- to posttest, the validity of this instrument as an outcome measure is once again called into question. Lastly, it is disappointing that Kendall and Braswell perpetuate the notion that selection criteria need only be intuitively (or face) valid (i.e., teacher referral for "nonself-controlled" behavior).

Summary and Recommendation for Treatment

In prior critical reviews of the cognitive-behavioral literature pertaining to impulsive children, Kendall and Braswell (1985) and Whalen, Henker, and Henshaw (1985) concluded that research findings are at best mixed. They noted that the efficacy of cognitive-behavioral interventions with impulsive children has been documented only for limited behavioral domains, in narrow ranges of context, and for short-term intervals. In addition, they noted that only a few studies have assessed the long-term durability of treatment gains, and these studies have shown limited maintenance. It should be noted, however, that it is often difficult to compare studies within this area because the treatment components used seem to vary with the therapist, and few studies incorporate adequate controls to make possible the evaluation of individual treatment components as well as their additive contributions. On the whole, however, Kendall and Braswell note that interventions that involve much therapist/child interaction, child involvement in the problem-solving process, and behavioral contingencies produce more gains than programs in which one of these components is missing.

As noted previously, research difficulties arise because there seems to be no consensus among researchers as to how impulsive children should be identified and selected for research. The MFFT is often used as a selection or outcome measure, although there is controversy over this instrument's construct validity for this purpose (Bentler & McClain, 1976; Block, Block, & Harrington, 1974; Kagan & Messer, 1975; Messer, 1976; Reynolds & Stark, 1986). In addition, Hobbs, Moguin, Tyroler, and Lahey (1980) insightfully note that cognitive-behavioral treatment studies at times use larger numbers of dependent measures than subjects. Regardless of the statistical procedeure implemented, numerous dependent measures inflate alpha levels to the extent that some significant findings may be anticipated by chance alone.

It is encouraging, however, that cognitive interventions are beginning to affect impulsive children's behavior in a meaningful way. Investigators are designing programs to enhance generalization and are achieving such goals on at least a short-term basis. Kendall and Braswell (1985) note some considerations for enhancing the impact of cognitive-behavioral interventions with individual children, which merit mention here. They emphasize the importance of appropriate and thorough assessment practices aimed at accurately identifying the particular nature of the child's difficulties. As in all therapeutic endeavors, an optimal match between presenting problem and treatment intervention is of paramount importance, because these diagnostic assumptions form the very basis for all subsequent therapeutic efforts. Well thought-out combinations of the assessment techniques previously discussed should give the school psychologist some indications of the degree of impulsivity present as well as the factors that mediate the impulsive behavior.

In addition, Kendall and Braswell stress that one of the therapist's primary goals must be to establish a cooperative, collaborative working relationship with the client. This is of special concern when participation in the therapeutic process has been "forced" on the child by significant others in his or her environment. Optimal treatment results require that the therapist and child work together towards mutually agreed upon (or at least previously stated) goals. The therapist may initially lay the foundation for a collaborative exchange by sharing treatment duties with the child (i.e., recording training responses, tallying numbers of tokens earned), by taking turns with the child in formulating and reciting the self-instructive statements, and by eliciting the child's input (and often acting on these suggestions) concerning the content of the problem situations to be role-played. Braswell, Kendall, Braith, Carey, and Vye (1985) indicate that children with increased "ownership" of the therapeutic program experience optimal treatment gains.

Impulsive children often come to therapy with a history of academic failure and interpersonal rejection. Therefore, these children seem predisposed to "throwing in the towel" when they encounter adversity. These issues were alluded to earlier when discussing the inclusion of coping statements within the constellation of self-instructive verbalizations. It is imperative that the therapist build a relapse-preventative component into the cognitive-behavioral program, which insulates the child from the detrimental effects of negative self-attributions associated with failure to perform training (and later real-life) tasks adequately. The therapist can initiate this relapse-preventative training by serving as a coping, verbalizing model. The therapist should set the occasion for personal failure as she or he takes turns problem-solving with the child. When these errors occur, the therapist should engage in appropriate coping verbalizations, which model the attitude that when problem-solving attempts result in failure, the problematic situation should be reassessed, strategy implementation deficiencies remediated, and the task approached again (i.e., the therapist might say . . .) "Oop, I guess I messed up. I'll have to remember to go slower and stop to think next time. Then I'll get the problem right"). Similarly, if the child has not yet begun to provide his own coping statements spontaneously when encountering failure, the therapist might provide appropriate coping statements for him, such as:

> Oh, was that one too difficult? Maybe he did go too fast and that may have been the reason. I know he can do better when he takes his time. We have to practice going slower (Kendall and Braswell, 1985:147).

In addition, it is important to instill the child with the knowledge (through direct instruction or modeling) that certain aspects of task performance (in training and in life) are related to chance and are not under his or her direct control. When playing games with the child that contain an element of chance, the therapist might model coping behaviors relevant to situations in which adverse consequences are due to chance occurrences, as for example:

> Heck, that sets me back a lot. You're gonna win. Darn, I was trying too hard too! (pause) All I can do is answer the questions—I can't control the roll of the dice. That wasn't my fault, it was just bad luck. (pause) I'll keep trying so maybe when my luck is good I can maybe win the game (Kendall and Braswell, 1985:148).

Similarly, if the child fails to fulfill a homework assignment, the therapist relates a message such as:

> Last week you told me about how you used the steps to think about making your lunch for the bike ride. That was a terrific example. This week you don't have one, but maybe next week you will. I'll remind you at the end of today's meeting. You did well last time so I'm sure you can do it again. This one time doesn't mean you can't do it later on (Kendall and Braswell, 1985:148).

The primary goal of relapse training is to assist the child in identifying errors in problem solving and in taking steps to remediate these situations, without emotional devastation.

Finally, Kendall and Braswell insightfully point out that therapy termination should not mean the end of therapeutic contact with the child. The researchers suggest routine follow-up assessments and booster sessions when the child encounters a particularly difficult problem situation with a negative outcome.

As noted in the previous discussion, intervention strategies with impulsive children often produce short-term gains, yet fail to provide long-term, generalizable, socially meaningful improvement. Several efforts have been meritorious and collectively point to a potentially fruitful area of applied research designed to optimize generalization and persistence of therapeutic gains.

9
Aggressive and Conduct-Disordered Children and Adolescents

CONCEPTUAL AND DEFINITIONAL ISSUES

Prevalence and Definitions

Children presenting with aggressive and antisocial behaviors comprise between one third and one half of all child referrals for psychological services (Achenbach & Edelbrock, 1978; Gilbert, 1957; Herbert, 1978; Robins, 1974). In this chapter, aggression is used to describe a variety of acting-out behaviors that have in common an intrusive demand and aversive effect on others (Olweus, 1979). Aggressive acts include physically and verbally aggressive behaviors (e.g., threatening others, purposefully disturbing others, being verbally combative, making derogatory remarks, hitting, shoving) as well as destruction of property. In the schools, aggressive children are described by teachers as "starting fights," "mean," "argumentative," "teases others," and "rebellious." The aggressive child disrupts classroom activities and places excessive demands on teacher time and resources. The child who is repeatedly aggressive at school is likely to be diagnosed as conduct disordered and placed in special education classes for severely emotionally disturbed children.

Conduct disorder is a diagnostic category representing a constellation of behaviors that has been identified in multivariate investigations (Achenbach & Edelbrock, 1978; Quay, 1979). The major feature of the conduct-disordered child or adolescent is "a persistent pattern of conduct in which either the basic rights of others or major age-appropriate societal norms or rules are violated" (American Psychiatric Association, 1987, p. 53). Within the conduct-disorder diagnostic classification both aggressive and non-aggressive subtypes as well as socialized and unsocialized subtypes are distinguished. Unsocialized types are characterized by a failure to establish a normal degree of affection and emotional closeness with others. Unsocialized conduct-disordered children are unconcerned with the effects of their behavior on others and feel little remorse or guilt over their actions. The socialized types establish close attachments to others. However, they are callous and manipulative towards others who are not considered members of an insiders' group. In DSM-III-R (American Psychiatric Association, 1987), the terms solitary aggressive type and group type correspond, roughly, to the DSM-III undersocialized aggressive and socialized non-aggressive types.

Clinical Significance of Aggression

Aggressive behavior that is not severe or persistent enough to meet diagnostic criteria for conduct disorder is still of concern to educators and psychologists. Several lines of research demonstrate the clinical significance of aggression in children. These research findings support the view that aggression is stable over time, interferes with normal social development and satisfactory peer relationships, predicts social maladjustment in later adolescence and adulthood, and is related to poor academic outcomes, including school failure and dropping out of school. Research supporting each of these deleterious outcomes will be discussed.

Stability of Aggressive Behavior

Unlike social withdrawal, fears, and other problems of childhood, aggression tends to be relatively stable over time. Children identified in elementary school years as having problems with aggression and poor peer relations are likely to have these same problems in high school, where they are accompanied by problems in school learning and delinquency (Gersten, Langer, Eisenberg, Simcha-Fagen, & McCarthy, 1976; Lefkowitz, Eron, Walder, & Huesman, 1977). In a review of 16 longitudinal studies on aggression, Olweus (1979) identified a large degree of stability in measured aggression, similar to that of measured intelligence.

Aggression and Peer Rejection

Not surprisingly, children who engage in high levels of negative social behavior are disliked by their peers. The overlap between aggressive-disruptive behavior and rejected sociometric status is so great that many reviewers treat aggression and peer rejection as isomorphic descriptors (Conger & Keane, 1981). Indeed, behavioral observations of sociometrically rejected children reveal that rejected children are active, aversive, and disruptive in their social interactions (Cantrell & Prinz, 1985; Coie & Kupersmidt, 1983; Dodge, Coie, & Brakke, 1982).

The consistent finding of a relationship between aggression and peer rejection does not establish a causal relationship between the two variables. Conceivably a child's aggression could be a result of peers' negative behavior and negative attitudes toward him or her. The view that peer rejection is a consequence of aggression and not a cause of it is supported by several studies. For example, Coie and Kupersmidt (1983) observed the social interactions of play groups of five fourth-grade boys who were unfamiliar with each other before the first play session. Boys met in play groups once a week for 6 weeks. Groups were comprised of different sociometric status types, based on sociometric measures taken in their classrooms. Rejected boys were extremely active and aversive in the group and were perceived by group members as starting fights. Similarly, Dodge (1983) observed the social interactions of groups of eight unfamiliar boys. He found that boys who became rejected in the group engaged in more aggression and inappropriate behavior, including physical and verbal aggression.

Although peer rejection appears to be a consequence of aggression, probably aggression and peer rejection form a self-maintaining system in which each contributes to the other (Bierman, 1986). In support of this reciprocal deterministic view, Bierman and Schwartz (1986) report that rejected children receive more negative interactions from peers, even when their own level of negative behavior is taken into consideration.

Long-Term Prediction

Related to the stability of aggressive behavior is the long-term prognosis of aggression and rejection in children and adolescence. Research consistently indicates that aggression and peer rejection are risk factors for serious maladjustment in later years. For example, childhood aggression predicts adult schizophrenia (Watt, 1978) and criminality (Robins, 1966). Aggression and antisocial behaviors predict delinquency and serious adult pathologies within social class and level of intelligence (Conger & Miller, 1966; Robins, 1979; Roff & Wirt, 1984). Peer rejection in childhood is associated with a wide range of pathologies in young adulthood (Cowen et al., 1973; Roff, 1972; Roff, Sells, & Golden, 1972). In a frequently cited longitudinal study, Cowen et al. (1973) found that the number of negative sociometric nominations received in the third grade was a better predictor of adult psychiatric disturbance than was a battery including school records, intelligence performance, and self-report data.

Aggression and Learning Problems

Consistently, research has documented that childhood aggression and antisocial behavior are associated with learning problems. Rutter, Tizard, and Whitmore (1970) found that one quarter of slow readers showed antisocial behavior and one third of conduct-disordered children were reading disabled. Several investigators found that peer rejection, a correlate of aggression, is associated with poor academic achievement and school failure (Green, Forehand, Beck, & Vosk, 1980; Laughlin, 1954; Muma, 1965; Ullmann, 1957). In addition to interfering with the aggressive child's learning, the disruption caused by a child's aggression in schools interferes with other students' learning. The teacher must focus energies on managing the disruptive and aggressive behavior instead of on imparting content-relevant knowledge and skills.

Developmental Issues

Age-Related Changes

Aggression in preschool children is developmentally normal and usually transient. Instrumental aggressive behaviors (e.g., hitting or grabbing to get a toy) increase in frequency between ages 2 and 4 and then decrease substantially by the early school years (Van Alstnyne & Hattwick, 1939; Hartup, 1974). Some types of aggression in the preschool years appear to be manifestations of social interest rather than hostile intent. For example, Waldrop and Halverson (1975) found a relationship between aggression and affiliative behaviors in 2½-year-olds. Furthermore, aggression and affiliative behavior during preschool years predict indexes of social competence at age 7. Matthews (1972, reported in Matthews & Brooks-Gunn, 1984) found that observed aggressive behavior and popularity were positively correlated in a preschool sample. These findings suggest that the observed measures of aggression did not distinguish between rough and tumble play, which may have been coded as aggression, and maliciously intended aggressive behavior. In any event, by kindergarten, observed aggression correlates positively with peer rejection (Rubin & Daniels-Beirness, 1983).

Family Influences

Numerous investigators (i.e., Kazdin & Frame, 1983) have documented differences between families of nonaggressive and those of aggressive children. Patterson, Reid, Jones, and Conger (1975) conducted a particularly useful line of research on family interactional styles of families with aggressive children and families with nonaggressive children. Family interaction in families with aggressive children is characterized by a higher frequency of negative and hostile exchanges. Aggressive children engage in more irritating and aversive behaviors towards their parents. Their parents, in turn, respond with aversive control methods (e.g., hitting, threatening, yelling). A reciprocally coercive interactional style develops in which family members attempt to influence others by exercising aversive control.

Bierman (1986) suggests that aggressive children get caught in a negative socializing cycle. Family factors, such as parental coercive behavior, inconsistent discipline practices, inadequate reinforcement for positive behavior, and marital discord, make it likely that a child will engage in aggressive behaviors when he or she enters public school. Peers' response to the aggressive behavior excludes the child from the positive social interactions that are necessary for the development of prosocial behaviors. Additionally, peers' expectations for aggressive children to behave aggressively cause peers to respond selectively to the aggressive child's negative behavior and to fail to reward positive behaviors. As a result of hostile interactions and inadequate learning opportunities, aggressive children develop deviant social expectations and social-cognitive skill deficits. In turn, these deviant expectations and social-cognitive deficits contribute to a maladaptive socialization cycle.

Aggressive Subtypes

Coie and Dodge (1986) have distinguished two types of aggressive/rejected children. The *dominant aggressive child* uses aggression instrumentally to get his or her own way. This child has learned that aggression is positively reinforced. The *reactive aggressive child* overreacts to others, provocations and misinterprets peers' intentions by overinferring hostility. Coie and Dodge found that they could distinguish two types of aggressive boys based on a teacher rating scale consisting of items depicting angry, reactive aggressive behaviors and bullying, instrumentally aggressive behaviors. Black rejected boys in grades 3 to 6 were classified as high in dominant aggression, high in reactive aggression, high in both types of aggression, or low in both types of aggression. Dominant aggressive boys, although rejected, were viewed by peers as having some positive qualities (i.e., leadership and a sense of humor). Reactive aggressive boys were not only rejected but also viewed as having a poor sense of humor and poor leadership qualities. Of special interest is their finding that reactive aggressive boys were deficient in their ability to accurately interpret peers' intentions and tended to overattribute hostile intent. Dominant aggressive boys, however, were as accurate as nonrejected controls in interpreting peers' intentions. Coie and Dodge (1986) concluded that the reactive aggressive boys' aggression is a result, at least in part, of their social cognitive deficits and distortions. Specifically, they overperceive hostile intent in peers' social behavior and react to the perceived hostility with aggression. Dominant aggressive boys' aggression is a result of a social learning history that has taught them aggression is rewarded, at least in the short run. They use aggression strategically to obtain some desired goal. They are accurate in interpreting peers' social interactions.

Efforts to distinguish subtypes of aggressive children should lead to interventions that more closely match the reason for the aggressive behavior. In this regard, the dominant aggressive child might benefit from an intervention designed to teach problem-solving skills, including consequential thinking. Specifically, these children may not consider the less immediate consequences of their aggressive behavior and/or may be unable to generate effective, nonaggressive alternatives for obtaining a desired goal. Conversely, reactive aggressive children would be expected to benefit from an intervention that stresses accurate interpretation of others' behaviors. Social insight, empathy, and perspective-taking skills would be emphasized in an intervention program for them.

SOCIAL-COGNITIVE CORRELATES OF AGGRESSION AND REJECTION

The view of the aggressive, antisocial child as deficient in social cognition is not new. For example, Chandler (1971, 1973) documented differences in role-taking skills between delinquent and nondelinquent youths. Spivack, Shure, and their colleagues (Shure & Spivack, 1978; Spivack, Platt, & Shure, 1976) reported a series of studies showing that specific social problem-solving skills are associated with adjustment outcomes in children. These early studies stimulated research interest in social-cognitive correlates of maladjustment. Some of the most productive research on the role of social-cognitive processes in childhood psychopathology has been conducted with aggressive and rejected children. These research investigations have documented differences between aggressive/rejected children and adaptive children in role-taking (Chandler, 1971, 1973; Gurucharri, Phelps, & Selman, 1984), social knowledge (Asher & Renshaw, 1981; Ladd & Oden, 1979), the ability to generate effective alternatives to social problem situations (Spivack et al., 1976; Richard & Dodge, 1982), self-efficacy for aggressive versus assertive responding (Deluty, 1979, 1981a,b; Perry, Perry, & Rasmussen, 1986), expectations regarding the positive outcomes of aggressive versus assertive responding (Perry et al., 1986; Asarnow & Callan, 1985), attributional biases (Dodge, Murphy, & Buchsbaum, 1984; Nasby, Hayden, & DePaulo, 1980), and errors and distortions in attending to social cues (Dodge & Newman, 1981; Dodge & Frame, 1982). A comprehensive review of social-cognitive correlates of aggression and rejection is beyond the scope and goals of this chapter. However, selected studies that illustrate the importance of social-cognitive mediators in childhood aggression will be discussed.

Role Taking

Role taking, also referred to as social perspective-taking ability, is the ability to take the point of view of another person. It involves the ability to recognize the perceptions, thoughts, and feelings of another person. A frequently used measure of role-taking ability is Chandler's Bystander Cartoons (Chandler, 1971, 1973). Children are presented with 10 to 12 short stories, each consisting of a series of cartoon sequences that show a character experiencing an affectively laden event (e.g., fear at accidently breaking a window with a baseball) in the first several frames. In the next frame, another character is introduced (e.g., the first child is at home with his father after breaking the window when a knock at the door causes him to feel afraid). The test child is asked to retell the story from the point of view of the late arriving bystander (e.g., the boy's father who did not know about his son's mishap with the baseball). Perspective-taking is measured by the extent to which the tested child avoids including "privileged information" from the first several frames in his retelling of the story.

Chandler (Chandler, 1973; Chandler, Greenspan, & Barenboim, 1974) found deficits in social perspective-taking ability among 8- to 15-year-old antisocial children compared with normal control subjects. Using another measure of perspective-taking, Selman and his colleagues found deficits in perspective-taking among 7- to 13-year-olds described as having poor peer relationships (Selman, 1980). Among clinic-referred 6- to 12-year-olds, Cohen, Kershner, and Wehrspann (1985) found an association between externalizing symptoms on the Child Behavior Checklist (Achenbach & Edelbrock, 1983) and deficits in perspective-taking ability. It is important to note that deficits in perspective-taking ability are not specific to aggressive children but are also found in other groups of socially deviant children (Waterman et al., 1981).

Social Problem Solving

Aggressive/rejected children generate fewer solutions to hypothetical social dilemmas (Richard & Dodge, 1982; Asarnow & Callan, 1985) and their solutions are less effective and more aggressive than are those of nonaggressive children (Asarnow & Callan, 1985; Deluty, 1981b; Lochman, & Lampron, 1986; Richard & Dodge, 1982). In the Richard and Dodge study, groups of popular, aggressive, and isolated boys at two grade levels (second/third grades and fourth/fifth grades) were presented with six hypothetical problem situations and asked to generate alternative solutions to the problem. Three situations concerned a conflict with a peer and three concerned a situation in which the child wanted to initiate a friendship with an unfamiliar peer. Popular children generated more solutions than did either the aggressive or isolated groups, which did not differ. Although initial solutions generated by all groups were equally effective, subsequent solutions varied as a function of subject status. Popular children continued to generate effective solutions, whereas aggressive and isolated children's subsequent solutions were ineffective and aggressive. The premise that deviant boys are deficient in the specific skill of generating effective solutions and not in evaluating solutions was supported by the finding that groups did not differ in their ratings of effectiveness of solutions presented to them by the experimenter.

Asarnow and Callan (1985) investigated five social-cognitive skills in fourth- to sixth-grade boys with positive and negative (rejected) peer status. The five processes were (1) ability to generate a number of alternative solutions to social problems, (2) ability to generate nonaggressive, positive solutions to problems, (3) ability to evaluate possible solutions, (4) ability to plan adaptively, and (5) ability to make accurate attributions. After being presented with four social vignettes representing both aggressive and friendship situations, children were asked to generate solutions to the problem. Next, children were asked to evaluate solutions to the vignette problems. After children's responses to the situations and evaluations of responses to the four vignettes were obtained, the same situations were presented again, and each child was asked to describe what he would "feel and think" in each situation. Finally, the child was presented with six possible self-statements that the "child in the story might be thinking and feeling" and asked to rate each one in terms of how likely the story child would be to feel and think that way. Compared with popular boys, rejected boys generated fewer solutions to the hypothetical problems, generated less mature, prosocial, and assertive solutions, generated more aggressive solutions, evaluated aggressive strategies more positively and prosocial strategies more negatively, and showed less adaptive and more maladaptive planning. Thus, Asarnow and Callan (1985) not only replicated the finding that rejected children generate fewer and more negative solutions, but also documented differences in rejected and popular children's characteristic planning, or means-end thinking. Specifically rejected children were less likely to give a response indicating consequential thinking (e.g., "If I hit him, I'd get in trouble), anticipation of obstacles to a solution, reference to social rules, or goal setting.

Aggressive children's social problem-solving deficiencies do not occur equally in all types of situations. Researchers have found that aggressive/rejected children are especially likely to experience problems in situations involving peer provocation (Lochman & Lampron, 1986; Dodge, McClaskey, & Feldman, 1985). For example, Dodge and his colleagues (1985) found that aggressive/rejected children's role-play responses to different social situations were overall less competent than were the responses of nonaggressive, adaptive children. However, the deficiencies of aggressive/rejected children were most evident in situations involving being provoked by peers and in response to meeting social expectations. In addition to marked group differences in responding to problematic situations, low consistency of responding across situations among aggressive children was found. The researchers concluded that although general social problem-solving deficiencies characterize aggressive/rejected children, individual aggressive children will have particular problems with some situations and not with others. Because of the low cross-situational consistency of responding, assessments of aggressive/rejected children's social problem-solving skills require an assessment of these skills in different situations. Therefore a skill X situation assessment approach is recommended.

Self-Efficacy and Outcome Expectancies for Aggression

One reason that aggressive children respond with more aggressive and fewer assertive and prosocial solutions to hypothetical conflicts may be that aggressive children value assertive solutions more negatively and aggressive solutions more positively than do other children (Asarnow & Callan, 1985). Recently, Perry, et al. (1986) found that aggressive children, compared with nonaggressive children, are more confident that aggression would produce tangible rewards and would reduce aversive treatment by others. Additionally, aggressive children reported that it is easier to perform aggressive acts and more difficult to inhibit aggressive impulses. In social learning theory terms, aggressive children have higher self-efficacy for aggressive behaviors (they are more confident that they could perform the aggressive response) and more positive outcome expectancies for aggressive responses (they are more likely to believe that aggressive responses will lead to desirable outcomes). Although the correlational design of the study did not permit a determination of causal relations among self-efficacy, outcome expectancies, and aggressive behavior, the obtained relationships are consistent with a social learning theory view of aggression. According to this view, aggressive responding is a result of a child's self-efficacy and outcome expectancies. These expectations are the result of one's learning history (i.e., past experiences).

Attributional Biases

Several researchers have consistently found that aggressive children demonstrate a systematic bias to infer hostile intent in ambiguous social situations (Nasby et al., 1980; Dodge, et al., 1984; Waldman, 1986; Dodge, 1980; Steinberg & Dodge, 1983). Steinberg and Dodge had pairs of same-sex children compete in a block-building task. Each subject discovered that some of his or her blocks had fallen before the prize was awarded. The cause of the blocks falling was ambiguous. Aggressive subjects were more likely to attribute their misfortune to the hostile behavior of peers than were non-aggressive subjects. In a second study (Dodge et al., 1984) children were presented with videotaped vignettes depicting peer provocations. In each vignette, the peer's intent was depicted as hostile, prosocial, accidental, ambiguous, or merely present. For example, one vignette depicted a peer accidently knocking down a child's blocks. Another vignette depicted a peer purposefully knocking down a child's blocks. The vignettes were presented to groups of popular, average, rejected, and neglected children. Socially deviant children (rejected and neglected children) were less accurate than were normal children in identifying prosocial and accidental intentions for the provocations. Furthermore, when these children misidentified prosocial and accidental provocations, they were highly likely to label these acts as hostile. Especially significant is the finding that children's choices of a behavioral response to the provocations by peers were a direct function of their perception of the intent of the peer but not a function of the actual intention portrayed by the peer. The researchers concluded that, "It is a child's perception of a peer's intention, not the peer's actual intention, that determines that child's behavioral response to a provocation. This finding is strong evidence of the critical role that children's perceptions play in determining their behavior" (Dodge et al., 1984:71).

Attentional and Memory Deficits

Dodge and his colleagues (Dodge & Newman, 1981; Dodge & Frame, 1982) hypothesized that aggressive children's attributional bias was related to two aspects of their cognitive processing. Specifically, they predicted that aggressive children would respond more quickly to social situations, without taking advantage of all the available social cues, and would demonstrate selective recall of hostile cues. Both hypotheses were supported in research investigations. Additionally, the tendency for aggressive children to overattribute hostile intent to peers' actions was evident only when aggressive children made their decision quickly as to the peer's intent. Aggressive boys who did not respond quickly made decisions that were not biased or different from those of nonaggressive boys. Furthermore, subjects tended to make decisions as to intent (hostile or benign) that were consistent with the kinds of cues they recalled. These findings support the view that aggressive boys' tendency to overattribute hostile intent is mediated by their tendency to respond impulsively and to selectively recall cues consistent with hostile intent, compared with cues consistent with benign intent. The researchers suggest that their findings are consistent with a reciprocally deterministic cognitive model of aggressive behavior. Specifically, aggressive boys have acquired an expectation that peers will behave towards them in hostile ways. This expectation causes them to respond quickly and to attend selectively to hostile cues, thus overattributing hostility to peers' behaviors towards them. The biased attribution causes them to respond aggressively, which, in turn, leads to retaliatory aggression from peers. The retaliatory aggression confirms the original expectation.

COGNITIVE BEHAVIORAL ASSESSMENT OF AGGRESSIVE/REJECTED CHILDREN

An Information-Processing Assessment Model

Hughes and Hall (1987) and Dodge and his colleagues (Dodge, 1986; Dodge et al., 1985; Dodge & Murphy, 1984) have recommended a social-information processing model of social competence that is particularly applicable to assessing aggressive/rejected children. Both models attempt to identify the social situations in which the child's performance is deficient and the specific cognitive and behavioral skills that lead to judgments of competence. Both models conceptualize social competence as involving the exercise of specific skills at three sequential stages. These stages are labeled Reading, Generating, and Applying by Hughes and Hall (1987) and Decoding, Decision-making, and Enactment by Dodge and Murphy (1984). Although both models recognize the importance of identifying practical social tasks that are problematic for the individual, they differ in the relative emphasis on specific situations versus generalizable skills. The Dodge and Murphy model reflects a bottom-up processing or building-block approach to the identification of social-cognitive deficits, whereas the Hughes and Hall model places greater emphasis on generalizable skills.

Hughes and Hall conceptualize social problem-solving as a function of the appropriate application of cognitive and behavioral skills to social problem situations. A person's social performance is judged competent when the person's perception of a social situation is accurate and a strategic behavioral repertoire appropriate to the social problem is applied. Socially competent outcomes, then, require that an individual accurately interpret social cues (*Read* the situation), generate appropriate social responses (*Generate*), and effectively implement the selected response in the situation (*Apply*). An individual child may have deficits at one or more stages in the social problem-solving process. The child who demonstrates deficits in interpreting social cues or in generating effective responses has social-cognitive deficits, whereas the child who has deficits in enacting a selected response has a behavioral deficit.

Theoretically, this model allows a division of social incompetence into three major categories: behavioral skill deficits, cognitive deficits, and cognitive/behavioral deficits. Some examples may be helpful (Figure 9.1). The girl with a behavioral skill deficit (Type II) encounters an unfamiliar peer at soccer practice. The girl would like to get acquainted with the peer and knows that introducing herself and initiating conversation would be an effective strategy. However, her execution of that strategy is flawed by nervous mannerisms, poor eye contact, and mild stuttering. The boy who has a cognitive skill deficit (Type III) invites a classmate to his house to play a game. The boy construes the goal of the game as winning rather than as making friends. Therefore, he engages in highly competitive behaviors. Finally, a girl with cognitive and behavioral skill deficits is accidently bumped by a classmate while standing in the lunch line. The girl mislabels the peer's behavior as intentional and responds by shoving the peer.

According to the model, competent social performance requires three component skills. Figure 9.2 depicts a schematic of the social decision-making process starting from a social problem situation and moving through componential choice points to behavioral subtypes.

The first component in the decision-making process addresses the question, "Does the child have problems related to 'reading' the social situation?" Greenspan (1981) has referred to this component of social awareness as social sensitivity and defines it as "the individual's ability to label accurately the meaning of a social object or event, at a given moment in time" (p. 18). "Reading" a social event is understood to mean the ability to identify accurately personal states of others (i.e., role-play) and to identify accurately social situations (i.e., social inference). Hughes and Hall go beyond Greenspan's definition to include, under the general heading of "reading," problems analogous to "reading comprehension" or what Greenspan calls problems of social insight. Social insight refers to the ability to understand the underpinnings or nuances associated with particular social situations. In Greenspan's model, these nuances have labels such as psychological insight, moral judgment, and social comprehension. These latter areas reflect a deeper, more causal understanding as opposed to a surface

Social Cognition		Appropriate Skills	Inappropriate Skills
	Correct	Type I No Error	Type II Behavioral Skill Deficit
Person's Perception of the Social Situation	Incorrect	Type III Cognitive Deficit	Type IV Cognitive/ Behavioral Deficit

FIGURE 9.1. Cognitive and behavioral skills used in social situations. *Source*: J. N. Hughes and R. J. Hall, "A Proposed Model for the Assessment of Social Competence," *Professional School Psychology*, 1987, *2*, 252.

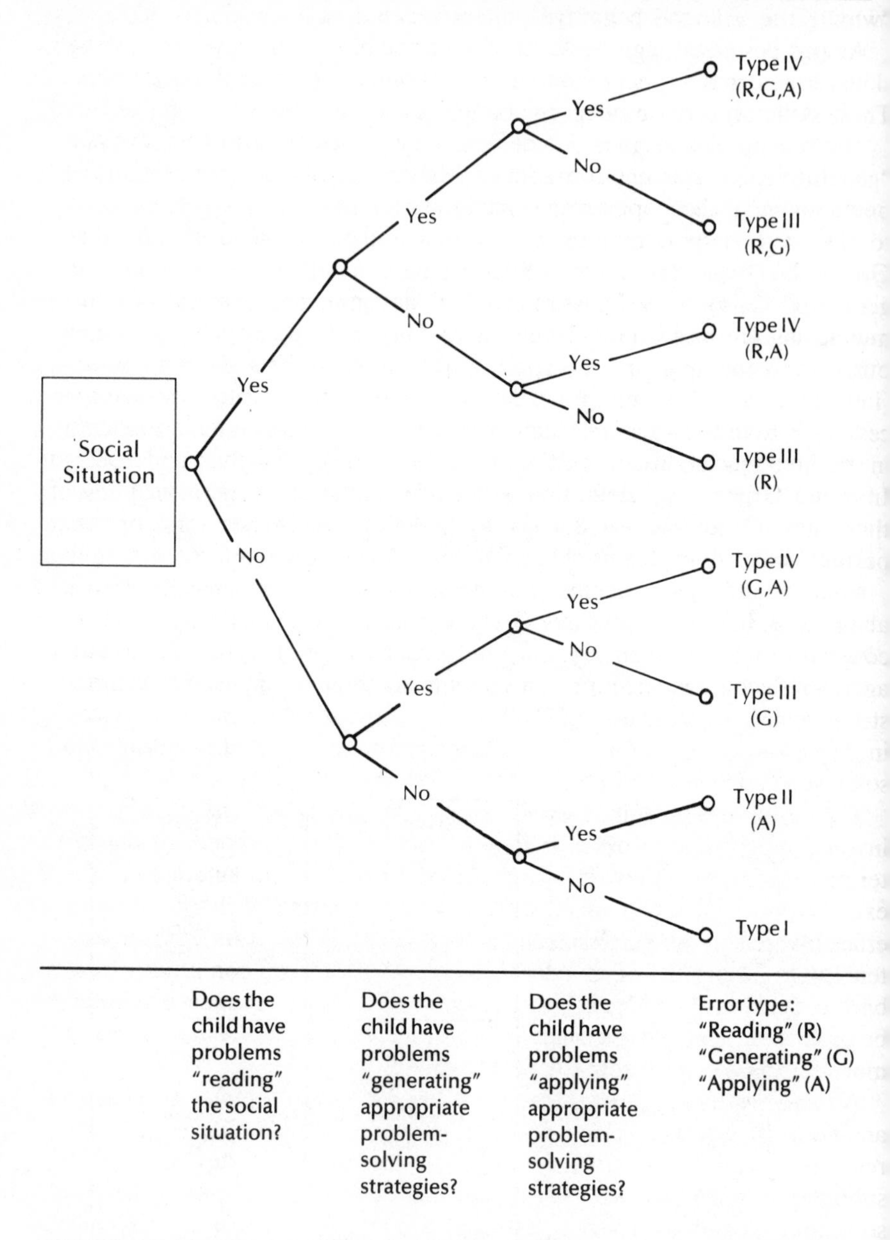

FIGURE 9.2. Schematic of social decision-making process. *Source*: J. N. Hughes and R. J. Hall, "A Proposed Model for the Assessment of Social Competence," *Professional School Psychology*, 1987, *2*, 252.

understanding of an event and are captured by questions pertaining to the "why" rather than the "what" of a social situation.

As just described, aggressive children are deficient in social role-taking skills, in interpreting peers' intentions, and in using available social cues. These skills fall into the category of reading skills.

The second choice point in the schematic is anchored to the keyword "generating." The question posed at this point is, "Does the child have problems generating appropriate problem-solving strategies?" In contrast to the more passive reading phase, the generating phase entails what Greenspan (1981) refers to as social communication. Strategic behaviors are generated to intervene intentionally with others for the purpose of communicating (i.e., referential communication) or to attempt to persuade others to change their behaviors to meet the problem-solver's needs (i.e., social problem-solving). Although this phase of information processing is active in that an individual is acting on information gathered in the reading phase, it still represents internal cognitive processing. In other words, the child may know how to behave effectively, but there are no guarantees that knowing how will translate directly into performance.

As discussed earlier, aggressive children as a group are deficient in their ability to generate many effective solutions to social problems, are more confident of their ability to implement aggressive solutions, and expect aggressive responses to result in more positive outcomes. Thus, they demonstrate several processing differences relevant to the second major step in processing social information, generating solutions, and selecting one solution to try.

The third component linking assessment to treatment/intervention involves the translation of knowledge into action. This component is characterized by the fluency with which skilled behaviors are summoned and executed in accord with some strategic plan and by the ability to monitor efficiently one's own performance. Self-monitoring for errors and inconsistencies in actions and/or reactions allows one to provide continuous feedback to the reading and generating components. New information then can be used to update strategic plans and to modify behaviors in order to obtain more desirable results from social encounters.

Although the proposed choice points represent continuous dimensions and not dichotomous decisions, they are depicted in the schematic as yes/no responses to enhance testability of the model and to illustrate the different subtypes of individuals with social competence problems. As in Figure 9.2, some individuals would be characterized as having only reading, generating, or applying problems. Interventions for these children should be different from one another and should be different from those constructed for individuals having difficulty in more than one phase of the overall process.

In either case, it is proposed that by systematically addressing questions posed at each point along the schematic, social competence problems can be specified more accurately and child progress can be documented more directly.

Implications of Model of Assessment

Consistent with assessment practices recommended throughout this book, the assessment of aggressive/rejected children should include impact and specifying assessment procedures. The child's impact on others is assessed most effectively by sociometric procedures and teacher and parent rating scales. The specific skills that need to be assessed are suggested by the social information-processing model (i.e., the component skills at each of the three stages of the model).

To accomplish both impact and specifying assessment objectives, a three-step assessment model is recommended. First, whether or not a social competence problem exists is determined through sociometric measures and parent and teacher ratings. Second, hypothesized skill deficits and problematic social situations are identified through child interviews. Third, these hypothesized cognitive and behavioral skill deficits are assessed with a battery of tests. The result is a typology of social problem-solving deficits and a description of the social situations in which the child displays deviant behavior. Next, these three assessment stages are applied to assessment of the rejected/aggressive child.

Stage 1 Assessment: Assessing Others' Perceptions of Aggressive/Rejected Children

Peer Sociometrics

Peers' perceptions of the aggressive child can be obtained through sociometric procedures. Because aggressive behavior leads to peer rejection, aggressive children are likely to receive a high number of rejected nominations and a low number of acceptance nominations. To distinguish between rejected and neglected children, it is important to use both positive and negative nomination questions, as in the Coie, Dodge, & Coppotelli (1982) classification system. As described in chapter 3, rejected children are children whose social preference scores (i.e., positive nominations minus negative nominations, or liking minus disliking nominations) are at least 1 standard deviation below the mean for a group of peers. If rejection nominations are objected to in the school situation, the evaluator can use a combination of a peer rating scale and a positive nomination question, as described by Asher and Dodge (1986). In Asher and Dodge's alternative classification system, a liking rating of 1 on a 1 to 5 rating scale (with a 1 response indicating "I don't like to play with" and a 5 rating indicating "I like to play with a lot") is treated as a rejection nomination in computing social preference scores. Agreement between the two methods in classifying rejected children is very high (91 percent).

Peers' perceptions of children's aggression can also be obtained with peer behavioral descriptions. The peer behavioral description method is a more structured peer nomination procedure. The best example of this sociometric procedure is the Class Play (Bower, 1969; Lambert & Bower, 1961). Children pretend to be directors of an imaginary play and "cast" their classmates into a variety of positive and negative roles. Example roles are "Someone who is the leader. When we do something in class or on the playground, someone everybody listens to" and "A bully, someone who picks on smaller boys and girls." The Revised Class Play (Masten, Morison, & Pellegrini, 1985) consists of 30 roles, 15 positive and 15 negative, and yields three scores identified through factor analysis: sociability-leadership, aggressive-disruptive, and sensitive-isolated. The eight items comprising the aggressive-disruptive scale are listed in Table 9.1. For each factor, Masten et al. (1985) report good internal consistency as well as good stability for intervals of 6 to 17 months.

In his research with aggressive children, Dodge (Dodge, 1980; Dodge & Newman, 1981) has used a combination of like most and like least nominations plus peer behavior descriptions. Nomination scores on peer behavioral descriptions of aggression (i.e., this child starts fights and hits other kids) have evidenced good short-term and long-term stability (Coie & Dodge, 1983; Dodge & Newman, 1981). To be selected as aggressive, a child must be rejected (i.e., receive a high number of peer nominations as disliked and a low number of peer nominations as liked), receive a high number of nominations on the aggressive behavior description, and score above the median of his or her teacher's ratings of aggression.

Table 9.1. Items on an Aggressive Subscale of Revised Class Play

Items
Picks on other kids
Too bossy
Teases other children too much
Gets into a lot of fights
Loses temper easily
Shows off a lot
Interrupts when other children are speaking
Acts like a little kid

Source: A. S. Masten, P. Morison, and D. Pellegrini, "A Revised Class Play Method of Peer Assessment" 1985, *Developmental Psychology, 21*, 527. Copyright 1985 by the American Psychological Association. Adapted by permission.

Teacher Ratings

Factor analyses of comprehensive teacher rating scales consistently find an aggressive/acting out factor (e.g., Child Behavior Checklist, Achenbach & Edelbrock, 1983; Behavior Problem Checklist, Quay & Peterson, 1983; Walker Problem Behavior Identification Checklist, Walker, 1976). Extensive research on teacher ratings support the view that ratings of children's social behaviors are reliable and valid (Hughes, in press-a; Hops & Greenwood, in press). Comprehensive rating scales like the Child Behavior Checklist as well as ratings of specific social skills (e.g., Stephen's Social Behavior Assessment, Stephens, 1981; Teacher Rating of Social Skills-Children; Clark, Gresham, & Elliott, 1985) are important to the identification of aggressive children. Because teachers' perceptions of a child are frequently the basis for referral to special services and predict other socially important outcomes, they are important indexes of the impact or social validity of intervention programs with aggressive children.

Both peer ratings and teacher ratings can help answer the questions "Is there a problem?" and "Did the problem improve?" Neither teacher ratings nor peer sociometric measures are useful for specifying the specific cognitive and behavioral deficits that account for a child's aggressive behavior or the situations in which these deficits are most apparent.

Stage 2: Interviewing the Child

The psychologist proceeds to the child interview when social skills problems based on results from the sociometric and rating scale assessments are suspected. Bierman (1983:218) states that the purpose of the child interview is to assess cognitive and affective variables that may mediate behavioral difficulties: "Like adults, children have thoughts and feelings about their emotional and interpersonal experiences, and their interpretations of various social and emotional events may directly affect their reactions to such events and their subsequent attitudes and behaviors." The recommended approach is similar to the reflective reasoning interviews used by Selman (1980) and Renshaw (reported in Renshaw & Asher, 1982), structured around such problem-solving contexts as making friends, resolving conflicts, and joining in. The social contexts that are most problematic for the child can be identified through interviews with the teacher. In this regard, a taxonomy of problematic social situations for children (TOPS), developed by Dodge and his colleagues (Dodge et al., 1985), would be useful in identifying the social situations in which an aggressive child is most likely to display incompetent performance.

Selman, Jaquette, and Bruss-Saunders (1979) provide an in-depth discussion of the hypothetical-reflective interview method. In brief, the psychologist presents a series of social problem situations by means of stories representing different social problem-solving contexts. The child is asked a number of questions about each story. These questions are designed to obtain information on children's problem-solving processes, such as those outlined in the RGA model. For example, children who have difficulty responding to peer provocations can be told a story about a child who is walking home from school one rainy day and a classmate rides by him on his bike. When the boy rides by, mud is splashed on the child's pants. The psychologist then asks the child a series of questions, such as the following (Hughes & Hall, 1987):

I. What is the story about?
R What happened?
e Why did that happen?
a Does the child have a problem? What is the problem?
d What is the child thinking and feeling?

II. What could the child do to solve the problem?
G
e
n What might happen next if the child did that?
e What else could the child do?
r 1. What might happen if the child did that?
a 2. What would be the best thing to do? Why?
t
e

III. Is that what you would do?
A
p How good are you at doing that?
p Show me how you would do that.
l
y

Stage 3: Specifying Component Skills

At the third stage of assessment, a screening battery comprised of procedures designed to assess the hypothesized skill deficits is selected. At this stage, the psychologist attempts to collect information for purposes of decision making at different junctures in the proposed model (Figure 9.2). The model is built around a series of questions pertinent to each of the decision-making points. Table 9.2 lists assessment procedures and archival sources (where available) that will be helpful in answering questions pertinent to each decision point in the model.

It is important to note that clinically adequate measures of many of the constructs summarized in Table 9.1 do not currently exist. Therefore, conclusions reached on the basis of these measures should be treated as hypotheses. In this regard, clinical decision making involves a process of collecting the best available data in order to characterize how the child solves

Table 9.2. Sample Questions, Procedures, and References for the RGA Model

Questions	Assessment Procedure	Reviews
Phase 1. Does the child have problems "reading" the social situation?		
1. Does the child accurately label others' intentions?	*Intention-Cue Discrimination Task (Dodge et al., 1984)	
2. Does the child accurately label others' emotions?	*Affective Perspective Taking Task (Marsh et al., 1980)	
3. Does the child sense social problems?	PEPSI (Feldhusen et al., 1972)	Butler and Meichenbaum (1981)
4. What goals does the child construct in social situations?	*Goals Interview (Renshaw, 1981)	
5. Does the child see the problem from multiple and differing social perspectives?	Chandler Role Taking Task (Chandler, 1971)	Enright and Lapsley (1980); Kendall et al. (1981)
	Interpersonal Understanding Interview (Selman et al., 1979)	Selman, 1980
6. Does the child seek information that would be useful in clarifying the problem?	PEPSI (Feldhusen et al., 1972)	Butler and Meichenbaum (1981)
Phase 2. Does the child have problems "generating" appropriate problem-solving strategies?		
1. Does the child generate different solutions to problems?	PIPS (Shure & Spivack, 1974)	Spivack et al. (1976); Butler and Meichenbaum (1981)
	Problem Solving Measure (Allen et al., 1976)	Butler and Meichenbaum (1981)
2. Does the child make step-by-step plans for achieving given problem resolutions?	MEPS (Platt & Spivack, 1975) and Children's MEPS (Shure & Spivack, 1972; Spivack et al., 1985)	Kendall and Braswell (1985)
3. Does the child anticipate consequences of different solutions to problems?	What Happens Next? Game (Spivack & Shure, 1974); The Awareness of Consequences Test (Shure & Spivack, 1978)	
4. Does the child use the evaluation of consequences in selecting a plan?		
Phase 3. Does the child have problems "applying" appropriate problem-solving strategies?		
1. Does the child "stop and think" before responding in social situations?	Teacher Self Control Rating Scale (Humphrey, 1982); direct observation; Conners Parent and Teacher Rating Scales (Goyette et al., 1978)	Reynolds and Stark (1986); Barton and Ascione (1984); McMahon (1984)

Table 9.2. *continued*

Questions	Assessment Procedure	Reviews
	Self Control Rating Scale (Kendall & Wilcox, 1979)	Reynolds and Stark (1986)
2. Does the child verify whether his or her solution was effective (self-monitoring)?	PEPSI (Feldhusen et al., 1972); direct observation	Butler and Meichenbaum (1981); Barton and Ascione (1984)
3. Does the child engage in the behavioral skills necessary to successfully carry out the solution?	Direct Observation Procedures; BAT-C (Bornstein et al., 1977) Waksman Social Skills Rating Scale (1985)	Barton and Ascione (1984); Michelson et al. (1981)

Notes: The assessment procedures and reviews of assessment procedures are for purposes of illustration and are not presented as an exhaustive listing.
Procedures preceded by an asterisk (*) have been developed for research and are not easily available.
Source: J. N. Hughes and R. J. Hall, "A Proposed Model for the Assessment of Social Competence" *Professional School Psychology*, 1987, 254–255. Reprinted by permission.

social problems. Therefore, results from the assessment represent maps of children's social problem-solving difficulties, the accuracy of which is best tested by documentation and evaluation of child progress before, during, and after the implementation of an intervention (Evans, 1985).

Results obtained at the third stage of assessment serve two purposes. First, they provide confirming or disconfirming evidence and additional detail regarding hypothesized cognitive and behavioral skill deficits. Second, they provide a preintervention baseline for the specific skills to be targeted in the intervention. The intervention can be evaluated by analyzing changes in the child's peer acceptance and behavioral adjustment (Stage 1) and/or changes in the specific skills targeted for intervention (Stage 3). The use of both impact assessment measures (i.e., sociometrics and teacher rating scales) and specifying assessment measures (i.e., interview and skill battery) helps to document changes in specific skills resulting from the intervention as well as how those changes impact on others' perceptions of the child.

COGNITIVE BEHAVIORAL INTERVENTIONS FOR AGGRESSIVE/REJECTED CHILDREN

Cognitive behavioral interventions with aggressive/rejected children can be grouped into four intervention approaches. These approaches are self-instructional training, anger management, social skills training, and social-cognitive skill training.

Self-Instructional Training

Self-instructional training (SIT) with aggressive children attempts to remediate their impulsivity. It is assumed that the impulsive/aggressive child responds aggressively because he or she does not "stop and think" before responding to an anger-provoking situation. The self-control approach to treating aggressive children teaches children to engage in coping self-talk. Training in self-instruction is modeled on Meichenbaum and Goodman's (1971) training procedures. Because these procedures are discussed in considerable detail in chapter 8, they are not elaborated here.

Several researchers have investigated the efficacy of SIT with aggressive children. Schneider (1974; Robin, Schneider, & Dolnick, 1976; Schneider & Robin, 1976) developed a SIT procedure called the turtle technique to help emotionally disturbed, aggressive children to inhibit aggressive responses. Children are taught the "turtle response" of pulling in one's limbs and lowering the head to withdraw from a provoking situation. Next, children are taught relaxation skills they can use while "doing the turtle." Whereas studies present evidence that the turtle reduces aggressive behavior, the lack of an attention control group and the improbability that classroom observers were blind to subjects' conditions (i.e., doing the turtle is a noticeable activity) limit confidence in these findings.

In a multiple baseline design, Goodwin and Mahoney (1975) investigated the efficacy of SIT training in decreasing hyperactive boys' aggressive responses to peers' verbal taunts. Baseline observations were taken during a taunting game in which each of three hyperactive boys, aged 6 to 11 years, was, in turn, verbally taunted by the other subjects. All boys had marked difficulty remaining calm and responding nonaggressively. One week after baseline, subjects viewed a film of a boy participating in the verbal taunting game. The boy remained calm and modeled adaptive coping self-talk (e.g., "I'm not going to let them bug me"). After viewing the modeling film, the boys' behavior during the taunting game did not improve. A few days later the boys viewed the modeling film again, but this time the therapist pointed out and discussed the model's coping self-talk. The boys were asked to recall as many coping self-statements as they could before participating in the taunting game again 1 week later. Following the second viewing of the modeling film, the boys' behavior in the taunting game improved. A limitation of this study is the lack of a control for habituation to the taunting game. It may be that the boys just got used to verbal taunts.

Using behavioral rehearsal and SIT, Kettlewell and Kausch (1983) taught coping skills to aggressive boys aged 7 to 12 years attending a summer day camp. Training occurred in a group that met twice weekly for 4 weeks, with each session lasting 60 minutes. Additionally, each child participated in 30 minutes of individual training per week. The behavioral rehearsal procedures used in group sessions included practicing nonaggressive responses to the taunting game (Goodwin & Mahoney, 1975) and role plays of situations in which aggressive behavior is a frequent occurrence. Children observed models demonstrate nonaggressive responses to these situations and practiced nonaggressive responses in role plays. Relative to subjects in a no treatment control group, subjects receiving the coping skills training improved on performance in the taunting game and on measures of problem-solving ability. No improvement was found on three of four measures of naturalistic aggressive behavior. Although the frequency of physical and verbal aggression and peer ratings of aggression showed no improvement, treated subjects required less discipline for fighting. Therefore, the study offers very modest support for the efficacy of SIT in changing aggression in real-life situations. The treatment may have decreased the frequency of more severe aggressive behaviors, behaviors that are likely to result in disciplinary action.

Camp, Blom, Hebert, and Van Doorninck (1977) developed the Think Aloud program to teach coping self-talk to second-grade boys. Treatment included SIT with cognitive and social tasks as well as problem-solving training. The SIT attempted to teach boys to ask and answer questions in a problem-solving sequence involving questions pertinent to identifying the problem, generating alternative solutions, evaluating solutions, and monitoring implementation of their solution plan. The Think Aloud program has been evaluated in several studies (Camp et al., 1977; Camp, 1980; Camp & Bash, 1980). Dependent measures in each study included measures of cognitive change and teacher ratings of classroom behavior. Additionally, some studies included behavioral observations. Overall, Think Aloud produces changes in cognitive measures (e.g., paper-and-pencil measures of problem-solving and impulsivity). However, evidence of improvement in real-life aggression has not been demonstrated. In one study (Camp & Bash, 1981), boys receiving a self-esteem enhancing program conceptualized as a control treatment decreased their aggressive behaviors more than did boys in the Think Aloud program. With respect to problem-solving measures, boys in the Think Aloud program had an increase in the number of alternatives given to interpersonal problems, but the quality of the alternatives produced continued to be aggressive. Considering the length of the program (30 half-hour sessions with two to three children in a group) and the very modest improvement obtained, the use of the Think Aloud program with aggressive children is not warranted. Similar programs with aggressive children have also failed to demonstrate improvement in classroom behavior (e.g., Coats, 1979). In an extensive review of SIT with impulsive children, Kendall and Braswell (1985) concluded that SIT produces significant treatment effects on measures of cognitive impulsivity and classroom ratings of self-control in non-self-controlled, nonaggressive children. However, it does not decrease the aggressive behaviors of children who manifest their lack of self-control in aggressive acting out. These children need different or additional procedures.

Anger Management

Subsumed under the category of anger management are cognitive-behavioral programs that combine self-control, interpersonal problem solving, and cognitive restructuring approaches.

Hughes (in press-b) reports a case study of anger management intervention in an aggressive 12-year-old girl. This case is presented here to illustrate the treatment components in anger management intervention. Julie, a 12-year-old Caucasian girl of average intelligence, was referred by the school counselor for aggressive outbursts.

> Julie frequently had temper tantrums at school when frustrated, fought with her classmates, and used foul language. On two occasions during the first two months of the school year, Julie physically assaulted her teacher. Julie's mother stated that she and her husband could not control Julie when she had one of her "fits" and that they were ready to "send Julie to a home for bad girls." Julie's father, a recovering alcoholic, worked on an oil rig in a city a three hours drive from home, and was home only 2 days a week. Because Julie's parents frequently argued and were considering divorcing for the second time, family therapy was not considered a good choice.
>
> Julie received 12 one-hour sessions twice a week. During the first session, the therapist interviewed Julie and her mother and stated the treatment goals as teaching Julie ways to control her temper and alternatives to aggressive behavior. To increase Julie's motivation to learn anger control skills, the disadvantages of Julie's temper were discussed. The therapist saw Julie individually for the sessions; however, the therapist spent approximately 15 minutes with Julie's mother at the beginning of each hour session, explaining the treatment, obtaining information regarding Julie's behavior at home and at school, and teaching parent management approaches. During sessions 2–4, Julie learned relaxation skills, using progressive muscle relaxation and positive visual imagery. Julie received a notebook in which she recorded her relaxation practices at home, and the therapist rewarded her with a grab bag of toys for completing relaxation homework. During sessions 3 and 4, Julie completed an anger hierarchy, indicating on an anger thermometer how angry she felt when different things happened. Body cues associated with angry feelings were identified. The items for the anger hierarchy were obtained from Julie's diary of anger-arousing situations as well as from teacher and parent reports. During sessions 5 and 6, Julie learned coping self-statements to help her stay cool when starting to feel angry (e.g., "Relax, calm down"; "I can feel angry without blowing up"; "Blowing up will not help me get what I want"; "I am in control of me. I do not have to fight"; "I can solve this problem if I think it out"). Julie continued practicing relaxation at home and in the sessions. During session 7, Julie was instructed to relax and then to imagine an incident low on the anger hierarchy. If she started to feel tense and angry, she was instructed to practice coping self-statements and to relax until she no longer felt tense and angry.

During sessions 7–9, Julie practiced coping self-statements and relaxation while imagining increasingly arousing situations. Specific coping self-statements that were most helpful in reducing angry feelings were identified. In addition, Julie was given a notebook in which she recorded her use of relaxation and coping self-statements in anger-arousing situations outside the clinic. She recorded the situation, her use of coping statements and relaxation, and the outcomes (What happened? How did I feel? What did I do? What happened next?). Beginning during session 8 and continuing through session 12, Julie practiced social problem-solving steps. Specifically, the therapist taught Julie to think of different ways she could solve problems (alternative thinking) and to anticipate the consequences of different solutions (consequential thinking). These problem-solving steps were incorporated into the coping self-statements. Julie continued to record her use of the skills taught and received rewards for bringing the recordings to each session.

At posttreatment and at 3-month follow-up, Julie's teacher reported an improvement in Julie's disruptive behaviors, according to the Conners Teacher Rating Questionnaire (Goyette, Conners, & Ulrich, 1978). Fortunately, the teacher had kept frequency counts for Julie's aggressive behaviors for a 6-week period just prior to treatment and, at the therapist's request, continued to count aggressive behaviors until 6 weeks after treatment. The number of aggressive behaviors at posttreatment was 23% of the pretreatment level and 28% of the pretreatment level at 6-week follow-up. Julie's parents also reported a noticeable improvement. Near the end of treatment, Julie proudly told the therapist about provocations during the week to which she had responded "cool as a cucumber."[1]

Several researchers have conducted controlled studies investigating the efficacy of anger management with aggressive children. Lochman and his colleagues (Lochman, Nelson, & Sims, 1981; Lochman, Burch, Curry, & Lampron, 1984) developed an anger control program that attempts to teach children to inhibit initial aggressive reactions, to cognitively relabel stimuli perceived as hostile, and to solve problems by generating alternative coping responses. Children are instructed in these cognitive skills during 12 40-minute small group sessions held twice weekly. The goals and activities planned for each session are included in Table 9.3.

In the 1981 study (Lochman et al., 1981), 12 children referred by their teachers as the most aggressive and disruptive in class were placed in two treatment groups (the design did not include a control group). Teachers' behavior ratings were used to measure treatment outcomes. Following treatment, children's acting out and aggressive classroom behaviors decreased and their on-task behavior increased. These encouraging results were extended in a second, better designed study. The 76 subjects in this study were boys who received the highest teacher ratings of aggression. Boys were assigned randomly to one of four conditions: anger coping program,

[1]From "Brief Psychotherapies" by J. N. Hughes. In T. Gutkin & C. R. Reynolds (Eds.), *Handbook of school psychology* (2nd ed.). New York: John Wiley & Sons, in press.

Table 9.3. Goals and Activities for Anger Management Program

Session 1. Goals: (a) Introduce group rules, and (b) promote self-awareness by noting differences and similarities between group members physically, behaviorally, emotionally, and attitudinally. Activities included taking pictures of each group member with an instant camera, body tracings of numbers on large pieces of paper, and perception of the Gestalt Vase/Face design.
Session 2. Goal: Explore children's reactions to cooperating with, being controlled by, and being distracted by peers. Activities included acting as pairs of robots and building domino towers while being verbally distracted by peers.
Session 3. Goal: Problem identification. Learn which specific aspects of a situation create a problem and lead to anger arousal. Activities included identifying problems in brief stories and in role-played situations.
Session 4. Goal: Generate alternative solutions to problems. Activities included cartoon sequences for interpersonal problem solving (e.g., children fighting over a bicycle) and role playing.
Sessions 5 and 6. Goal: Evaluate alternative solutions by identifying positive and negative consequences and making a decision about the relative value of the alternatives. Activities included cartoon sequences and role playing.
Session 7. Goal: (1) Increase physiological awareness of anger arousal with increased awareness acting as a cue for problem solving, and (2) to use positive self-statements when provoked. The primary activity was viewing a modeling videotape, which depicted a young boy telling an offscreen narrator how he physically felt about being reprimanded by his mother for not doing his homework. The child also described his internal negative self-statements that he had when he was angry (e.g., "I want to get back at my mother and teacher for making me miss a television show"), and positive self-statements he could use to decrease his anger arousal (e.g., "If I stick to the homework rules, I can watch TV sooner").
Session 8. Goal: To integrate techniques of physiologic awareness, self-talk, and social problem solving. The self-talk techniques included positive self-statements and covert inhibiting speech (e.g., "Stop! Think! What Should I Do?"). Activities included viewing of three modeling videotapes in which children were experiencing reactive anger to being punished by a teacher for something they did not do, to peer teasing, and to being ignored by peers. After each problem situation, the children in the group were encouraged to identify the problem and generate alternative solutions. Several typed alternate solutions were then presented for each problem, prefaced by the use of covert inhibiting speech to disrupt the reflexive aggressive response. The group children evaluated the various alternatives.
Session 9. Goal: To integrate and practice techniques modeled in Session 8. Activities included role-playing and beginning the development of two anger arousal "scenes" that the group will videotape themselves in the format of the modeling tape.
Session 10, 11, and 12. Goal: Integrate and practice techniques modeled in Session 8. Activities included role plays, completion of the group's videotape, and discussion of anger control efforts in school and at home.

Source: J. E. Lochman, W. M. Nelson, III, and J. P. Sims, "A Cognitive Behavioral Program for Use with Aggressive Children," 1981, *Journal of Clinical Child Psychology, 10*: 147. Copyright 1981 by Section on Clinical Child Psychology, American Psychological Association. Reprinted by permission.

goal-setting intervention, combination anger coping and goal-setting intervention, and an untreated control group. In goal-setting intervention, which was conceptualized as minimal treatment, children's weekly behavior goals were established in a group that met for 8 weeks. Their goals were monitored daily by the classroom teacher, and the boys received contingent reinforcement for obtaining their weekly goals. Dependent measures included classroom observations, teacher ratings of aggression, measures of interpersonal cognitive problem solving, self-reported self-esteem, and peer acceptance and aggression nominations. Subjects in the anger coping conditions (with and without goal setting) decreased their aggressive/disruptive behaviors in the classroom and were rated by their parents as less aggressive. The addition of goal-setting intervention tended to augment the treatment effects in the classroom. Additionally, the anger coping condition resulted in improved self-esteem. There were no other significant group differences. Given the improvement in the boys' behavior, it is disappointing that teachers' and peers' perceptions of the treated boys did not change. It may be that significant others' perceptions of the boys are relatively rigid and do not change in response to an improvement in the child's behavior. This finding of improved social skills with no concomitant improvement in peer acceptance is consistent with results of research on social skills training with aggressive/rejected children (Bierman & Furman, 1984). Unless interventions include opportunities for target children's peers to interact with them in a positive social context, peers' perceptions of treated children do not change, even when the target child's behavior improves (Bierman & Furman, 1984).

Forman (1980) compared the relative effectiveness of cognitive restructuring and an externally controlled response cost intervention in reducing students' aggressive classroom behavior. The subjects were 18 students from the third, fourth, or fifth grades referred to the school psychologist for aggressive behavior. Students were randomly assigned to response cost, cognitive restructuring, or attention control conditions. Dependent measures included teacher ratings of aggressive/disruptive behaviors, teacher recordings of the frequency of aggressive behaviors, and classroom behavioral observations.

The cognitive restructuring procedure was modeled on rational-emotive therapy (Ellis, 1962, 1973; Knaus, 1974). Specifically, children were taught that persons control their feelings and behavior through their thoughts, or self-talk. Situations that children reported as provoking aggression were discussed, and children were asked to describe thoughts that would cause them to get angry and thoughts that would help them not to get angry. A script of thoughts that help children not to get angry included statements that objectively describe the situation without exaggeration or distortion, show consideration of possible reasons for the other person's behavior, anticipate consequences for aggressive and nonaggressive responses, acknowledge that each person controls his or her own emotions and behavior, generate nonaggressive solutions, and provide self-reinforcement. After the script for an anger-provoking situation was constructed, the children relaxed and imagined themselves in the situation, thinking the adaptive thoughts as the group leader read the script. Children were asked to practice these thoughts while imagining these situations at home and to practice these thoughts in anger-provoking situations.

In the response cost procedure, the teacher fined the child for each incident of aggressive behavior. Each fine resulted in a loss of 2 minutes of recreational time. Both cognitive restructuring and response cost programs produced a decrease in aggressive behaviors and were significantly more effective than the control program. The two treatment groups did not differ in effectiveness; however, the response cost program produced a greater reduction in teacher recorded incidences of aggression. This finding is not surprising, considering that the response cost program involved the greatest teacher participation, which may have led to bias in teacher recordings of the frequency of aggressive behavior. Additionally, because the response cost program was implemented in the classroom and cognitive restructuring outside the classroom, classroom measures of improvement assess a lesser degree of generalization for the response cost program relative to the cognitive restructuring program.

The studies by Lochman and his colleagues and Forman demonstrate the effectiveness of anger management programs with aggressive elementary school children. Feindler, Marriott, and Iwata (1984) evaluated the effectiveness of a group anger control program with 36 adolescents attending a junior high school behavior modification program for multisuspended delinquents. Students were randomly assigned to one of three anger control treatment groups or to a no treatment control group. Training over 10 hour-long sessions consisted of relaxation training, self-control training, and problem-solving training. Training procedures included didactic presentations of rational emotive therapy theory, physiologic cues associated with anger, and techniques for controlling aggressive responses. Conflict situations were presented in a role-play format. The trainer modeled different anger coping techniques, and students practiced these techniques in the role plays. Additionally, students were exposed to graduated presentations of specific provocations, with decreasing warnings or prompts to prepare them for the provocation. Students recorded their attempts to practice anger control techniques in situations outside training. Compared with nontreated control subjects, trained subjects improved on measures of self-control and problem solving. Additionally, treated subjects tended to reduce their severely aggressive behaviors in school.

Social Skills Training

The view of aggressive children as deficient in social skills is supported by numerous studies reporting relationships between aggression and rejection (Coie & Dodge, 1983). Social skills training with aggressive/rejected children attempts to remediate the social skill deficits that lead to negative social interactions and peer rejection. Earlier studies on effectiveness of social skills training in improving unpopular children's social skills and peer acceptance did not distinquish between rejected children (who tend to be aggressive) and neglected children. Because the skill deficits in these two types of unpopular children are different, it is not surprising that these intervention studies produced mixed evidence of the effectiveness of social skills training in improving children's social skills and social competence (Hughes, 1986; Hughes & Sullivan, in press). When researchers select children for training based not only on low peer acceptance but also on low pretreatment rates of the skills targeted in the intervention, social skills training often leads to increased skill performance and peer acceptance (Bierman & Furman, 1984; Bierman, Miller, & Stabb, 1987; Ladd, 1981). Although social skills training may improve the social competence of some unpopular children, its use with rejected/aggressive children has been investigated only recently (Bierman, et al., 1987; Kazdin, Esveldt-Dawson, French, & Unis, 1987).

Bierman et al. (1987) compared the effectiveness of instructions (social skills training) and prohibitions (response cost) and combined instructions and prohibitions in improving peer interactions and sociometric ratings of rejected boys in grades 1 to 3. Subjects were 32 boys selected because they received a high number of rejection peer nominations and high levels of observed negative peer interaction. Subjects were randomly assigned to one of the three treatment conditions or to a no treatment control condition. Each treatment condition consisted of 10 half-hour sessions, during which a target child engaged in a series of cooperative tasks with nontarget classmates.

The instruction condition was similar to Ladd's (1981) coaching program. The adult coach began each session with a brief discussion of the target skill and elicited behavioral examples from the group. The target skills were (1) questioning others for information, clarification, and invitation, (2) helping, including giving support and suggestions and cooperating in play, and (3) sharing. After discussion of the target skill, children were instructed to practice the skill in a cooperative play activity. Postplay reviews of performance of the target skill were led by the therapist. In a departure from Ladd's program, the therapist rewarded skillful performance of the target skill with tokens during the play activity. Additionally, the therapist praised skillful performance of the target skills.

In the prohibition condition, the therapist presented a set of rules to control the children's negative behavior during the session. The children played the same cooperative games as in the instruction condition; however, they received no instructions in specific social skills and did not receive token reinforcement for specific skills. Instead, the experimenter provided random reinforcement as long as the children did not break the rules.

Whenever a child violated a rule, the experimenter removed his cup for 1 minute.

In the combination condition, children were instructed in specific skills and praised and given token reinforcement for performance of target skills. They also were told what behaviors were prohibited and lost their token cup for 1 minute for engaging in the prohibited behavior. In all conditions, tokens were exchanged for a snack at the end of each session.

Dependent measures included behavioral observations, teacher and peer ratings of aggression, peer play ratings, and peer positive and negative nominations.

The investigators predicted that the instructions and prohibition conditions would have differential effects on rejected-aversive children's negative and positive behaviors. As expected, the coaching program increased prosocial behaviors but did not decrease negative behaviors. The prohibitions condition decreased negative behaviors but did not increase prosocial behaviors. The combined program (instructions plus prohibitions) produced immediate and sustained improvement in boys' positive and negative behaviors and on peers' reactions to them. Despite their improved behavior, these rejected-aversive children did not gain greater peer acceptance immediately after treatment or at the 6-week or 1-year follow-up. One exception to this statement was a decreased disliking on the part of classmates who served as partners in the play session for boys in the combined treatment condition. Apparently, unless a child's classmates have opportunities to work cooperatively with the disliked child, classmates are unlikely to increase their liking for previously disliked peers. The difficulty in changing peers' acceptance for rejected-aversive children may reflect peer reputational factors. Children continue to view a child according to the child's reputation instead of according to the child's current behavior.

Social-Cognitive Skills Training

Research has consistently demonstrated deficits in social-cognitive skills in aggressive children. Recently, interventions attempting to remediate these social-cognitive deficits were evaluated; Kazdin et al. (1987) compared the effectiveness of training in interpersonal problem-solving skills and relationship therapy in treating severely aggressive children aged 7 to 13 years. Children were inpatients of a psychiatric facility where children are hospitalized for 2 to 3 months for acute disorders, including highly aggressive and destructive behavior. Parent and teacher ratings of aggressive behavior were collected when the child was admitted to the hospital and at follow-up assessments up to 1 year after discharge. The problem-solving program was modeled after treatment procedures developed by Spivack, Platt, and Shure (1976) and Kendall, Padawer, Zupan, and Braswell (reported in Kendall &

Braswell, 1985). Treatment was administered individually in 20 sessions, each lasting 45 minutes and administered two or three times per week. Interpersonal problem-solving skills were taught through the application of verbal instruction to the child, modeling, discussion of hypothetical problem situations, enactment of skills in role-plays, corrective feedback, and social reinforcement. Token reinforcement for completion of homework and response cost procedures for errors in carrying out the problem-solving approach were used during the treatment sessions.

The relationship therapy program also involved 20 individual sessions. The focus of the program was to build a close relationship with the child and to provide empathy, unconditional positive regard, and warmth.

The interpersonal problem-solving program significantly improved behavior at school and at home, and this program was superior to relationship therapy. Furthermore, treatment effects in the children's home schools were maintained up to 1 year after treatment. The researchers concluded that "The results suggest that cognitive-behavior problem-solving skills training can effect changes in a seriously disturbed clinical population, that the changes are evident in community-based measures, and that changes are sustained at least up to 1 year" (Kazdin et al., 1987, p. 84).

A very different social-cognitive intervention for antisocial youth was implemented in a school setting with behavior problem adolescents (Arbuthnot & Gordon, 1986). The adolescents had been identified by their teachers as aggressive, disruptive, or both. Treatment consisted of a discussion of moral dilemmas for 45 minutes each week for 16 to 20 weeks. Discussions took place during one class period at school. Dependent measures included measures of sociomoral reasoning and behavioral measures including behavioral referrals, tardiness, academic performance, and police and court contacts. Compared with subjects in a no treatment control group, treated subjects demonstrated advances in moral reasoning and improvements in behavioral measures. For the most part, these effects were maintained for 1 year. Evidence that behavioral improvement was mediated by advances in moral reasoning was supported by a significant relationship between advances in moral reasoning and behavioral improvement. That is, those students who improved the most on behavioral measures also improved the most on measures of moral reasoning.

The results of the Arbuthnot and Gordon (1986) study are especially promising because the moral reasoning program can be incorporated into ongoing classroom curricular activities, "thereby obviating negative labelling effects and providing developmental benefits for all students rather than only for those with behavioral problems" (p. 215). Although the subjects in this study included behavior problem adolescents, some of whom were aggressive, the effectiveness of a moral reasoning intervention with severely aggressive adolescents has not yet been investigated.

SUMMARY

Cognitive behavioral approaches with aggressive and rejected children have achieved some notable successes. The successful programs include more than self-instructional training. They differ, however, in their other treatment components. Interpersonal problem-solving training that involves instruction, modeling, and behavioral rehearsal, multicomponent anger management programs, and moral reasoning programs have resulted in meaningful treatment gains on measures of both the impact of treatment and the specific component skills.

It is likely that different interventions are differentially effective with different types of aggressive children. The model of social information-processing described in this chapter suggests the marker variables that would be useful in identifying subtypes of aggressive children. Children who are deficient in social perception and social reasoning would be likely to benefit from programs that teach these skills, such as Kazdin's (1987) interpersonal problem-solving skills training and Arbuthnot and Gordon's (1986) moral reasoning program. Children who are deficient in the behavioral skills necessary to enact social solutions would benefit from social skills training programs similar to the program of Bierman et al. (1987). Finally, children who have adequate social reasoning and behavioral skills but who respond impulsively to social problems might benefit from self-instructional training that emphasizes verbal mediation of behavior.

SECTION III

COGNITIVE-BEHAVIORAL APPROACHES AND INDIRECT INTERVENTIONS

10
Cognitive-Behavioral Approaches to Prevention in Schools

Definitions and Conceptual Overview

The notion that the prevention of disorders is a cost-effective and efficient alternative to treatment is neither new nor controversial. The value of the prevention of mental health problems is widely accepted by both professionals and lay persons. Furthermore, this acceptance is not of recent origin (remember Ben Franklin's aphorism, "an ounce of prevention is worth a pound of cure").

To the layperson, the term prevention means "to stop something from happening in the first place." It is in this sense of the term that we say we vaccinate our children to prevent the occurrence of rubella. Mental health professionals have defined prevention more specifically. Gerald Caplan (1964:16), a pioneer in the field of primary prevention of mental and emotional disorders, delineated three levels of prevention (primary, secondary, and tertiary), defined as:

> programs for reducing (1) the incidence of mental disorders of all types in a community ("primary prevention"), (2) the duration of a significant number of those disorders which do occur ("secondary prevention"), and (3) the impairment which may result from these disorders ("tertiary prevention").

According to Caplan's terminology, primary prevention refers to efforts to keep a problem from occurring. Therefore, primary prevention efforts come closest to the layperson's definition of prevention. Primary prevention efforts attempt to reduce the incidence of problems in a community by keeping the problems from occurring in the first place. Teaching disadvantaged preschool children interpersonal problem-solving skills to help them establish satisfactory peer relationships exemplifies the primary prevention of emotional and behavioral problems. Strengthening the factors in a community that promote mental health and lessening factors that contribute to psychopathology are primary prevention efforts. Therefore, efforts to humanize education (Schmuck & Schmuck, 1974) by increasing democratic processes and decreasing authoritarian control may be conceptualized as primary prevention programs.

Secondary prevention efforts attempt to keep mild to moderate problems from becoming severe. Programs that screen children for maladapting behavioral and emotional patterns and that provide early intervention to children identified as maladaptive illustrate the secondary prevention of emotional and behavioral problems. Therefore, secondary prevention efforts are based on early detection of individuals who possess indicators of risk for later serious maladjustment. Those individuals identified through a systematic population-wide case-finding approach must be provided prompt and effective intervention for the effort to be a secondary prevention one. In contrast to primary prevention, which is directed towards essentially nondysfunctional populations, secondary prevention programs involve individuals who are already manifesting maladaptive behaviors to a mild or moderate degree. It is expected that without prompt intervention, the behavior of these individuals would worsen with time. Teaching self-control to children rated by teachers as impulsive and teaching friendship-making skills to shy and withdrawn children are examples of secondary mental health prevention programs.

Tertiary prevention is not prevention at all, in the ordinary sense of that term, because a significant problem already exists. The before-the-fact aspect of prevention does not apply to tertiary prevention. Instead, tertiary prevention efforts aim to limit the severity of the outcomes and to change the course of the disorder's sequelae. In physical health, the term refers to efforts to restore physical functioning following injury or illness. In the mental health field, the term tertiary prevention has limited use. Therefore, prevention usually refers only to primary and secondary prevention efforts. "In essence, prevention primarily refers to actions taken to avoid the development of a disorder or problem, or secondarily, to identify potential problems early in their development and to take actions to minimize negative effects" (Roberts & Peterson, 1984:1).

Emory Cowen, another pioneer in preventive mental health, elaborated on Caplan's definition of prevention. Specifically, Cowen posited that preventive efforts must be population focused (rather than individually focused), have a before-the-fact quality, and be based on a solid knowledge base suggesting that the program does indeed hold potential for preventing maladjustment (Cowen, 1982). Cowen criticizes programs touted as primary or secondary prevention programs that lack documentation of their effectiveness in reducing the incidence or severity of emotional and behavioral problems in the targeted population.

George Albee also has made a valuable contribution to the field of prevention. Albee believed that conceptualizations of prevention based on medical models were not appropriate to mental illness prevention. Albee's conceptualization of emotional disturbance stresses socially learned behaviors and sources of stress in a community. Albee (1982) proposed a formula relating the incidence of emotional problems to organic factors and difficult life circumstances, on the one hand, and individual strengths and social support, on the other:

$$\frac{\text{Incidence of}}{\text{Psychopathology}} = \frac{\text{Organic Factors} + \text{Stress}}{\text{Coping Skills} + \text{Self-Esteem} + \text{Support Groups}}$$

This formula provides a framework for prevention efforts. For example, school-based programs that attempt to improve children's self-esteem, skills for relating to others, and capabilities for handling crises increase individuals' resources for coping with organic problems and environmental stress, resulting in a lower incidence of psychopathology. Other efforts might attempt to lessen organic factors, such as malnutrition or lead poisoning, or to reduce social stressors, such as inadequate housing or social isolation.

Two other terms relevant to primary prevention that need to be defined are "risk factors" and "promotion of mental health." Primary prevention efforts are directed toward at-risk groups. These groups are defined as at risk because of a statistical association between some experience, condition, or behavior and the development of a disorder (Commission on the Prevention of Mental-Emotional Disabilities, 1987). Poverty, single parent families, low reading achievement, and low birth weight are all risk factors because individuals so characterized have a higher-than-average incidence of mental-emotional disabilities.

Efforts in promoting mental health are directed to population groups without defined risk. In actual practice, promotion and prevention form a service continuum, and distinctions between the two types of programs are often difficult to make. As more risk factors are identified, the number of individuals who are not at risk for maladjustment becomes smaller. Roberts and Peterson (1984) suggest that childhood is a developmental stage during which individuals are particularly vulnerable to stressors that may have far-reaching and negative consequences. Therefore, promoting children's psychosocial competence both promotes mental health and prevents later mental/emotional disabilities.

HISTORICAL OVERVIEW

Despite the wide acceptance of the notion that the prevention of a disorder is a cost effective and efficient alternative to treatment, community-based mental health prevention programs are not highly visible in most communities. This disappointing state of affairs is not solely the result of the public's lack of awareness of the need for preventing mental disorders. In 1963, federal legislation was passed establishing community mental health centers. John F. Kennedy advocated strongly for a prevention role for these new community mental health centers (Roberts & Peterson, 1984).

Unfortunately, only 5 percent of funds for the operation of community mental health centers were allocated to the prevention of emotional problems through consultation and education programs. With few resources committed to prevention, tremendous press for direct services, and a fee-for-service model of reimbursement, few clinics established viable prevention programs (Roberts & Peterson, 1984). Fifteen years after passage of the Community Mental Health Centers Act of 1963, the President's Commission on Mental Health, appointed by Jimmy Carter, stated:

> At present our efforts to present mental illness or to promote mental health are unstructured, unfocused, and uncoordinated. They command few dollars, limited personnel, and little interest at levels where resources are sufficient to achieve results. If we are to change this state of affairs, as we believe we must, the prevention of mental illness and the promotion of mental health must become a visible part of national policy (President's Commission on Mental Health, 1978:53).

Since 1978, research in the prevention of mental/emotional disabilities has increased steadily, contributing to a rapidly expanding knowledge base to direct prevention efforts (Commission on the Prevention of Mental-Emotional Disabilities, 1987). In 1984, the National Mental Health Association established the Commission on the Prevention of Mental-Emotional Disabilities to review the status of prevention within the mental health field. The Commission concluded that based on existing knowledge, availability of existing organizational structure, and urgency of need, four areas have immediate potential for preventing mental/emotional disabilities: wanted and healthy babies, prevention of adolescent pregnancy, school-based competency-building programs, and support, information, and training for those in situations of extreme stress. Certainly school-based prevention programs are relevant to each of these four areas.

SCHOOL-BASED PREVENTION

The Commission on the Prevention of Mental-Emotional Disabilities (1987:39) acknowledged the critical role of the school in preventing emotional/mental disabilities.

> The Commission is especially concerned that the nation's schools have the mental health resources and expertise they need. Mental health professionals bear a special responsibility to help school administrators and teachers develop competent individuals.
>
> *Competence and mental health are inseparable.* Children must learn academic skills to succeed and feel confident; they must learn how to get along with others to succeed in school and later in life. The school's job *is* enormous and critical. Teaching children interpersonal skills and providing health education, including coping skills and sex education, are as essential as teaching reading, writing, arithmetic and science.

Schools offer the greatest opportunity for population-focused prevention efforts. School-based prevention programs can be implemented in a cost-effective manner because the organizational structure necessary to support programs already exists. Schools could offer programs that are less intrusive and stigmatizing, because schools serve a broad cross-section of children in the community. Schools also could intervene at developmentally critical times such as the entrance to first grade or the transition to middle school. Finally, because school personnel are often the first persons outside the home to notice problems, schools are critical in the early detection of children's problems.

FRAMEWORK FOR REVIEWING SCHOOL-BASED PREVENTION PROGRAMS

A wide range of school-based prevention programs are in existence today. Population-focused primary prevention programs include affective education programs, such as Developing Understanding of Self and Others (DUSO, Dinkmeyer, 1970), mental health consultation to teachers (Conoley & Conoley, 1982; Brown, Pryzwansky, & Schulte, 1987), alcohol and drug education programs in classrooms (Severson, 1984), school-wide screening for depression (Reynolds, 1984), compensatory education programs for economically disadvantaged preschoolers, pregnancy prevention programs (Schinke, Blythe, & Gilchrist, 1981), and problem-solving training with inner-city high school students (Sarason & Sarason, 1981). Secondary prevention programs are also prevalent in schools. Secondary prevention programs attempt to intervene early in the developmental course of emotional/mental disabilities. The most well-known school-based secondary prevention program is the Primary Mental Health Project (PMHP) in Rochester, New York (Cowen, Trost, Dorr, Lorion, Izzo, & Isaacson, 1975). A primary objective of this very large project is the broad dissemination of its model to schools across the nation. The PMHP model has four components: (1) a focus on young children, (2) population-based screening to detect early signs of school maladjustment, (3) the use of paraprofessionals to work with maladapting students, and (4) a shift from an assessment and therapy role to an indirect service role for mental health specialists in the schools (Cowen et al., 1975). A 1977 survey found that over 35 school districts had implemented the PMHP model (Cowen, Davidson, & Gesten, 1980), and since 1977, many more schools have implemented programs based on this model (Durlak & Jason, 1984). The PMHP model emphasizes program evaluation, with many evaluation studies reported in the *American Journal of Community Psychology*.

Whereas the PMHP programs target children who are showing signs of school maladjustment, other secondary prevention programs target specific subpopulations of children with adjustment problems, including socially isolated children (e.g., Oden & Asher, 1977), nonself-controlled children (e.g., Kendall & Zupan, 1981), and aggressive children (e.g., Lochman, Nelson, & Sims, 1981). Many school-based interventions with specific groups that are reviewed in this book could be appropriately cast in the secondary prevention mold, because these programs attempt to intervene with maladapting children who are detected early.

A comprehensive review of school-based prevention research is beyond the scope and goals of this chapter. Consistent with the goal of this book, the intent of this chapter is to describe the most promising strategies for preventing emotional and behavioral disabilities that are clearly based on cognitive behavior theory. Furthermore, to reduce the overlap with other chapters, programs that attempt to intervene early in the development of specific disorders (e.g., conduct disorder, social withdrawal) are not reviewed in this chapter.

This review is organized according to three approaches to prevention in the schools. Cognitive-behavioral programs that represent each of these three approaches are reviewed. In the *milestone approach*, the prevention program is provided at particular developmental points considered to be important to later functioning. Programs that teach interpersonal problem-solving skills to economically disadvantaged preschoolers (Spivack & Shure, 1974) and programs that teach problem-solving skills to middle school students (Elias, Gara, Ubriaco, Rothbaum, Clabby, & Schuyler, 1986) exemplify the milestone approach. The *problem-focused approach*, exemplified by PMHP, is based on early intervention for school maladjustment problems. Within the PMHP model, several progams have emphasized the enhancement of children's problem-solving and coping skills, and these programs are reviewed in the second section. The third approach is a *population-wide approach* to prevention. Included in this section are programs that attempt to improve the learning environment by reducing teacher stress and increasing cooperative learning experiences.

MILESTONE APPROACH

"The milestone approach has as its main thrust an orientation toward intervening at different developmental levels, when the individual might be thought to be particularly at risk for certain problems" (Roberts & Peterson, 1984:18). Certainly childhood is a developmental stage during which many developmental tasks crucial for future healthy adjustment are accomplished. During childhood, an individual develops a self-concept that influences the child's current and future emotional, social, and behavioral adjustment and work mastery. During childhood, children develop psychosocial competencies and coping skills that are important to current and future adaptive functioning. A large body of research convincingly demonstrates the relationship between early school maladjustment, as evidenced by low achievement or unsatisfactory interpersonal relationships, and later maladjustment (Cowen et al., 1975). Prevention programs that are population-wide and directed toward building children's psychosocial competencies are considered milestone approaches.

ICPS Training

The interpersonal problem-solving training approach developed by Spivack and Shure (1974) and their associates at the Hahnemann Medical College illustrates the milestone approach to preventing emotional/mental disabilities. This approach is based on research demonstrating the relation between specific interpersonal cognitive problem-solving (ICPS) skills and adjustment during childhood (Spivack & Shure, 1982). Since 1974, there have been a plethora of research studies evaluating the effect of ICPS training on social-cognitive skills and behavioral adjustment. (See Urbain & Savage, in press, for a comprehensive review.) Because the results of these studies generally support the beneficial effects of training, ICPS approaches are being recommended as among the most promising formats for prevention efforts (President's Commission on Mental Health, 1978; Commission on the Prevention on Mental-Emotional Disabilities, 1987).

Rather than providing a comprehensive review of the ICPS literature, this section attempts to accomplish two less ambitious objectives. First, empirical support for the crucial role of ICPS skills in behavioral and social adjustment is summarized. Second, selected ICPS intervention programs are critically reviewed. These intervention studies are representative of ICPS training at each of three age levels: early childhood (preschool and kindergarten), middle childhood, and preadolescence and adolescence. Four criteria were used in selecting studies for inclusion in this review: (1) ICPS training was the primary intervention component, (2) the length and duration of the training permitted an adequate test of the effectiveness of training, (3) training was conducted in classrooms (in vivo), and (4) outcome assessment measures permit documentation of the hypothesized link between improved problem-solving skills and improved behavior.

Empirical Support for the Role of ICPS Skills in Adjustment

Developmentally, ICPS skills are hypothesized to play a crucial role in adjustment, in that if a person can solve interpersonal problems, he or she is likely to succeed at important personal and interpersonal tasks. Success at these tasks, in turn, leads to enhanced self-esteem and self-efficacy (Spivack & Shure, 1974). Spivack and Shure (1982) described six ICPS skills they believe are important to adjustment, recognizing that the relative importance of these skills may differ at different developmental stages. These ICPS skills are:

1. *Generation of alternate solutions*: the ability to generate a variety of solutions to problems.
2. *Consideration of consequences of social acts*: the tendency to consider the consequences of one's social actions on oneself and others and the ability to generate a range of possible consequences for a completed action.
3. *Development of means-end thinking*: the ability to generate the step-by-step means by which an interpersonal problem could be resolved.
4. *Development of social causal thinking*: the recognition that one's actions and feelings are reciprocally related to the actions and feelings of others.
5. *Sensitivity to problems*: the awareness of the variety of problems that arise in human interactions in general and in a particular interaction.
6. *Dynamic orientation*: the recognition that behavior may reflect motives or antecedents that are not discerned readily or easily.

Various measures of ICPS skills have been developed. Although the format differs somewhat for different skills, the assessment generally involves the initial presentation of a hypothetical story or dilemma to a child, followed by questions to the child. Depending on the specific skill being assessed, the child is asked to generate several solutions to problems, discuss consequences of acts, delineate the steps in implementing the solution, or describe what is wrong about an interpersonal exchange.

The theory that ICPS skills mediate adjustment from age 4 on has obtained some empirical support. Two ICPS skills have consistently been found to relate to adjustment-alternative thinking and means-end thinking. The capacity to generate alternative solutions to problems has been related to adjustment in preschoolers (Spivack & Shure, 1974; Shure & Spivack, 1978, 1980), in kindergarteners (Shure & Spivack, 1980), in elementary school children (Richard & Dodge, 1982; Shure, 1980), and in adolescents (Platt, Spivack, Altman, Altman, & Peizer, 1974). It is the most important ICPS skill among 4- and 5-year-olds, differentiating adaptive children from inpatient-impulsive and inhibited-withdrawn children and differentiating the latter two groups (inhibited-withdrawn children are the more deficient) (Spivack et al., 1976). The hypothesis that alternative thinking ability mediates behavioral adjustment is supported by the finding that improvement in alternative thinking following ICPS training is associated with improved behavioral adjustment (Shure & Spivack, 1978). However, this relationship between improved scores on measures of alternative thinking and improved behavioral adjustment has not been replicated consistently (e.g., Gesten, de Apodaca, Rains, Weissberg, & Cowen, 1979; Olexa & Forman, 1984). The role of alternative thinking in adolescents is less clear (Spivack & Shure, 1982; Kendall & Fischler, 1984).

Means-end thinking, the ability to articulate the sequence of step-by-step means that may be necessary to carry out a particular solution to an interpersonal problem, has received a great deal of research attention. The process of means-end thinking requires an ordering of steps to be taken, some recognition that such planning takes time, and the possibility that there may be obstacles that will require attention. Unlike alternative and consequential thinking, which emerge as significant for adjustment in young children, means-end thinking becomes significant for adjustment after age 8 to 10 (Pellegrini, 1980; Shure & Spivack, 1972; Platt & Spivack, 1972). The finding that aggressive and inhibited second-grade boys are less proficient on a measure of means-end thinking than are average boys, with inhibited children more deficient than aggressive boys (Gouze, Rayias, & Bieber-Schneider, 1983), is a typical research finding with children in this age group and with older children.

In reviewing the evidence for the theory that ICPS skills mediate adjustment, Kendall and Fischler (1984) conclude that alternative thinking skills differentiate adjusted and maladjusted children in early childhood. Both alternative thinking and means-end thinking are significant for adjustment in middle childhood, and only means-end thinking is consistently related to adjustment in adolescence. The roles of causal and consequential thinking are less clearly established.

An important aspect of ICPS theory is its emphasis on thinking *processes*, not thinking *content*.

> We wish to emphasize the *process* quality of such cognition. ICPS skills define *how* people think in the area of interpersonal problems, specifically in appreciating and coping with problems . . . The working assumption underlying this orientation is that although the success with which a problem is solved on any given occasion may be determined by *what* the person thinks, over the long run the person will come up with the right *what* when ICPS processes have been learned and brought to bear (i.e., the person knows how to think problems through when they arise). A child's social adjustment will be more in his or her control when the child is well oriented to interpersonal problems and known how to think than when the child has learned a specific list of solutions to specific classes of problems that may arise (Spivack & Shure, 1982:331).

Other researchers present evidence that the content as well as thinking processes are important to adjustment (Ladd & Oden, 1979; Richard & Dodge, 1982). For example, several researchers have found that aggressive children's solutions to interpersonal problems are more aggressive (Richard & Dodge, 1982; Asarnow & Callan, 1985). Ladd and Oden (1979) found that unpopular third- and fifth-grade children's solutions to a problem requiring offering assistance to a child tended to be more unique. They concluded that low accepted children are less aware of peer norms or values for helpful social behaviors. Well-accepted children have greater shared knowledge regarding situationally appropriate helpful behaviors. In their study, they found a negative relation between the number of different types of strategies and popularity among girls, but not among boys.

Considering all the evidence, both thinking processes and content (social knowledge) are important to social adjustment. Emphasis on processes without considering content is not supported by the literature. Increasingly, researchers are attending to social problem-solving as a process comprised of several sequential skills rather than as a set of discrete skills (Dodge & Murphy, 1984; Hughes & Hall, 1987). This process involves appropriate encoding of social cues, the generation and evaluation of strategies for solving interpersonal problems, and the behavioral enactment of the selected skill.

ICPS Training with Young Children

Spivack and Shure (1974; Shure, 1981) taught ICPS skills to black inner-city 4-year-olds attending a federally funded day care program. Of 219 children attending the program, 113 received training, with the remaining children comprising a control group. Some of these control and experimental children received ICPS training the next year in kindergarten. Instructed children and control children were studied over a 2-year period from just before nursery school entrance to immediately after kindergarten. Training was presented by teachers in the form of 46 structured daily training lessons, consisting of daily activities and discussion. The first few lessons taught linguistic concepts such as same-different and if-then thought to be prerequisite to problem-solving. Following lessons taught three skills: enumerating alternatives, enumerating consequences, and pairing specific solutions with specific consequences. Teacher demonstration, puppet play, and stories were used to illustrate ICPS skills, and whenever possible, the problem-solving methods were applied to actual problems arising among the children during the day.

Nursery-trained youngsters improved significantly more than did matched controls on measures of alternative thinking and consequential thinking. Regarding behavior, significantly more of the children initially rated as impulsive or withdrawn who received training improved on teacher ratings of adjustment, compared with similar children in the control group.

Of critical importance to the mediating role ICPS skills are assumed to lay is the finding that those children who improved the most in ICPS skills /ere the same ones whose behavior improved the most.

Because teachers provided training and rated behavior, the possibility of ater bias cannot be ruled out. However, these same children were rated as mproved the following year by kindergarten teachers who were not aware f their treatment status. Children receiving training in kindergarten for the irst time benefited from ICPS training relative to never trained control ubjects, as evidenced by improved teacher ratings of adjustment. Whereas lternative thinking mediated improvement in kindergarten, both alterna- ive thinking and consequential thinking mediated improvement in the indergarten group.

The evidence that ICPS training prevented later behavioral problems is trong. Whereas 86 percent of the children initially rated as adjusted in ursery school and trained in ICPS skills were rated as adjusted 6 months fter training, in kindergarten, only 58 percent of the control children nitially rated as adjusted maintained that adjustment. At 1 year follow- p, 8 of 9 trained children were adjusted compared with 4 of 10 control ubjects. Additionally, trained children initially rated as maladjusted were ignificantly less likely to continue to be rated as maladjusted at 1-year ollow-up, compared with control children initially rated as maladjusted Shure & Spivack, 1982).

Efforts to extend and replicate Spivack and Shure's findings have met with neven success (Gillespie, Durlak, & Sherman, 1982; Rickel & Burgio, 982). For example, Winer, Hilpert, Gesten, Cowen, and Schubin (1982) aught ICPS skills to predominantly white, middle-class children. Trained hildren improved on ICPS measures and on teacher ratings of behavioral djustment. However, evidence of a direct link between ICPS skills and djustment gains was not found.

Taken together, evidence supports the view that ICPS training with reschool and kindergarten children improves skills and behavior. Further- nore, these gains are durable and generalize to new settings. Evidence of a irect link between ICPS skills and behavioral adjustment in early childhood s inconsistent.

CPS Training with Children in Middle Childhood

Most ICPS training studies have been conducted with elementary school hildren. Seven studies utilizing a control group and based on Spivack and hure's (1974) work are listed in Table 10.1. All studies listed improved CPS skills. Findings of a link between improved skills and gains in ehavioral adjustment are, however, inconsistent. Some studies found an mprovement in ICPS skills but no gain in behavioral and sociometric neasures (Larcen reported in Allen et al., 1976; Gesten et al., 1979; Olexa & Forman, 1984). Two studies documented an improvement in both ICPS

Table 10.1. Sample ICPS Training Studies

Study	Subjects	Duration	Posttreatment Measure[a]	Follow-up
Larcen (reported in Allen et al., 1976)	150 males and females, grades 3–4	24 sessions, 30 minutes each	Self-esteem, *locus of control, level of aspiration, sociometrics, teacher ratings (not blind), *problem-solving measures, *attitude toward school	None
Elardo & Caldwell, 1979	68 males and females, grades 4–5	56 lessons, 25 minutes each	*Role-taking test, *alternative thinking test, *teacher ratings (not blind)	None
Gesten et al., 1982	8 males and females grades 2–3	17 sessions, 30–40 minutes each	*Tests of problem-solving, *simulated problem-solving measure, teacher ratings (not blind), sociometrics	One year, *teacher ratings of social competence (blind), *sociometric measures
Gesten et al., 1979	All 2nd and 3rd grade males and females in 9 classrooms (*n* not specified)	17 sessions, 20–30 minutes each	*Tests of problem-solving, simulated problem-solving task, sociometrics, locus of control; self-esteem, teacher ratings, IQ tests	None
McClure et al., 1978	185 males and females, grades 3–4	20 sessions, 30 minutes each	*Problem-solving test, *simulated observations, *locus of control	6 months, no treatment effects
Olexa & Forman, 1984	64 urban males and females, grades 4–5	8 sessions, 50 minutes each	*Tests of ICPS skills, teacher ratings (not blind), naturalistic observations	5 weeks, same results as at posttreatment
Weissberg et al., 1981a	563 males and females, grades 2–4	42 sessions, 20–30 minutes each	*Tests of ICPS skills, *simulated problem-solving, interview, *teacher ratings (not blind), sociometrics	None

[a]Significant treatment effect on posttreatment measure is indicated by an asterisk.

skills and behavior but did not document a link between skills and behavior (Gesten et al., 1982; McClure, Chinsky, & Larcen, 1978). Of the two studies that correlated gains in ICPS skills with behavioral gains, one found evidence for the mediating hypothesis (Elardo & Caldwell, 1979) and one did not (Weissberg et al., 1981a). Studies falling in each of these categories are reviewed next.

Studies Reporting Improved Skills Only. Larcen (reported in Allen et al., 1976) taught ICPS skills to third- and fourth-grade children. Classroom teachers presented the 24 half-hour lessons. Specific skills taught were divergent thinking, problem identification, alternative thinking, consequential thinking, and means-end problem-solving. Instructional techniques included modeling, role-play, and discussion of hypothetical problems. Additionally, children were encouraged to apply their problem-solving skills to real-life interpersonal problems arising in school and to give each other feedback on their problem-solving behavior. Compared with children in a no treatment control group, trained children improved on measures of problem-solving skills and developed a more internal locus of control. However, no effect of training was evident on teacher ratings of behavioral adjustment or on peer sociometric measures.

Similarly, Gesten et al. (1979) found improvement on measures of problem-solving but no improvement on behavioral or sociometric measures among third-grade children participating in 17 short (20- to 30-minute) ICPS lessons conducted in classrooms by teachers. Olexa and Forman (1984) compared the effects of problem-solving training with and without operant procedures (response cost). Disadvantaged fourth- and fifth-grade children attending an urban school were assigned to one of the following treatment conditions: problem-solving training, response cost, problem-solving and response cost, or no treatment control. Treatment outcome measures included measures of problem-solving skills, behavioral observations, and teacher behavior ratings. Training was based on Spivack and Shure's (1974) procedures and occurred in children's title 1 classrooms for 50 minutes per week for 8 weeks. Training was implemented by a school psychologist and a school social worker, but the title 1 teacher participated in the group. The response cost procedure involved losing a point for each violation of a group rule. Points could be exchanged at the end of each class period for a reward. Although students in the problem-solving group (with and without response cost) acquired the targeted skills, significant changes in teacher ratings of behavior or observed classroom behavior were not found. The researchers noted an unexplained tendency towards an increase in observed aggression for the problem-solving only group. They suggested that although the children in the problem-solving condition learned to generate alternatives, they tended to generate aggressive alternatives because of their lack of knowledge of nonaggressive solutions. Children in the combined problem-solving and response cost treatment groups did not manifest an increase in aggressive behavior, presumably because the response cost procedures taught them which types of solution were unacceptable. These findings support the view that problem-solving training should be concerned with the content of thinking (products) as well as thinking processes. Failure to find evidence of behavioral improvement following training may be a result of the brevity of training (eight lessons compared with between 17 and 56 for similar programs) and the low level of teacher involvement in training.

Studies Reporting Improved Skills and Behavior. In an especially well-implemented study, Gesten et al. (1982) evaluated long-term effects of a 17-lesson, classroom-based problem-solving intervention with second- and third-grade suburban children. The problem-solving curriculum trained three problem-solving skills: problem identification, alternative solution generation, and anticipation of consequences. Children were taught to engage in a six-step problem-solving process:

> (a) Know exactly what the problem is; (b) Decide on your goal; (c) Stop and think before you act; (d) Think of as many solutions as you can; (e) Think of the different things that might happen next after each solution; (f) When you think you have a good solution, try it! (Gesten et al., 1982:98).

Two trained undergraduates assisted the teacher in the training, and teachers and aides received training in 2-hour weekly sessions. At posttesting, students receiving the full program improved more on problem-solving measures, including a simulated problem situation, than did students receiving an abbreviated training package or no treatment. The simulated problem-solving task involved asking the child to retrieve a marker from a child in the next room. The second child was a confederate and had been instructed to politely refuse the request. Adjustment results, by contrast, generally indicated that control children improved more than did those in either training group. The researchers explain this unexpected finding by bias on the part of teachers caused by instructions to teachers to rate trained children harshly (in an attempt to reduce a bias on the part of teachers to rate trained children as improved). This explanation is supported by data obtained the next year, in new classrooms. Children receiving training (full or abbreviated versions) did better than did control subjects in 7 of 10 teacher-rated adjustment factors. On most adjustment measures, trained children either held their own or improved at follow-up, whereas control children's behavior deteriorated. Additionally, trained children were rated as better liked than control children the next year and reported liking their new fourth-grade classmates more than the control subjects.

The pattern of correlations between cognitive skills acquired and adjustment gains combined with the likely response bias in the first year of the program did not permit any clear interpretations of the mediating role of cognitive skills. The study does demonstrate the preventive impact of problem-solving training. New teachers and peers, unaware of the prior year's intervention, viewed trained children as better adjusted and more likable. Whereas control children deteriorated on teacher-rated adjustment, experimental children held their own or improved.

McClure and associates (1978) taught problem-solving to third- and fourth-grade children attending a suburban school. Classroom training was divided into six components:

> The *problem-solving orientation* component included the following: (a) the expectancy that problems are a normal part of life, (b) the expectancy that children can solve many of their own problems, (c) an awareness of affect as a problem cue, and (d) an inhibitory set to "stop and think" before responding impulsively to problems. The *problem identification* component included the following: (a) discriminating relevant from irrelevant elements of the problem, (b) the importance of accurately identifying the problem, and (c) setting short- and long-term goals. The *alternative solutions* component encouraged the subjects to generate many possible solutions to each problem. The *considera-tion-of-consequences* component taught the child to consider the potential obstacles and opportunities associated with each solution before deciding on a course of action. The *elaborations* component emphasized the concrete, step-by-step process of planning necessary to implement a solution. Finally, the *integration* component presented all of these social problem-solving features as a unified set of strategies that one might apply to a problem (p. 505).

Three training groups were used: videotape modeling only, videotape nodeling and discussion, and videotape modeling and role-play. A control group received no training. At posttest, trained subjects evidenced an mprovement in problem-solving skills and locus of control (toward greater nternality). These gains, however, had disappeared 6 months following raining. Two months after treatment, trained subjects in the videotape and ole-play training condition demonstrated improved problem-solving in a structured group peer interaction measure, the Friendship Club Interaction FCI). For the FCI, children were asked to participate in a contest in which in award was promised to the team that gave the best answer to a series of questions about "how to make friends." In addition to the contest questions he children were confronted with a number of actual problems embedded n the FCI setting. For example, although the groups had six children, only ive chairs were present. The group had to decide how to distribute officer itle cards (president, vice-president, etc.). Children's interactions were videotaped for later scoring. Children in the modeling plus role-play condition exhibited better problem-solving behaviors in the FCI. Because the FCI appears a good substitute for naturalistic observations, these results provide evidence that the taught skills generalized to real-life settings. An unexpected finding was a low but significant negative correlation between he problem-solving measures and FCI. This finding casts doubt on the validity of the measures used to assess cognitive problem-solving skills.

Elardo and Caldwell (1979) evaluated the effects of a 56-lesson problem-solving curriculum on role-taking, problem-solving skills, and classroom adjustment of 9- and 10-year-old children attending regular classes in an urban school. Lessons were taught by classroom teachers and focused on role-taking ability and problem-solving skills. The curriculum, titled Project Aware, included classroom opportunities for children to exchange ideas and feelings, to discuss interpersonal problems and alternatives for dealing with each problem, and to consider the consequences of each alternative. The teachers and the principal received extensive in-service training on the Project Aware curriculum, meeting with the experimenter weekly for 5 months for training. An emphasis in training was discussion of ways to incorporate the curriculum's objectives into everyday social situations. For the first month of training, the experimenter conducted classroom discussion, with the teacher as a participant. The teacher then assumed responsibility for discussion. Experimental children improved, relative to the control subjects in 3 of 11 factors of a teacher rating scale and on measures of alternative thinking ability. The relationship between cognitive and behavioral gains was not reported.

Studies Reporting Relationship Between Skills and Behavior. Gesten and his colleagues (Gesten et al., 1982) replicated and extended findings of an earlier study (Weissberg, Gesten, Rapkin, Cowen, Davidson, De Apodaca, & McKim, 1981b). Although the earlier intervention improved the performance of program children on several cognitive and behavioral problem-solving measures, the effects on teacher adjustment ratings differed for urban and suburban groups. Although suburban program children improved more than did control children, the reverse was true for urban youngsters. The second study built on the first study.

The problem-solving curriculum was presented in 42 structured lessons led by classroom teachers. Small group role play, videotape modeling, cartoon workbooks, and class discussion were used to teach children a six-step problem-solving process similar to that of McClure et al. (1978). The curriculum was taught three times a week for 14 weeks. Teachers were encouraged to apply the problem-solving approach to everyday problems and to use problem-solving dialoguing to help children resolve everyday problems. Training was conducted in suburban and urban second-, third-, and fourth-grade classrooms. Program trainers periodically observed lessons and consulted with the teachers regarding program implementation and problems. The effects of training were assessed with measures of problem-solving skills, an analogue problem-solving situation, teacher behavior ratings scale, and classroom sociometric ratings. Although trained children in urban and suburban schools improved on measures of alternative thinking and teacher ratings, gains in problem-solving were not related to behavior gains. These results support the notion that children do learn the skills and generalize them to real-life behavioral performance outside the classroom, as demonstrated by the analogue behavioral measure. Because only alternative thinking was assessed in this study, the role of other cognitive skills, such as means-end thinking, in adjustment was not examined. For latency-aged children, alternative thinking does not mediate social adjustment. A critical remaining issue is the identification of those cognitive problem-solving skills that actually mediate healthy adjustment in this age group.

ICPS Training with Preadolescents and Adolescents

Compared with the number of ICPS training studies with latency-aged children, there are relatively few social problem-solving studies with preadolescents and adolescents that are conceptualized as primary prevention efforts (Sarason & Sarason, 1981; Marsh, Serafica, & Barenboim, 1980). An intervention study conducted by Elias, Gara, Ubriaco et al. (1986) is an especially important social problem-solving study with preadolescents. This well-designed study is noteworthy in several respects. First, the study was clearly conceptualized as a primary prevention effort. Social problem-solving skills were taught to fifth graders to improve their ability to adapt successfully to the stressors involved in making the transition from elementary to middle school. Previous research (Elias, Clabby, Dorr, Ubriaco, & Schuyler,1982) had documented that middle school is a time of great turmoil for children. Furthermore, the outcome of the middle-school years is important in the subsequent adjustment of children as they move into adolescence and adulthood (Kendall, Lerner, & Craighead, 1984). The purpose of the year-long social problem-solving curriculum taught in fifth grade was to provide children with social problem-solving skills and strategies that would place them "in a position to experience the stressors of middle school in a more calm, controlled, and less problematic manner than children who were less able to access such a strategy" (p. 262). Specific hypotheses were that there would be a direct relation between the amount of social problem-solving training and children's (a) perceptions of middle school as a favorable environment and (b) ability to cope with stressors adaptively. Additionally, a mediating role for social problem-solving skills was hypothesized.

Also contributing to its primary prevention impact is the population-wide nature of the program. The training was provided to all fifth-grade children for whom parental permission was given in all four of the elementary schools within the school district. Ninety-eight percent of the possible sample received the training. These children formed a cohort that will stay largely intact over the course of the following 8 years. The possibility that the program's impact will be durable is greatly enhanced by the population-wide focus, especially considering that the program emphasized the application of social problem-solving skills to everyday problems and to helping other children apply the social problem-solving steps.

A second exemplary aspect of the study is the attention given to ensure that the social problem-solving curriculum was fully implemented. The researchers suggest that uneven implementation of training curricula by teachers in other studies may account for the often inconsistent results both within studies as well as between studies. In the Elias et al. (1986) study, psychological consultants worked with teachers to ensure their understanding of upcoming lessons, to model appropriate instructional strategies (e.g., dialoguing, life space interviewing, and role-plays), and to monitor and provide feedback to teachers about the performance of the lessons. Data collected by classroom observers indicated that the majority of teachers spontaneously used the problem-solving approach to mediate conflicts between students with an average frequency of three times per week.

Third, the program included several design features intended to promote generalization of the skills taught: (a) The program was extensive. The full program was implemented over the course of the academic year. (b) The program emphasized the application of skills. This emphasis was achieved by separating instructional and application phases in the full program (a partial program condition included only the instructional phase, taught from January to May). In the instructional phase (October to December), eight problem-solving skills grouped into three sets of social problem-solving skills were taught in 20 lessons averaging approximately 40 minutes each, conducted twice per week. The eight skills were introduced sequentially, with the last two lessons devoted to helping children integrate all eight steps around specific problem situations. The application phase (January to May) consisted of two main parts. First, teachers were instructed in the "life space intervention technique," in which teachers attempt to mediate everyday conflicts between students by engaging them in a problem-solving process rather than by stepping in and solving the dispute themselves. Second, teachers were instructed in techniques for bringing problem-solving into the regular classroom routine. Teachers generally were presented with a wide range of application strategies and activities to use during the application stage to promote generalization of skills learned in the first semester. (c) The program format for the instructional phase incorporated a number of instructional design elements intended to promote generalization. Each session followed the format outlined here:

1. Group sharing of any occurrences or feelings children would like to share,
2. Brief presentation of the skill to be covered in the lesson,
3. Presentation of a sample situation to provide context for the featured skill,
4. Dialoguing-based discussion of the situation and the skill,
5. Role-play of the situation and skill, and
6. Summary and review.

Three experimental conditions were employed in a quasiexperimental design. Childen in two schools received the full program, and children in the remaining two schools received the partial program. A control group consisted of children entering middle school during the year before the treated children's entrance to middle school. The program's impact was assessed by two primary instruments: The Survey of Middle School Stressors (SMSS) and the Group Social Problem Solving Assessment (GSPSA). Each instrument consists of several subparts. The first part of the SMSS assesses children's perceptions of their adjustment to middle school, and the second part assesses children's perceptions of middle school. In the second part, children rate middle school by 15 bipolar adjectives (e.g., dangerous-safe, friendly-unfriendly). The third section of the SMSS consists of 28 stressful situations commonly occurring in middle school (e.g., forgetting one's locker combination, getting more homework, being teased). Students rate the extent to which each stressor was a problem for them in middle school.

The GSPSA consists of two parts: knowledge of problem-solving steps and problem-solving in response to hypothesized problem situations. The instrument yields two total scores: Primary Social Problem-Solving (Problem Analysis and Action, Specificity of Planning, and Interpersonal Sensitivity) and Obstacle Social Problem-Solving (Expectancies, Alternatives, and Planning in Response to Obstacles).

Results support the conclusion that the full program was superior to the partial program. Children receiving full training reported experiencing fewer and less intense stressors in middle school, compared with children in the partial training condition. For 24 of the 28 stressors, children in the full training condition reported that stressors were less of a problem than were children receiving partial training. However, partial training was superior to no training in reducing the number and intensity of middle school stressors. Full and partial training generally resulted in better adjustment to middle school, relative to no treatment, and the full training program was superior to partial training.

Because prior studies with elementary school children resulted in inconsistent findings regarding the link between improved cognitive problem-solving skills and improved adjustment, the researchers were interested in determining the relation between social problem-solving skills and the experience of school stressors. The findings were supportive of the hypothesized mediating role for social problem-solving skills. The greater the children's problem-solving skills, the less they reported difficulty with school stressors. Interpersonal Sensitivity and Problem Analysis and Action were most productive of difficulty with school stressors. Children with poor social problem-solving skills were likely to experience many intense stressors; however, good problem solvers did not necessarily experience few stressors.

Besides demonstrating that social problem-solving skills intervention prevents difficulties with stressors in middle school, the study provides convincing evidence of the mediating role of problem-solving skills in adjustment. Furthermore, the specific skills that contribute to adjustment were identified (e.g., Problem Analysis and Action and, to a lesser degree, Planning and Consequential Thinking).

EARLY INTERVENTION WITH MALADAPTING CHILDREN

Many of the school-based intervention studies reviewed in earlier chapters in this book could be conceptualized as secondary prevention interventions. These interventions attempt to intervene early in the developmental course of an emotional/behavioral disability. Specific types of child problems targeted in these interventions include depression (Butler, Miezitis, Friedman, & Cole, 1980), social withdrawal (Ladd, 1981), aggression (Camp et al., 1977; Lochman et al., 1981), and school phobia (Kennedy, 1965). Whereas these previously discussed studies targeted specific types of maladapting children, the studies reviewed in this section intervene with a wider spectrum of children who evidence signs of school maladaptation.

Certainly the singular most important and best known school-based secondary prevention program is the Primary Mental Health Project (PMHP, Cowen et al., 1975). As already noted, the PMHP is based on four core characteristics: a focus on primary grade children, the systematic use of screening and detection procedures to identify early school adjustment problems, the use of nonprofessional personnel to expand the availability of services, and a changing role for school mental health professionals, moving from direct services to staff training and consultation and resource functions (Cowen et al., 1980).

For the first 11 years, the PMHP existed as a pilot project in schools in Rochester, New York. In 1969 it was expanded to 11 schools in Rochester and several nearby county schools. Between 1972 and 1977 the project undertook a successful nationwide dissemination program with funding from the National Institute of Mental Health (Cowen et al., 1980). In 1977, 30 school districts nationally had developed programs that met at least three of the four structural emphases of the PMHP. Since 1977, additional programs have been added each year (Durlak & Jason, 1984). The results of the extensive outcome studies support the effectiveness of the PMHP model in improving school adjustment (e.g., Cowen, Dorr, Trost, & Izzo, 1972; Lorion & Cowen, 1976).

Although the Rochester program is the prototype PMHP program, different schools have developed different intervention foci and techniques (Kirschenbaum & Ordman, 1984). For example, some programs emphasize individually oriented, nondirective counseling and the establishment of warm, trusting, and empathic relationships (Cowen, et al., 1972), whereas other programs emphasize behavioral techniques (social and token reinforcement for positive behavior) (Durlak, 1977). Consistent with the goals of this chapter, an intervention program patterned on the PMHP model that uses cognitive-behavioral procedures is reviewed.

In 1977, Durlak and Mannarino (1977) designed a program that combined social skills training and behavioral techniques. In 1980 Durlak compared their behaviorally oriented social skills training intervention with relationship-oriented counseling. Consistent with the PMHP model, high risk children were selected by screening all 226 children in grades 1 through 3 in a suburban, working-class elementary school. Screening was accomplished with two teacher rating scales, and 64 children were identified as shy, withdrawn, or acting out and therefore at high risk for school maladjustment. Children were randomly assigned to the social skills training group or the control group. Training was provided in a small group led by undergraduate students (instead of housewives, as in the Rochester model). Groups met weekly for 14 weeks. Lessons focused on three skills: identification of interpersonal problems, generation of alternative solutions, and anticipation of consequences of these solutions. These skills were taught through puppet scenarios, role-play exercises, stories, and group discussion. Additionally, leaders applied social skills to problems that arose in the group.

Children in the social skills training group made greater improvements on teacher ratings of adjustment than did control children. Unfortunately, teachers were not blind to treatment status, and their ratings may have been biased. The view that improved ratings reflected improved child behavior is supported by sociometric data. Children who participated in social skills training gained significantly more in sociometric acceptance than did control children. Although the results lend support to the view that social skills training is effective with maladapting young children, the absence of an attention control limits confidence in the conclusion that improvement was a result of social skills training and not of nonspecific treatment factors, such as attention. This methodological shortcoming is compounded by the fact that outcome measures did not include a measure of specific skills taught in the program.

POPULATION-WIDE APPROACH

Population-wide preventive approaches in the school attempt to ameliorate those environmental factors thought to negatively affect children's growth and development and to promote those conditions thought to be conducive to growth and development (Roberts & Peterson, 1984). This ecological orientation to prevention is illustrated by attempts to increase democratic decision-making in school, to improve social-emotional climate in classrooms, to improve teachers' effectiveness as mental health agents, to increase the opportunities for students to engage in cooperative learning strategies, and to improve racial relations. It is certainly beyond the scope and goals of this book to provide even the sketchiest review of population-wide prevention efforts in schools. The reader is referred to a review of ecologically oriented school-based prevention programs by Jason, Durlak, and Holton-Walker (1984). In this section, one cognitive-behavioral intervention program is described that illustrates this third and last approach to school-based prevention programming. This approach is a cognitive-behavioral intervention intended to reduce teachers' stress and improve teachers' ability to cope with stressors.

Teacher anxiety is one environmental factor that may negatively affect students' learning and adjustment. When a teacher is anxious, the classroom climate is not conducive to optimal learning (Keavney & Sinclair, 1978). Specifically, teacher stress has been linked to poor teacher performance, negative student affect, and poor student achievement (see Coates & Thoresen, 1976).

Forman (1982) reported the results of an 18-hour cognitive-behavioral stress management program provided to 12 urban secondary school teachers. Forman's stress management program was patterned on Meichenbaum's (1977) stress inoculation model. Meichenbaum's stress inoculation procedure consists of three stages: (a) an educational phase during which the client is provided with a conceptual understanding of his or her response to stress; (b) a rehearsal phase during which the client is instructed in cognitive and behavioral coping techniques; and (c) an application phase during which the individual has the opportunity to practice the coping techniques in response to stressors. Forman's program also included a cognitive restructuring component. Teachers who volunteered for the program participated in six 3-hour Saturday morning sessions. During the first session, a cognitive framework for understanding stress was provided, and teachers identified situations that were particularly stressful for them during the school day. The second session focused on progressive muscle relaxation. The third and fourth sessions were devoted to understanding the tenets of rational-emotive therapy (Ellis, 1962), and the ABC model of emotions was applied to commonly occurring stressful situations in the schools. During the fifth and sixth sessions, teachers practiced identifying their usual thoughts, feelings, and behaviors in specific stress situations and practiced different coping techniques, such as substituting rational for irrational thoughts and relaxing, through role play and imagery.

A total of 12 teachers participated in the program, and another 12 teachers who also volunteered for the training comprised a control group. Teachers receiving the training improved on self-report measures of stress and anxiety, whereas the control group did not. Additionally, program participants showed decreases in motoric manifestations of anxiety in the classroom after treatment, whereas the control group did not. Particularly encouraging is the finding that program teachers continued to show large reductions in self-reported anxiety and stress level from posttreatment to 6-week follow-up. Because daily practice was emphasized and teachers were instructed to continue using the techniques after completion of training, urther reductions seem to indicate that the teachers continued to use the elf-management techniques.

The results of Forman's stress management program for teachers suggests hat cognitive-behavioral procedures are effective in helping reduce teacher nxiety and stress levels. Unanswered in Forman's study, however, is the ffect of reduced anxiety and stress on classroom climate and student earning and adjustment. Although teacher anxiety is related to classroom limate and student outcomes, the effectiveness of stress management rograms on climate and student outcomes has not been demonstrated onclusively.

References

Abidin, R. R., Jr. (1975). Negative effects of behavioral consultation: I know I ought to, but it hurts too much. *Journal of School Psychology, 13*, 51–56.

Achenbach, T. M., & Edelbrock, C. S. (1978). The classification of child psychopathology: A review and analysis of empirical efforts. *Psychological Bulletin, 85*, 1275–1301.

Achenbach, T. M., & Edelbrock, C. (1983). *Manual for the Child Behavior Checklist and Revised Child Behavior Profile*. Burlington, VT: University Associates in Psychiatry.

Achenbach, T. M., & Edelbrock, C. (1986). *Manual for the teacher's report form and teacher's version of the Child Behavior Profile*. Burlington, VT: University Associates in Psychiatry.

Albee, G. W. (1982). Preventing psychopathology and promoting human potential. *American Psychologist, 37*, 1043–1050.

Alberto, P. A., & Troutman, A. C. (1982). *Applied behavior analysis for teachers*. Columbus, OH: Merrill.

Allen, G., Chinsky, A., Larcen, S., Lochman, J., & Selinger, H. (1976). *Community psychology and the schools: A behaviorally oriented multi-level preventive approach*. Hillsdale, NJ: Lawrence Erlbaum.

Allen, G., Elias, M. J., & Zlotlow, S. F. (1980). Behavioral interventions for alleviating test anxiety: A methodological overview of current therapeutic practices. In I. G. Sararon (Ed.). *Test anxiety: Theory research and applications* (pp. 155–186). Hillsdale, NJ: Lawrence Erlbaum.

Allen, K. E., Hart, B., Buell, J. S., Harris, F. R., & Wolf, M. M. (1964). Effects of social reinforcement on isolate behavior of a nursery school child. *Child Development, 35*, 511–518.

American Psychiatric Association (1980). *Diagnostic and statistical manual of mental disorders* (3rd Ed.). Washington, DC: American Psychiatric Association.

American Psychiatric Association (1987). *Diagnostic and statistical manual of mental disorders* (3rd Ed., Revised). Washington, DC: American Psychiatric Association.

Ames, R., Ames, C., & Garrison, W. (1977). Children's causal ascriptions for positive and negative interpersonal outcomes. *Psychological Reports, 41*, 595–602.

Arbuthnot, J., & Gordon, D. A. (1986). Behavioral and cognitive effects of a moral reasoning development intervention for high-risk behavior-disordered adolescents. *Journal of Consulting and Clinical Psychology, 54*, 208–216.

Arkin, R., Kolditz, T. A., & Kolditz, K. K. (1983). Attributions of the test-anxious student. *Personality and Social Psychology Bulletin, 9*, 271–280.

Asarnow, J. R., & Callan, J. W. (1985). Boys with peer adjustment problems: Social cognitive processes. *Journal of Consulting and Clinical Psychology, 53*, 80–87.

Asarnow, J. R., & Carlson, G. A. (1985). Depression self-rating scale: Utility with child and psychiatric inpatients. *Journal of Consulting and Clinical Psychology, 53*, 491–499.

Asher, S. R., & Dodge, K. A. (1986). Identifying children who are rejected by their peers. *Developmental Psychology, 22*, 444–449.
Asher, S. R., & Hymel, S. (1981). Children's social competence in peer relations: Sociometric and behavioral assessment. In J. D. Wine & M. D. Smye (Eds.), *Social competence* (pp. 125–157). New York: Guilford.
Asher, S. R., Hymel, S., & Renshaw, P. P. (1984). Loneliness in children. *Child Development, 55*, 1456–1464.
Asher, S. R., & Renshaw, P. D. (1981). Children without friends: Social knowledge and social skill training. In S. R. Asher & J. M. Gottman (Eds.), *The development of children's friendship*. New York: Cambridge University Press.
Asher, S. R., Singleton, L. C., Tinsley, B. R., & Hymel, S. (1979). A reliable sociometric measure for preschool children. *Developmental Psychology, 15*, 443–444.
Atkeson, B. M., & Forehand, R. (1978). Parent behavioral training for problem children: An examination of studies using multiple outcome measures. *Journal of Abnormal Child Psychology, 6*, 449–460.
Ayllon, T., & Rosenbaum, M. S. (1977). The behavioral treatment of disruption and hyperactivity in school settings. In B. B. Lahey & A. E. Kazdin (Eds.), *Advances in child clinical psychology*. New York; Plenum Press.
Ayllon, T., Smith, P., & Rogers, M. (1979). Behavioral management of school phobia. *Journal of Experimental Psychiatry, 1*, 125–138.
Bandura, A. (1969). *Principles of behavior modification*. New York: Holt, Rinehart & Winston.
Bandura, A. (1976). Self-reinforcement: Theoretical and methodological considerations. *Behaviorism, 4*, 135–155.
Bandura, A. (1977). *Social learning theory*. Englewood Cliffs, NJ: Prentice-Hall.
Bandura, A., Grusec, J., & Menlove, F. (1967). Vicarious extinction of avoidance behavior. *Journal of Personality and Social Psychology, 5*, 16–23.
Bandura, A., & Kupers, C. J. (1964). The transmission of patterns of self-reinforcement through modeling. *Journal of Abnormal and Social Psychology, 69*, 1–9.
Bandura, A., & McDonald, F. J. (1963). The influence of social reinforcement and the behavior of models in shaping children's moral judgements. *Journal of Abnormal and Social Psychology, 67*, 274–281.
Bandura, A., & Menlove, F. (1968). Factors determining vicarious extinction of avoidance behavior through symbolic modeling. *Journal of Personality and Social Psychology, 8*, 99–108.
Bandura, A., & Perloff, B. (1967). Relative efficacy of self-monitored and externally imposed reinforcement systems. *Journal of Personality and Social Psychology, 7*, 111–116.
Barabasz, A. F. (1973). Group desensitization of test anxiety in elementary school. *Journal of Psychology, 83*, 295–301.
Barkley, R. (1981). *Hyperactive children*. New York: Guilford.
Bartell, N. P., & Reynolds, W. M. (1986). Depression and self-esteem in academically gifted and nongifted children. A comparison study. *Journal of School Psychology, 24*, 55–61.
Barton, E. J., & Ascione, F. R. (1984). Direct observation. In T. H. Ollendick and M. Hersen (Eds.), *Child behavioral assessment* (pp. 166–194). New York: Pergamon Press.
Beck, A. T. (1967). *Depression: Causes and treatment.* Philadelphia: University of Pennsylvania Press.
Beck, A. T. (1976). *Cognitive therapy and the emotional disorders*. New York: International Universities Press.

Beck, A. T., Rush, J. J., Shaw, B. F., & Emery, G. (1979). *Cognitive therapy of depression*. New York: Guilford.

Beck, A. T., Ward, C., Mendelson, M., Mock, J., & Erbaugh, J. (1961). An inventory for measuring depression. *Archives of General Psychiatry, 4*, 53–63.

Beck, A. T., Weissman, A., Lester, D., & Trexler, L. C. (1974). The measurement of pessimism: The Hopelessness Scale. *Journal of Consulting and Clinical Psychology, 42*, 861–865.

Becker, W. C., Engelmann, S., & Thomas, D. R. (1971). *Teaching: A course in applied psychology*, Chicago: Science Research Associates.

Begelman, D. A., & Hersen, M. (1971). Critique of Obler and Terwilliger's "Systematic desensitization with neurologically impaired children with phobia disorders." *Journal of Consulting and Clinical Psychology, 37*, 10–13.

Beinfeld, G., & Peters, R. (1986). Social reasoning and social behavior in reflective and impulsive children. *Journal of Clinical Child Psychology, 15*, 221–227.

Bentler, P., & McClain, J. (1976). A multitrait-multi-method analysis of reflection-impulsivity. *Child Development, 47*, 218–226.

Bernfeld, G., & Peters, R. (1986). Social reasoning and social behavior in reflective and impulsive children. *Journal of Clinical Child Psychology*, 15(3), 221–227.

Bettes, B. A., & Walker, E. (1986). Symptoms associated with suicidal behavior in childhood and adolescence. *Journal of Abnormal Child Psychology, 4*, 591–604.

Bierman, K. L. (1983). Cognitive development and clinical interviews with children. In B. B. Lahey & A. E. Kazdin (Eds.), *Advances in clinical child psychology*, Vol. 6 (pp. 217–250). New York: Plenum.

Bierman, K. L. (1986). The relation between social aggression and peer rejection in middle childhood. In R. J. Prinz (Ed.), *Advances in behavioral assessment of children and families*, Vol. 2 (pp. 151–178). New York: JAI Press.

Bierman, K. L., & Furman, W. (1984). The effects of social skills training and peer involvement on the social adjustment of preadolescents. *Child Development, 55*, 151–162.

Bierman, K. L., & McCauley, E. (1987). Children's descriptions of their peer interactions: Useful information for clinical-child assessment. *Journal of Abnormal Child Psychology*.

Bierman, K. L., Miller, C. L., & Stabb, S. D. (1987). Improving the social behavior and peer acceptance of rejected boys: Effect of social skill training with instructions and prohibitions. *Journal of Consulting and Clinical Psychology, 55*, 194–200.

Bierman, K. L., & Schwartz, L. A. (1986, August). *Selecting social intervention techniques for aggressive rejected boys.* Paper presented at meeting of the American Psychological Association, Washington, DC.

Bierman, K. L., & Schwartz, L. A. (1987). Clinical-child interviews: Approaches and developmental considerations. *Journal of Child and Adolescent Psychotherapy*.

Bijou, S. W. (1966). A functional analysis of retarded development. In N. R. Ellis (Ed.), *International review of research in mental retardation*. New York: Oxford University Press.

Birnbrauer, J. S., Wolf, M. M., Kidder, J. D., & Tague (1965). Classroom behavior of retarded pupils with token reinforcement. *Journal of Experimental Child Psychology, 2*, 219–325.

Block, J., Block, J., & Harrington, D. (1974). Some misgivings about the Matching Familiar Figures Test as a measure of reflection-impulsivity. *Developmental Psychology, 10*, 611–632.

Bolstad, O. P., & Johnson, S. M. (1977). The relationship between teachers' assessment of students and students' actual behavior in the classroom. *Child Development, 48*, 570–578.

Bonney, M. (1943). The relative stability of social, intellectual and academic status in grades II to IV, and the interrelationships between these various forms of growth. *Journal of Educational Psychology, 34*, 88–102.

Bornstein, M., Bellack, A. S., & Hersen, M. (1977). Social skills training for unassertive children: A multiple-baseline analysis. *Journal of Applied Behavior Analysis, 10*, 183–195.

Bornstein, M., Bellack, A. S., & Hersen, M. (1980). Social skills training for highly aggressive children. *Behavior Modification, 4*, 173–186.

Bower, E. M. (1969). *Early identification of emotionally handicapped children in school* (2nd Ed.). Springfield, IL: Charles C Thomas.

Braswell, L., Kendall, P., Braith, J., Carey, M., & Vye, C. (1985). "Involvement" in cognitive behavioral therapy with children: Process and its relationship to outcome. *Cognitive Therapy and Research, 9*, 611–630.

Brown, A. L. (1975). The development of memory: Knowing, knowing about knowing, and knowing how to know. In H. W. Reese (Ed.), *Advances in child development and behavior,* Vol. 10. New York: Academic Press.

Brown, D., Pryzwansky, W. B., & Schulte, A. C. (1987). *Psychological consultation: Introduction to theory and practice*. Newton, MA: Allyn and Bacon.

Brown, R. (1985). The validity of teacher ratings in differentiating between two subgroups of attention deficit disordered children with or without hyperactivity. *Educational and Psychological Measurement, 45*, 661–669.

Bugental, D. B., Whalen, C. K., & Henker, B. (1977). Causal attributions of hyperactive children and motivational assumptions of two behavior-change approaches: Evidence for an interactionist position. *Child Development, 48*, 874–884.

Burns, H. (1972). The effect of self-directed verbal commands on arithmetic performance and activity level. *Dissertation Abstracts International, 33*, 1782B.

Busk, P., Ford, R., & Schulman, J. (1973). Stability of sociometric responses in classrooms. *Journal of Genetic Psychology, 123*, 69–84.

Butler, L., & Meichenbaum, D. (1981). The assessment of interpersonal problem-solving skills. In P. C. Kendall & S. D. Hollon (Eds.), *Assessment strategies for cognitive-behavioral interventions* (pp. 197–225). New York: Academic Press.

Butler, L., Miezitis, S., Friedman, R., & Cole, E. (1980). The effect of two school-based intervention programs on depressive symptoms in preadolescents. *American Educational Research Journal, 17*, 111–119.

Cairns, E., & Cammock, T. (1978). Development of a more reliable version of the Matching Familiar Figures Test. *Developmental Psychology, 5*, 555–560.

Camp, B. W. (1980). Two psychoeducational treatment programs for young aggressive boys. In C. K. Whalen & B. Henkler (Eds.), *Hyperactive children: The social psychology of intervention for children and adults.* New York: Pergamon Press.

Camp, B. W., & Bash, M. A. (1980). Think aloud: Improving self-control through training in problem-solving. In D. P. Rathjen & J. P. Foreyt (Eds.), *Social competence: Intervention for children and adults.* New York: Pergamon Press.

Camp, B. W., & Bash, M. A. (1981). *Think aloud: Increasing social and cognitive skills: A problem-solving program for children (primary level).* Champaign, IL: Research Press.

Camp, B. W., Blom, G. E., Hebert, F., & Van Doorninck, W. J. (1977). "Think aloud": A program for developing self-control in young aggressive boys. *Journal of Abnormal Child Psychology, 5*, 157–169.

Campbell, D. T., & Fiske, D. W. (1959). Convergent and discriminant validation by the multitrait and multimethod matrix. *Psychological Bulletin, 56*, 81–105.
Cantrell, V. L., & Prinz, R. J. (1985). Multiple perspectives of rejected, neglected, and accepted children: Relation between sociometric status and behavioral characteristics. *Journal of Consulting and Clinical Psychology, 53*, 884–889.
Caplan, G. (1964). *Principles of preventive psychiatry*. New York: Basic Books.
Carlson, C. (1986). Attention deficit disorder without hyperactivity: A review of preliminary experimental evidence. In B. Lahey & A. Kazdin (Eds.) (pp. 153–176), *Advances in Clinical Child Psychology*. New York: Plenum Press.
Cartledge, G., & Milburn, J. F. (1986). *Teaching social skills to children: Innovative approaches* (2nd Ed.). New York: Pergamon Press.
Castaneda, A., McCandless, B., & Palermo, D. (1956). The children's form of the Manifest Anxiety Scale. *Child Development, 27*, 317–326.
Catania, A. C. (1975). The myth of self-reinforcement. *Behaviorism, 3*, 192–199.
Chandler, M. J. (1971, March). *Egocentrism and childhood psychopathology: The development and application of measurement techniques*. Paper presented at the biennial meeting of the Society for Research in Child Development, Minneapolis.
Chandler, M. J. (1973). Egocentrism and antisocial behavior: The assessment and training of social perspective-taking skills. *Developmental Psychology, 9*, 326–332.
Chandler, M. J., Greenspan, S., & Barenboim, C. (1974). Assessment and training of role-taking and referential communication skills in institutionalized emotionally disturbed children. *Developmental Psychology, 10*, 546–553.
Christoff, K. A., Scott, W. O., Kelley, M. L., Schlundt, D., Baer, G., & Kelly, J. (1985). Social skills and social problem-solving training for shy young adolescents. *Behavior Therapy, 16*, 468–477.
Ciminero, A. R., Calhoun, K. S., & Adams, H. E. (Eds.) (1977). *Handbook of behavioral assessment*. New York: John Wiley & Sons.
Clark, L., Gresham, F. M., & Elliott, S. N. (1985). Development and validation of a social skills assessment measure: The TROSS-C. *Journal of Psychoeducational Assessment, 4*, 347–356.
Coates, T. J., & Thoresen, C. E. (1976). Teacher anxiety: A review with recommendations. *Review of Educational Research, 46*, 159–184.
Coats, K. I. (1979). Cognitive self-instructional training approach for reducing disruptive behavior of young children. *Psychological Reports, 44*, 127–134.
Cohen, N. J., Kershner, J., & Wehrspann, W. (1985). Characteristics of social cognition in children with different symptom patterns. *Journal of Applied Developmental Psychology, 6*, 227–290.
Cohen-Sandler, R., Berman, A. L., & King, R. A. (1982). Life stress and symptomatology: Determinants of suicide behavior in children. *Journal of the American Academy of Child Psychiatry, 21*, 178–186.
Coie, J. D., & Dodge, K. A. (1983). Continuities and changes in children's social status: A five-year longitudinal study. *Merrill-Palmer Quarterly, 29*, 261–282.
Coie, J. D., & Dodge, K. A. (1986, August). *Hostile and instrumentally aggressive children: A social information processing perspective*. Paper presented at the annual meeting of the American Psychological Association, Washington, DC.
Coie, J. D., Dodge, K. A., & Coppotelli, H. (1982). Dimensions and types of status: A cross-age perspective. *Developmental Psychology, 18*, 557–570.
Coie, J. D., & Kupersmidt, J. B. (1983). A behavioral analysis of emerging social status in boys' groups. *Child Development, 54*, 1400–1416.
Cole, D. A., & Rehm, L. P. (1986). Family interaction patterns and childhood depression. *Journal of Abnormal Child Psychology, 14*, 297–314.

Collins, R. L., Rothblum, E. D., & Wilson, G. T. (1986). The comparative efficacy of cognitive and behavioral approaches to the treatment of obesity. *Cognitive Therapy and Research, 10*, 299–318.

Commission on the Prevention of Mental-Emotional Disabilities (1987). *The prevention of mental-emotional disabilities.* Alexandria, VA: National Mental Health Association.

Conger, A., Conger, J., Wallander, J., Ward, D., & Dygdon, J. (1983). A generalizability study of the Conners' Teacher Rating Scale—Revised. *Educational and Psychological Measurement, 43*, 1019–1031.

Conger, J. C., & Keane, A. P. (1981). Social skills intervention in the treatment of isolated or withdrawn children. *Psychological Bulletin, 90*, 478–495.

Conger, J. J., & Miller, W. C. (1966). *Personality, social class, and delinquency.* New York: John Wiley & Sons.

Conners, K. (1969). A teacher rating scale for use in drug studies with children. *American Journal of Psychiatry, 126*, 884–888.

Conners, K. (1970). Symptom patterns in hyperkinetic, neurotic and normal children. *Children Development, 41*, 667–682.

Conners, K. (1972). Pharmaco-therapy of psychopathology in children. In H. Quay & J. Werry (Eds.), *Psychopathological disorders of children.* New York: Wiley.

Conners, K. (1973). Rating scales for use in drug studies with children. *Psychopharmacology Bulletin* (*Special Issue, Pharmacotherapy with Children*), 24–84.

Conners, K. (1980). *Food additives and hyperactive children.* New York: Plenum Press.

Connolly, J., & Doyle, A. (1981). Assessment of social competence in preschoolers: Teachers versus peers. *Developmental Psychology, 17*, 454–462.

Conoley, J. C., & Conoley, C. W. (1982). *School consultation: A guide to practice and training.* New York: Pergamon Press.

Copeland, A., & Weissbrod, C. (1978). Behavioral correlates of the hyperactivity factor of the Conners Teacher Questionnaire. *Journal of Abnormal Child Psychology, 6*, 339–343.

Cowen, E. L. (1982). Primary prevention research: Barriers, needs and opportunities. *Journal of Primary Prevention, 2*, 131–137.

Cowen, E. L., Davidson, E. R., & Gesten, E. L. (1980). Program dissemination and the modification of delivery practices in school mental health. *Professional Psychology, 11*, 36–47.

Cowen, E. L., Dorr, D. A., Trost, M. A., & Izzo, L. D. (1972). Follow-up study of maladapting school children seen by nonprofessionals. *Journal of Consulting and Clinical Psychology, 39*, 235–238.

Cowen, E. L., Pederson, A., Barbigian, H., Izzo, L. D., & Trost, M. A. (1973). Long term follow-up of early detected vulnerable children. *Journal of Consulting and Clinical Psychology, 41*, 438–446.

Cowen, E. L., Trost, M. A., Dorr, D. A., Lorion, R. P., Izzo, L. D., & Isaacson, R. V. (1975). *New ways in school mental health: Early detection and prevention of school maladaptation.* New York: Human Sciences Press.

Coyne, J. C., & Gotlib, T. H. (1983). The role of cognition in depression: A critical appraisal. *Psychological Bulletin, 94*, 472–505.

Crandall, V. C., Katovsky, W., & Crandall, V. S. (1965). Children's beliefs in their control of reinforcements in intellectual-academic achievement situations. *Child Development, 36*, 91–109.

Csapo, M. (1983). Effects of social learning training with socially rejected children. *Behavioral Disorders, 8*, 199–208.

Cytryn, L., & McKnew, D. H., Jr. (1972). Proposed classification of childhood depression. *American Journal of Psychiatry, 29*, 149–155.

Cytryn, L., McKnew, D. H., Jr., & Bunney, W. E., Jr. (1980). Diagnosis of depression in children: A reassessment. *American Journal of Psychiatry, 137*, 22–25.

Deci, E. L. (1975). *Intrinsic motivation*. New York: Plenum Press.

Deffenbacher, J. L. (1980). Worry and emotionality in test anxiety. In I. G. Sarason (Ed.), *Test anxiety: Theory, research, and applications* (pp. 111–128). Hillsdale, NJ: Lawrence Erlbaum.

Deffenbacher, J. L., & Kemper, C. C. (1974). Systematic desensitization of test anxiety in junior high students. *The School Counselor, 22*, 216–222.

DeHass, P. (1986). Attention styles and peer relationships of hyperactive and normal boys and girls. *Journal of Abnormal Child Psychology, 14*(3), 457–467.

Delamater, A., Lahey, B., & Drake, L. (1981). Toward an empirical subclassification of "learning disabilities": A psychophysiological comparison of "hyperactive" and "nonhyperactive" subgroups. *Journal of Abnormal Child Psychology, 9*, 65–77.

Deluty, R. H. (1979). Children's action tendency scale: A self-report measure of aggressiveness, assertiveness, and submissiveness in children. *Journal of Consulting and Clinical Psychology, 47*, 1061–1071.

Deluty, R. H. (1981a). Adaptiveness of aggressive, assertive, and submissive behavior for children. *Journal of Clinical Child Psychology, 10*, 149–155.

Deluty, R. H. (1981b). Alternative-thinking ability of aggressive, assertive, and submissive children. *Cognitive Therapy and Research, 5*, 309–312.

Dember, W. N. (1965). The new look in motivation. *American Scientist, 53*, 409–427.

Dember, W. N. (1974). Motivation and the cognitive revolution. *American Psychologist, 29*, 161–168.

Diener, C. I., & Dweck, C. S. (1978). An analysis of learned helplessness: Continuous changes in performance, strategy, and achievement cognitions following failure. *Journal of Personality and Social Psychology, 36*, 451–462.

Dinkmeyer, D. (1970). *Developing understanding of self and others*. Circle Pines, MN: American Guidance Service.

Dodge, K. A. (1980). Social cognition and children's aggressive behavior. *Child Development, 51*, 162–170.

Dodge, K. A. (1983). Behavioral antecedents of peer social status. *Child Development, 54*, 1386–1399.

Dodge, K. A. (1986). A social information processing model of social competence in children. In M. Perlmutter (Ed.), *Cognitive perspective on children's social and behavioral development* (pp. 77–125). Hillsdale, NJ: Lawrence Erlbaum.

Dodge, K. A., Coie, J. D., & Brakke, N. P. (1982). Behavior patterns of socially rejected and neglected preadolescents: The roles of social approach and aggression. *Journal of Abnormal Child Psychology, 10*, 389–410.

Dodge, K. A., & Frame, C. L. (1982). Social cognitive biases and deficits in aggressive boys. *Child Development, 53*, 620–635.

Dodge, K. A., McClaskey, C. L., & Feldman, E. (1985). Situational approach to the assessment of social competence in children. *Journal of Consulting and Clinical Psychology, 53*, 344–353.

Dodge, K. A., & Murphy, R. R. (1984). The assessment of social competence in adolescents. In P. Karoly & J. J. Steffen (Eds.), *Adolescent behavior and contemporary concerns*, Vol. 3. Lexington, MA: Lexington Books.

Dodge, K. A., Murphy, R. R., & Buchsbaum, K. C. (1984). The assessment of intention-cue detection skills in children: Implications for developmental psychology. *Child Development, 55*, 163–173.

Dodge, K. A., & Newman, J. P. (1981). Biased decision-making processes in aggressive boys. *Journal of Abnormal Psychology, 90*, 375–379.

Dodge, K. A., Schlundt, D. C., Schocken, I., & Delugach, J. D. (1983). Social competence and children's sociometric status: The role of peer group entry strategies. *Merrill-Palmer Quarterly, 29*, 309–336.

Douglas, V. (1972). Stop, look and listen: The problem of sustained attention and impulse control in hyperactive and normal children. *Canadian Journal of Behavioral Science, 4*, 159–182.

Douglas, V. (1974). Sustained attention and impulse control: Implications for the handicapped child. In J. Swets & L. Elliot (Eds.), *Psychology and the handicapped child*. Washington, D.C.: U.S. Office of Education.

Douglas, V. I. (1975). Are drugs enough? To train or treat the hyperactive child. *International Journal of Mental Health, 5*, 199–212.

Douglas, V. I. (1976). Attention factors. In R. M. Knight & D. J. Baker (Eds.), *The neuropsychology of learning disorders*. Baltimore, MD: University Park Press.

Douglas, V. I. (1983). Attention and cognitive problems. In M. Rutter (Ed.), *Developmental neuropsychiatry*, 280–330. New York: The Guilford Press.

Douglas, V. I., & Parry, P. (1983). Effects of reward on delayed reaction time task performance of hyperactive children. *Journal of Abnormal Child Psychology, 2*, 313–326.

Douglas, V. I., Parry, P., Marton, P., & Garson, C. (1976). Assessment of a cognitive training program for hyperactive children. *Journal of Abnormal Child Psychology, 4*, 389–410.

Douglas, V. I., & Peters, K. (1979). Toward a clearer definition of the attention deficit of hyperactive children. In G. A. Hale & M. Lewis (Eds.), Attentional and cognitive development, 173–247. New York: Plenum Press.

Durlak, J. A. (1977). Description and evaluation of a behaviorally oriented school-based preventive mental health program. *Journal of Consulting and Clinical Psychology, 45*, 27–33.

Durlak, J. A. (1980). Comparative effectiveness of behavioral and relationship group treatment in the secondary prevention of school maladjustment. *American Journal of Community Psychology, 8*, 327–340.

Durlak, J. A., & Jason, L. A. (1984). Preventive programs for school-aged children and adolescents. In M. C. Roberts & L. Peterson (Eds.), *Prevention of problems in childhood: Psychological research and applications* (pp. 103–132). New York: John Wiley & Sons.

Durlak, J. A., & Mannarino, A. P. (1977). The Social Skills Development Program: Description of a school-based preventive mental health program for high-risk children. *Journal of Clinical Child Psychology, 6*, 48–52.

Durrell, D. (1955). *Durrell Analysis of Reading Difficulty*. New York: Harcourt, Brace & World.

Dusek, J. B. (1980). The development of test anxiety in children. In I. G. Sarason (Ed.), *Test anxiety: theory, research, and applications* (pp. 87–110). Hillsdale, NJ: Lawrence Erlbaum.

Dusek, J. B., Kermis, M. D., & Mergler, N. L. (1975). Information processing in low and high test anxious children as a function of grade level and verbal labeling. *Developmental Psychology, 11*, 651-652.

Dusek, J. B., Mergler, N. L., & Kermis, M. D. (1976). Attention, encoding, and information processing in low- and high-test, anxious children. *Child Development, 47*, 201–207.

Dweck, C. S. (1975). The role of expectations and attributions in the alleviation of learned helplessness. *Journal of Personality and Social Psychology, 31*, 674–685.

Dweck, C. S., & Reppucci, N. D. (1973). Learned helplessness and reinforcement responsibility in children. *Journal of Personality and Social Psychology, 25*, 109–116.

Eaton, W. D. (1980). Cross logged analysis of children's test anxiety and defensiveness. *Journal of Educational Psychology, 72*, 404–407.

Edelbrock, C., Costello, A. J., Dulcan, M. K., Kalas, R., & Conover, N. C. (1985). Age differences in the reliability of the psychiatric interview of the child. *Child Development, 56*, 265–275.

Edelson, J. L., & Rose, S. D. (1982). Investigations into the efficacy of short-term group social skills training for socially isolated children. *Child Behavior Therapy, 3*, 1–16.

Eisenberg, L., & Conners, K. (1971). Psychopharmacology in childhood. In N. B. Talbot, J. Kagan, & L. Eisenberg (Eds.), *Behavioral science and pediatric medicine.* Philadelphia: Saunders.

Eisenbruch, M. (1983). Affective disorders in parents: Impact upon children. In D. P. Cantwell & G. A. Carlson (Eds.), *Affective disorders in childhood and adolescence: An update* (pp. 276-333). New York: Spectrum.

Elardo, P. T., & Caldwell, B. M. (1979). The effects of an experimental social development program on children in the middle childhood period. *Psychology in the Schools, 16*, 93–100.

Elias, M. J., Clabby, J., Dorr, D., Ubriaco, M., & Schuyler, T. (1982). *The improving social awareness-social problem solving project: A case study in school-based action research* (Action Research Workshop Report No. 4). New York: William T. Grant Foundation.

Elias, M. J., Gara, M., Ubriaco, M., Rothbaum, P. A., Clabby, J. F., & Schuyler, T. (1986). Impact of a preventive social problem solving intervention on children's coping with middle school stressors. *American Journal of Community Psychology, 14*, 259–275.

Elias, M. J., Rothbaum, P. A., & Gara, M. (1986). Social-cognitive problem solving in children: assessing the knowledge and application of skills. *Journal of Applied Developmental Psychology, 7*, 77–94.

Ellis, A. (1962). *Reason and emotion in psychotherapy.* New York: Lyle Stuart.

Ellis, A. (1973). Rational-emotive therapy. In R. Corsini (Ed.), *Current psychotherapies.* Itasca, IL: Peacock.

Ellis, A. (1977). Rational-emotive therapy: Research data that supports the clinical and personality hypothesis of RET and other modes of cognitive-behavior therapy. *Counseling Psychologist, 7*, 2–42.

Enright, R. P., & Lapsley, D. K. (1980). Social role-taking: A review of the constructs, measures, and measurement properties. *Review of Educational Research, 50*, 647–674.

Eschenroeder, C. (1982). How rational is rational-emotive therapy? A critical appraisal of its theoretical foundations and therapeutic methods. *Cognitive Therapy and Research, 6*, 381–392.

Evans, I. M. (1985). Building systems models as a strategy for target behavior selection in clinical assessment. *Behavioral Assessment, 7*, 21–32.

Evers, W. L., & Schwartz, J. C. (1973). Modifying social withdrawal in preschoolers: The effects of filmed modeling and teacher praise. *Journal of Abnormal Child Psychology, 1*, 248–256.

Evers-Pasquale, W. L. (1978). The Peer Preference Test, a measure of reward value: Item analysis, cross-validation, concurrent validation, and replication. *Journal of Abnormal Child Psychology, 6*, 175–188.

Evers-Pasquale, W. L., & Sherman, M. (1975). The reward value of peers: A variable influencing the efficacy of film modeling in modifying social isolation in preschoolers. *Journal of Abnormal Child Psychology, 3*, 179–189.

Faust, J., Baum, C. G., & Forehand, R. (1985). An examination of the association between social relationships and depression in early adolescence. *Journal of Applied Developmental Psychology, 6*, 291–297.

Feindler, E. L., Marriott, S. A., & Iwata, M. (1984). Group anger control training for junior high school delinquents. *Cognitive Therapy and Research, 8*, 299–311.

Feld, S., & Lewis, J. (1967). Further evidence on the stability of the factor structure of the test anxiety scale for children. *Journal of Consulting Psychology, 31*, 434.

Feld, S. C., & Lewis, J. (1969). The assessment of achievement anxieties in children. In C. P. Smith (Ed.), *Achievement-related motives in children.* New York: Russell-Sage.

Feldhusen, J., Houtz, J., & Ringenbach, S. (1972). The Purdue Elementary Problem-Solving Inventory. *Psychological Reports, 31*, 891–901.

Ferritor, P. E., Buckholdt, D., Hamblin, R. L., & Smith, L. (1972). The non-effects of contingent reinforcement for attending behavior on work accomplished. *Journal of Applied Behavior Analysis, 5*, 7–18.

Fielstein, E., Klein, M. S., Fischer, M., Hanon, C., Koburger, P., Schneider, M. J., & Leitenberg, H. (1985). Self-esteem and causal attributions for success and failure in children. *Cognitive Therapy and Research, 9*, 381–398.

Finch, A. J., & Rogers, T. R. (1984). Self-report instruments. In T. H. Ollendick & M. Hersen (Eds.), *Child behavioral assessment: Principles and procedures.* New York: Pergamon Press.

Finch, A. J., & Saylor, C. F. (1984). An overview of child depression. In W. Burns & J. Lavigne (Eds.), *Progress in pediatric psychology* (pp. 201–239). New York: Grune & Straton.

Firestone, P., & Douglas, V. I. (1975). The effect of reward and punishment on reaction times and autonomic activity in hyperactive and normal children. *Journal of Abnormal Child Psychology, 3*, 201–216.

Forman, S. G. (1980). A comparison of cognitive training and response cost procedures in modifying aggressive behavior of elementary school children. *Behavior Therapy, 11*, 594–600.

Forman, S. G. (1982). Stress management for teachers: A cognitive-behavioral program. *Journal of School Psychology, 30*, 180–187.

Foster, S. L., & Ritchey, W. L. (1985). Behavioral correlates of sociometric status of fourth-, fifth-, and sixth-grade children in two classroom situations. *Behavioral Assessment, 7*, 79–93.

Frame, C., Matson, J. L., Sonis, W. A., Fialkov, M. J., & Kazdin, A. E. (1982). Behavioral treatment of depression in a prepubertal child. *Journal of Behavior Therapy and Experimental Psychiatry, 3*, 239–243.

Franco, D. P., Christoff, K. A., Crimmins, P. B., & Kelly, J. A. (1983). Social skills training for an extremely shy young adolescent: A case study. *Behavior Therapy, 14*, 568–575.

Friedlander, S., Philips, I., & Morrison, D. (1981). *Depression in childhood: An exploratory study*. Paper presented at the American Psychological Association, Los Angeles, California.

Furman, W., & Buhrmester, D. (1985). Children's perceptions of the personal relationships in their social networks. *Developmental Psychology, 21*, 1016–1024.

Furman, W., Rahe, D. F., & Hartup, W. W. (1979). Rehabilitation of socially withdrawn preschool children through mixed-age and same-age socialization. *Child Development, 50*, 915–922.

Garvey, W., & Hergrenes, J. (1966). Desensitization technique in the treatment of school phobia. *American Journal of Orthopsychiatry, 36*, 147–152.

Genshaft, J. L. (1982). The use of cognitive behavior therapy for reducing math anxiety. *School Psychology Review, 11*, 32–34.

Gersten, J. C., Langer, T. S., Eisenberg, J. B., Simcha-Fagen, O., & McCarthy, E. D. (1976). Stability and change in types of behavioral disturbance of children and adolescents. *Journal of Abnormal Child Psychology, 4*, 111–127.

Gesten, E. L., de Apodaca, R. F., Rains, M., Weissberg, R. P., & Cowen, E. L. (1979). Promoting peer related social competence in schools. In M. W. Kent & J. E. Rolf (Eds.), *Primary prevention of psychopathology,* (Vol. 3). *Social competence in children* (pp. 220–241). Hanover, NH: University Press of New England.

Gesten, E. L., Rains, M. H., Rapkin, B. D., Weissberg, R. P., de Apodaca, R. F., Cowen, E. L., & Bowen, R. (1982). Training children in social problem-solving competencies: A first and second look. *American Journal of Community Psychology, 10*, 95–115.

Gilbert, G. M. (1957). A survey of "referral problems" in metropolitan child guidance centers. *Journal of Clinical Psychology, 13*, 37–42.

Gillespie, J. F., Durlak, J. A., & Sherman, D. (1982). Relationship between kindergarten children's interpersonal problem-solving skills and other indices of school adjustment: a cautionary note. *American Journal of Community Psychology, 10*, 149–153.

Gjesme, T. (1983). Worry and emotionality components of test anxiety in relation to situational and personality determinants. *Psychological Reports, 52*, 267–280.

Glow, R., & Glow, P. (1982). The stability of child behavior disorders: A one year test-retest study of Adelaide versions of the Conners Teacher and Parent Rating Scales. *Journal of Abnormal Child Psychology, 10*, 33–60.

Goetz, T. E., & Dweck, C. S. (1980). Learned helplessness in social situations. *Journal of Personality and Social Psychology, 39*, 246–255.

Goldfried, M. R., & Merbaum, M. (1973). *Behavior change through self-control*. New York: Holt, Reinhart, & Winston.

Goldiamond, I. (1976). Self-reinforcement as an explanatory fiction. *Journal of Applied Behavior Analysis, 9*, 509–514.

Goodwin, S., & Mahoney, M. J. (1975). Modification of aggression through modeling: An experimental probe. *Journal of Behavior Therapy and Experimental Psychiatry, 6*, 200–202.

Gottman, J. M. (1977). The effects of a modeling film on social isolation in preschool children: A methodological investigation. *Journal of Abnormal Child Psychology, 5*, 69–78.

Gottman, J. M., Gonso, J., & Rasmussen, B. (1975). Social interaction, social competence, and friendship in children. *Child Development, 46*, 709–718.

Gottman, J. M., Gonso, J., & Schuler, P. (1976). Teaching social skills to isolated children. *Journal of Abnormal Child Psychology, 4*, 179–197.

Gouze, K., Rayias, M., & Bieber-Schneider, R. (August, 1983). *Cognitive correlates of aggression in second grade children.* Paper presented at the annual meeting of the American Psychological Association, Anaheim, California.

Goyette, C., Conners, K., & Ulrich, R. (1978). Normative data on revised Conners Parent and Teacher Rating Scales. *Journal of Abnormal Child Psychology, 6*, 221–236.

Graziano, A. M., & Mooney, K. C. (1980). Family self-control instruction for children's nighttime fear reduction. *Journal of Consulting and Clinical Psychology, 48*, 206–213.

Graziano, A. M., Mooney, K. C., Huber, C., & Ignasiak, D. (1979). Self-control instruction for children's fear reduction. *Journal of Behavior Therapy and Experimental Psychiatry, 10*, 221–227.

Green, K. P., Forehand, R., Beck, S. J., & Vosk, B. (1980). An assessment of the relationship among measures of children's social competence and children's academic achievement. *Child Development, 51*, 1149–1156.

Greenberg, L., & Erickson, W. (1982). Pharmacotherapy of children and adolescents. In C. Reynolds & T. Gutkin (Eds.), *The handbook of school psychology.* New York: Wiley.

Greenspan, S. (1981). *The clinical interview of the child.* New York: McGraw-Hill.

Greenwood, C. R., Walker, H. M., Todd, N. M., & Hops, H. (1979). Selecting a cost effective screening device for the assessment of preschool social withdrawal. *Journal of Applied Behavior Analysis, 12*, 639–652.

Gresham, F. M., & Nagle, R. J. (1980). Social skills training with children: Responsiveness to modeling and coaching as a function of peer orientation. *Journal of Consulting and Clinical Psychology, 48*, 718–729.

Grieger, R. M., & Boyd, J. D. (1983). Childhood anxieties, fears, and phobias: A cognitive-behavioral psychosituational approach. In A. Ellis & M. E. Bernard (Eds.), *Rational-emotive approaches to problems of childhood.* New York: Plenum Press.

Gronlund, N. E. (1959). *Sociometry in the classroom.* New York: Harper.

Gurucharri, C., Phelps, E., & Selman, R. (1984). Development of interpersonal understanding: A longitudinal and comparative study of normal and disturbed youths. *Journal of Consulting and Clinical Psychology, 52*, 26–36.

Halparin, J., Gittlemen, R., Klein, D., & Rudel. (1984). Reading-disabled hyperactive children: A distinct subgroup of attention deficit disorder with hyperactivity. *Journal of Abnormal Child Psychology, 12*(1), 1–14.

Hamilton, M. (1960). A rating scale for depression. *Journal of Neurology, Neurosurgery and Psychiatry, 23*, 56–62.

Hamilton, M. (1967). Development of a rating scale for primary depressive illness. *British Journal of Social and Clinical Psychology, 6*, 278–296.

Hart, B. M., Reynolds, N. J., Baer, D. M., Brawley, E. R., & Harris, F. R. (1968). Effect of contingent and noncontingent social reinforcement on the cooperative play of a preschool child. *Journal of Applied Behavior Analysis, 1*, 73–76.

Hartmann, D. P., Roper, B. L., & Bradford, D. C. (1979). Some relationships between behavioral and traditional assessment. *Journal of Behavioral Assessment, 1*, 3–21.

Hartup, W. W. (1974). Aggression in childhood: Developmental perspectives. *American Psychologist, 29*, 336–341.

Hartup, W. W., Glazer, J. A., & Charlesworth, R. (1967). Peer reinforcement and sociometric status. *Child Development, 38*, 1017–1024.

Hebb, D. O. (1960). The American revolution. *American Psychologist, 15*, 735–745.

Herbert, M. (1978). *Conduct disorders of childhood and adolescence: A behavioural approach to assessment and treatment.* Chichester, England: John Wiley & Sons.

Herjanic, B., & Reich, W. (1982). Development of a structured psychiatric interview for children: Agreement between child and parent on individual symptoms. *Journal of Abnormal Child Psychology, 10*, 307–324.

Herzog, D. B., & Rathbun, J. M. (1982). Childhood depression: Developmental considerations. *American Journal of the Disabled Child, 136*, 115–120.

Hobbs, S., Moguin, L., Tyroler, M., & Lahey, B. (1980). Cognitive behavior therapy with children: Has clinical utility been demonstrated? *Psychological Bulletin, 87*, 147–165.

Hodges, K., Kline, J., Stern, L., Cytryn, L., & McKnew, D. (1982). The development of a child assessment interview for research and clinical use. *Journal of Abnormal Child Psychology, 10*, 173–189.

Hodges, K., McKnew, D., Cytryn, L., Stern, L., & Kline, J. (1982). The Child Assessment Schedule (CAS) Diagnostic Interview: A report on reliability and validity. *Journal of the American Academy of Child Psychiatry, 21*, 468–413.

Holinger, P. C., & Offer, D. (1981). Perspectives on suicide in adolescents. In R. Simmons (Ed.), *Research in community mental health,* Vol. 2 (pp. 139–157). Greenwich, CT: JAI Press.

Hollandsworth, J., Glazeski, R., Kirkland, K., Jones, G., & Van Norman, L. (1979). An analysis of the nature and effects of text anxiety: Cognitive, behavioral, and physiological components. *Cognitive Therapy and Research, 3*, 165–180.

Holroyd, K. A. (1976). Cognition and desensitization in the group treatment of test anxiety. *Journal of Consulting and Clinical Psychology, 44*, 991–1001.

Homme, L. (1965). Perspectives in psychology: Control of coverants, the operants of the mind. *Psychological Record, 15*, 501–511.

Hops, H., Fleischman, D. H., Guild, J., Paine, S., Street, H., Walker, H. M., & Greenwood, C. R. (1978). *Program for establishing effective relationship skills (PEERS): Consultant manual.* Eugene: University of Oregon, Center at Oregon for Research in the Behavioral Education of the Handicapped.

Hops, H., & Greenwood, C. R. (in press). Social skill deficits. In E. J. Mash & L. G. Terdal (Eds.), *Behavioral assessment of childhood disorders* (2nd Ed.). New York: Guilford.

Hsia, H. (1984). Structural and strategic approach to school phobia/school refusal. *Psychology in the Schools, 21*, 360–367.

Hughes, J. N. (in press-a). Assessment of children's social competence. In C. R. Reynolds & R. L. Kamphaus (Eds.), *Handbook of psychological and educational assessment of children.* New York: Guilford.

Hughes, J. N. (in press-b). Brief psychotherapies In T. Gutkin & C. R. Reynolds (Eds.), *Handbook of school psychology* (2nd Ed.). New York: John Wiley & Sons.

Hughes, J. N. (in press-c). Interviewing children. In J. Dillard, & R. Reilley (Eds.), *Interviewing and communication skills.* New York: Charles Merrill.

Hughes, J. N. (1986). Methods of skill selection in social skills training: A review. *Professional School Psychology, 1*, 235–248.

Hughes, J. N., & Hall, D. M. (1985). Performance of disturbed and nondisturbed boys on a role play test of social competence. *Behavioral Disorders, 11*, 24–29.

Hughes, J. N., & Hall, R. J. (1987). A proposed model for the assessment of children's social competence. *Professional School Psychology, 2*, 247–260.

Hughes, J. N., & Sullivan, K. (in press). Outcome-assessment in social skills training with children. *Journal of School Psychology.*

Humphrey, L. L. (1982). Children's and teachers' perspectives on children's self-control: The development of two rating scales. *Journal of Consulting and Clinical Psychology, 50*, 624–633.

Hymel, S., & Asher, S. R. (March, 1977). *Assessment and training of isolated children's social skills.* Paper presented at the biennial meeting of the Society for Research in Child Development, New Orleans (ERIC Document Service Reproduction Service No. ED136930).

Jakibchuk, Z., & Smeriglio, V. L. (1976). The influence of symbolic modeling on the social behavior of preschool children with low levels of social responsiveness. *Child Development, 47*, 838–841.

Jason, L. A., Durlak, J. A., & Holton-Walker, E. (1984). Prevention of child problems in the schools. In M. C. Roberts & L. Peterson (Eds.), *Prevention of problems in childhood* (pp. 311–341). New York: John Wiley & Sons.

Jones, M. C. (1924). The elimination of children's fears. *Journal of Experimental Psychology, 7*, 383–390.

Jones, W. H., Hobb, S. A., & Hockenbury, D. (1982). Loneliness and social skill deficits. *Journal of Personality and Social Psychology, 42*, 682–689.

Joyce, B. B., & Weil, M. (1972). *Models of teaching.* Englewood Cliffs, NJ: Prentice-Hall.

Kagan, J. (1966). The generality and dynamics of conceptual tempo. *Journal of Abnormal Child Psychology, 71*, 17–24.

Kagan, J., & Messer, S. (1975). A reply to "Some misgivings about the Matching Familiar Figures Test as a measure of impulsivity." *Developmental Psychology, 11*, 244–248.

Kagan, J., Pearson, L., & Welch, L. (1966). Modifiability of an impulsive tempo. *Journal of Educational Psychology, 57*, 358–365.

Kagan, J., Rosman, B. L., Day, D., Albert, J., & Phillips, W. (1964). Information processing in the child: Significance of analytic and reflective attitudes. *Psychological Monographs* (Whole No. 578).

Kanfer, F. H. (1970). Self-regulation: Research, issues, and speculations. In C. Neuringer & J. L. Michael (Eds.), *Behavior modification in clinical psychology.* New York: Appleton-Century-Crofts.

Kanfer, F. H., & Karoly, P. (1972). Self-control: A behavioristic excursion into the lion's den. *Behavior Therapy, 3*, 398–416.

Kanfer, F. H., Karoly, P., & Newman, A. (1975). Reduction of children's fear of the dark by competence-related and situational threat-related verbal cues. *Journal of Consulting and Clinical Psychology, 43*, 251–259.

Kaplan, R. M., McCordick, S. M., & Twitchell, M. (1979). Is it the cognitive or the behavioral component that makes cognitive-behavior modification effective in test anxiety? *Journal of Counseling Psychology, 26*, 371–377.

Kashani, J. H., & Cantwell, D. P. (1983). Etiology and treatment of childhood depression: A biopsychological perspective. *Comprehensive Psychiatry, 24*, 476–486.

Kaslow, N. J., & Rehm, L. P. (1983). Childhood depression. In R. J. Morris and T. R. Kratochwill (Eds.), *The practice of child therapy* (pp. 27–51). New York: Pergamon Press.

Kaslow, N. J., Rehm, L. P., & Siegel, A. W. (1984). Social-cognitive and cognitive correlates of depression in children. *Journal of Abnormal Child Psychology, 12*, 605–620.

Kaslow, N. J., Tanenbaum, R. L., & Seligman, M. E. P. (1978). *The KASTAN: A children's attributional styles questionnaire*: Unpublished manuscript, University of Pennsylvania.

Kazdin, A. E. (1985). Selection of target behaviors: The relationship of the treatment focus to clinical dysfunction. *Behavioral Assessment, 7*, 33–47.

Kazdin, A. E., Colbus, D., & Rodgers, A. (1986). Assessment of depression and diagnosis of depressive disorder among psychiatrically disturbed children. *Journal of Abnormal Child Psychology, 14*, 499–515.

Kazdin, A. E., Esveldt-Dawson, K., French, N. H., & Unis, A. S. (1987). Problem-solving skills training and relationship therapy in the treatment of antisocial child behavior. *Journal of Consulting and Clinical Psychology, 55*, 76–85.

Kazdin, A. E., & Frame, C. (1983). Aggressive behavior and conduct disorder. In R. J. Morris & T. R. Kratochwill (Eds.), *The practice of child therapy* (pp. 167–192). New York: Pergamon Press.

Kazdin, A. E., French, N. H., Unis, A. S., & Esveldt-Dawson, K. (1983). Assessment of childhood depression: Correspondence of child and parent ratings. *Journal of the American Academy of Child Psychiatry, 22*, 157–164.

Kazdin, A. E., French, N. H., Unis, A. S., Esveldt-Dawson, K., & Sherick, R. B. (1983). Hopelessness, depression, and suicidal intent among psychiatrically disturbed inpatient children. *Journal of Consulting and Clinical Psychology, 51*, 504–510.

Kazdin, A. E., Rodgers, A., & Colbus, D. (1986). The Hopelessness Scale for Children: Psychometric characteristics and concurrent validity. *Journal of Consulting and Clinical Psychology, 54*, 241–245.

Keavney, G., & Sinclair, K. E. (1978). Teacher concerns and teacher anxiety: A neglected topic of classroom research. *Review of Educational Research, 48*, 273–290.

Keeney, T. J., Canizzo, S. R., & Flavell, J. H. (1967). Spontaneous and induced verbal rehearsal in a recall task. *Child Development, 38*, 953–966.

Keller, M. F., & Carlson, P. M. (1974). The use of symbolic modeling to promote social skills in preschool children with low levels of social responsiveness. *Child Development, 45*, 912–919.

Kendall, P., & Braswell, L. (1982). Cognitive-behavioral self-control therapy for children: A components analysis. *Journal of Consulting and Clinical Psychology, 50*, 672–689.

Kendall, P. C., & Braswell, L. (1985). *Cognitive-behavioral therapy for impulsive children*. New York: Guilford.

Kendall, P. C., & Finch, A. J., Jr. (1979). Developing nonimpulsive behavior in children: Cognitive-behavioral strategies for self-control. In P. C. Kendall & S. D. Hollon (Eds.), *Cognitive-behavioral interventions: Theory, research, and procedure*. New York: Academic Press.

Kendall, P. C., Finch, A. J., Little, V. L., Chirico, B. M., & Ollendick, T. H. (1978). Variations in a construct: Quantitative and qualitative differences in children's locus of control. *Journal of Consulting and Clinical Psychology, 46*, 590–592.

endall, P. C., & Fischler, G. L. (1984). Behavioral and adjustment correlates of problem solving: Validational analyses of interpersonal cognitive problem-solving measures. *Child Development, 55*, 879–892.

endall, P. C., & Hollon, S. D. (1979). Cognitive-behavioral interventions: Overview and current status. In P. C. Kendall & S. D. Hollon (Eds.), *Cognitive-behavioral interventions: Theory, research and procedures* (pp. 1–9). New York: Academic Press.

endall, P. C., Lerner, R., & Craighead, W. (1984). Human development and intervention in childhood psychopathology. *Child Development, 55*, 71–82.

endall, P. C., & Morrison, P. (1984). Integrating cognitive and behavioral procedures for the treatment of socially isolated children. In A. W. Meyers & W. E. Craighead (Eds.), *Cognitive behavior therapy with children* (pp. 261–288). New York: Plenum Press.

endall, P. C., Pellegrini, D. S., & Urbain, E. S. (1981). Approaches to assessment for cognitive-behavioral interventions with children. In P. C. Kendall & S. D. Hollon (Eds.), *Assessment strategies for cognitive-behavioral interventions.* New York: Academic Press.

endall, P., & Wilcox, L. (1979). Self-control in children: Development of a rating scale. *Journal of Consulting and Clinical Psychology, 47*, 1020–1029.

endall, P., & Wilcox, L. (1980). A cognitive-behavioral treatment for impulsivity: Concrete versus conceptual training in non-self-controlled problem children. *Journal of Consulting and Clinical Psychology, 48*, 80–91.

endall, P., & Zupan, B. (1981). Individual versus group application of cognitive-behavioral strategies for developing self-control in children. *Behavior Therapy, 12*, 344–359.

ennedy, W. A. (1965). School phobia: Rapid treatment of fifty cases. *Journal of Abnormal Psychology, 70*, 285–289.

eogh, B., & Hall, R. (1984). Cognitive training with learning-disabled pupils. In A. W. Meyers & W. E. Craighead (Eds.), *Cognitive behavior therapy with children* (pp. 163–191). New York: Plenum Press.

ettlewell, P. W., & Kausch, D. F. (1983). The generalization of the effects of a cognitive-behavioral treatment program for aggressive children. *Journal of Abnormal Child Psychology, 11*, 101–114.

irschenbaum, D. S., & Ordman, A. M. (1984). Preventive interventions for children: Cognitive behavioral perspectives. In A. W. Meyers & W. E. Craighead (Eds.), *Cognitive behavior therapy with children* (pp. 377–409). New York: Plenum Press.

naus, W. (1974). *Rational-emotive education: A manual for elementary school teachers.* New York: Institute for Rational Living.

ohn, M. (1977). The Kohn Social Competence Scale and Kohn Symptom Checklist for the preschool child: A follow-up report. *Journal of Abnormal Child Psychology, 5*, 249–263.

olb, K., & Whishaw, I. (1984). *Fundamentals of human neuropsychology.* San Francisco: W. H. Freeman.

omm, R. (1982). He's "LD"—I mean he's "ADD." *Academic Therapy, 17*(4), 431–435.

ondas, O. (1967). Reduction of examination anxiety and "stage fright" by group desensitization and relaxation. *Behavior Research and Therapy, 5*, 275–281.

ornhaber, R. C., & Schroeder, H. E. (1974). Importance of model similarity on extinction of avoidance behavior in children. *Journal of Consulting and Clinical Psychology, 43*, 601–607.

Kovacs, M. (1980/1981). Rating scales to assess depression in school-aged children. *Actor Paedopsychiatry, 46*, 305–315.

Kovacs, M. (1982). *The longitudinal study of child and adolescent psychopathology I. The semi-structured psychiatric interview schedule for children (ISC).* Unpublished manuscript. University of Pittsburgh School of Medicine-Western Psychiatric Institute.

Kovacs, M. (1983). *Children's Depression Inventory.* Available from Maria Kovacs University of Pittsburgh School of Medicine-Western Psychiatric Institute.

Kovacs, M., & Beck, A. T. (1977). An empirical-clinical approach toward a definition of childhood depression. In J. G. Schulterbrandt & A. Raskin (Eds.), *Depression in childhood: Diagnosis, treatment, and conceptual models.* New York: Raven Press.

Kratochwill, T. R. (1985). Selection of target behaviors in behavioral consultation. *Behavioral Assessment, 7*, 49–61.

Kupietz, S., Bailer, I., & Winsberg, B. (1972). A behavior rating scale for assessing improvement in behaviorally deviant children: A preliminary investigation. *American Journal of Psychiatry, 128*, 1432–1436.

Kuypers, D. S., Becker, W. C., & O'Leary, K. D. (1968). How to make a token system fail. *Exceptional Children, 35*, 101–109.

Ladd, G. W. (1981). Effectiveness of a social learning model for enhancing children's social interaction and peer acceptance. *Child Development, 52*, 171–178.

Ladd, G. W., & Mize, J. (1983). A cognitive-social learning model of social skill training. *Psychological Review, 90*, 127–157.

Ladd, G. W., & Oden, S. (1979). The relationship between peer acceptance and children's ideas about helpfulness. *Child Development, 50*, 402–408.

LaGreca, A. M., & Santogrossi, D. D. (1980). Social skills training with elementary school students: A behavioral group approach. *Journal of Consulting and Clinical Psychology, 48*, 220–228.

Lambert, N. M., & Bower, E. M. (1961). *A process for in-school screening of children with emotional handicaps.* Princeton, NJ: Educational Testing Service.

Landau, S., Milich, R., & Whitten, P. (1984). A comparison of teacher and peer assessment of social status. *Journal of Clinical Child Psychology, 13*, 44–49.

Lapouse, R., & Monk, M. A. (1959). Fears and worries in a representative sample of children. *American Journal of Orthopsychiatry, 29*, 803–818.

Laughlin, F. (1954). *The peer status of sixth- and seventh-grade children.* Bureau of Publication, Teachers College, Columbia University, New York.

Laxer, R. M., Quarter, J., Kooman, A., & Walker, K. (1969). Systematic desensitization and relaxation of high test-anxious secondary school students. *Journal of Counseling Psychology, 16*, 446–451.

Lazarus, A. A. (1960). The elimination of children's phobias by deconditioning. In H. J. Eysenck (Ed.), *Behavior therapy and the neuroses.* Oxford: Pergamon Press.

Lazarus, A. A., Davison, G. C., & Polefka, D. A. (1965). Classical and operant factors in the treatment of school phobia. *Journal of Abnormal Psychology, 70*, 225–229.

Leal, L. L., Baxter, E. G., Martin, J., & Marx, R. W. (1981). Cognitive modification and systematic desensitization with test anxious high school students. *Journal of Counseling Psychology, 28*, 525–528.

Lefebvre, M. F. (1981). Cognitive distortion and cognitive errors in depressed psychiatric and low back pain patients. *Journal of Consulting and Clinical Psychology, 49*, 517–525.

Lefkowitz, M. M., & Burton, N. (1978). Childhood depression: A critique of the concept. *Psychological Bulletin, 85*, 716–726.

Lefkowitz, M. M., Eron, L. D., Walder, L. O., & Huesman, L. R. (1977). *Growing up to be violent.* New York: Pergamon Press.

Leitenberg, H., Yost, L. W., & Carroll-Wilson, M. (1986). Negative cognitive errors in children: Questionnaire development, normative data, and comparisons between children with and without self-reported symptoms of depression, low self-esteem, and evaluation anxiety. *Journal of Consulting and Clinical Psychology, 54*, 528–536.

Lepper, M. R., & Greene, D. (1975). Turning play into work: Effects of adult surveillance and extrinsic rewards on children's intrinsic motivation. *Journal of Personality and Social Psychology, 31*, 479–486.

Lepper, M. R., Greene, D., & Nisbett, R. E. (1973). Undermining children's intrinsic interest with extrinsic reward: A test of the "overjustification" hypothesis. *Journal of Personality and Social Psychology, 28*, 129–137.

Lewinsohn, P. M. (1974). A behavioral approach to depression. In R. M. Friedman & M. M. Katz (Eds.), *The psychology of depression: Contemporary theory and research.* New York: John Wiley & Sons.

Little, S., & Jackson, B. (1974). The treatment of test anxiety through attentional and relaxation training. *Psychotherapy: Theory, research, and practice, 11*, 175–178.

Lloyd, J., & Loper, A. (1986). Measurement and evaluation of task-related learning behaviors: Attention to task and metacognition. *Psychology Review, 15*(3), 336–345.

Lobovits, D. A., & Handal, P. J. (1985). Childhood depression: Prevalence using DSM-III criteria and validity of parent and child depression scales. *Journal of Pediatric Psychology, 10*, 45–54.

Lochman, J. E., Burch, P. R., Curry, J. F., & Lampron, L. B. (1984). Treatment and generalization effects of cognitive behavioral and goal setting interventions with aggressive boys. *Journal of Consulting and Clinical Psychology, 52*, 915–916.

Lochman, J. E., & Lampron, L. B. (1986). Situational social problem-solving skills and self-esteem of aggressive and nonaggressive boys. *Journal of Abnormal Child Psychology, 14*, 605–617.

Lochman, J. E., Lampron, L. B., Burch, P. R., & Curry, J. F. (1985). Client characteristics associated with treatment outcome for aggressive boys. *Journal of Abnormal Child Psychology, 13*, 527–538.

Lochman, J. E., Nelson, W. M. III, & Sims, J. P. (1981). A cognitive behavioral program for use with aggressive children. *Journal of Clinical Child Psychology, 10*, 146–148.

Lorion, R. P., & Cowen, E. L. (1976). Comparison of two outcome groups in a school-based mental health project. *American Journal of Community Psychology, 4*, 56–63.

Lovaas, O. I. (1968). A program for the establishment of speech in psychotic children. In K. N. Sloane & S. P. MacAulay (Eds.), *Operant procedures in remedial speech and language training.* Boston: Houghton Mifflin.

Luria, A. (1959). The directive function of speech in development. *Werd, 18*, 341–352.

Luria, A. R. (1961). *The role of speech in the regulation of normal and abnormal behaviors.* New York: Liverwright.

McClure, L. F., Chinsky, J. M., & Larcen, S. W. (1978). Enhancing social problem-solving performance in an elementary school setting. *Journal of Educational Psychology, 70*, 504–513.

McFall, R. M. (1982). A review and reformulation of the concept of social skills. *Behavioral Assessment, 4*, 1–33.

McMahon, R. J. (1984). Behavioral checklists and rating scales. In T. H. Ollendick & M. Hersen (Eds.), *Child behavioral assessment* (pp. 80–105). New York: Pergamon Press.

McReynolds, R. A., Morris, R. J., & Kratochwill, T. R. (in press). In J. N. Hughes & R. J. Hall (Eds.), *Cognitive-behavioral approaches in educational settings*. New York: Guilford Press.

Mahoney, M. J. (1974). *Cognition and behavior modification*. Cambridge, MA: Ballinger.

Mahoney, M. J. (1976). On terminal terminology. *Journal of Applied Behavior Analysis, 9*, 515–517.

Mahoney, M. J. (1977). A critical analysis of rational-emotive theory and therapy. *Counseling Psychologist, 7*, 44–46.

Margolis, R. B., & Mynatt, C. R. (1986). The effects of external and self-administered reward on high base rate behavior. *Cognitive Therapy and Research, 10*, 109–122.

Marholin, D., & Steinman, W. M. (1977). Stimulus control in the classroom as a function of the behavior reinforced. *Journal of Applied Behavior Analysis, 10*, 465–478.

Marsh, D. T., Serafica, F. C., & Barenboim, C. (1980). Effect of perspective taking training on interpersonal problem solving. *Child Development, 51*, 140–145.

Masten, A. S., Morison, P., & Pellegrini, D. S. (1985). A revised class play method of peer assessment. *Developmental Psychology, 21*, 523–533.

Matthews, W. S., & Brooks-Gunn, J. (1984). Social development in childhood. In A. W. Meyers & W. E. Craighead (Eds.), *Cognitive behavior therapy with children* (pp. 19–44). New York: Plenum Press.

Meichenbaum, D. H. (1971). Examination of model characteristics in reducing avoidance behavior. *Journal of Personality and Social Psychology, 17*, 298–307.

Meichenbaum, D. H. (1972). Cognitive modification of test anxious college students. *Journal of Consulting and Clinical Psychology, 39*, 370–380.

Meichenbaum, D. H. (1977). *Cognitive-behavior modification: An integrative approach*. New York: Plenum Press.

Meichenbaum, D. H., Bowers, K. S., & Ross, R. R. (1968). Modification of classroom behavior of institutionalized female adolescent offenders. *Behavior Research and Therapy, 6*, 343–353.

Meichenbaum, D., & Cameron, R. (1981). Issues in cognitive assessment: An overview. In T. V. Merluzzi, C. R. Glass, & M. Genest (Eds.), *Cognitive assessment* (pp. 3–15). New York: Guilford Press.

Meichenbaum, D., & Genest, M. (1980). Cognitive behavior modification: An integration of cognitive and behavioral methods. In F. H. Kanfer & A. P. Goldstein (Eds.), *Helping people change* (2nd Ed.), New York: Pergamon Press.

Meichenbaum, D., & Goodman, J. (1969). Reflection-impulsivity and verbal control of motor behavior. *Child Development, 40*, 785–797.

Meichenbaum, D., & Goodman, J. (1971). Training impulsive children to talk to themselves: A means of developing self-control. *Journal of Abnormal Psychology, 77*, 115–126.

Melamed, B., & Siegel, L. (1975). Reduction of anxiety in children facing hospitalization and surgery by use of filmed modeling. *Journal of Consulting and Clinical Psychology, 43*, 511–521.

Messer, S. (1976). Reflection-impulsivity: A review. *Psychological Bulletin, 83*, 1026–1052.

Michelson, L., Foster, S., & Ritchey, W. (1981). Social skill assessment of children. In B. B. Lahey & A. E. Kazdin (Eds.), *Advances in Clinical Child Psychology* (pp. 119–165). New York: Plenum.

Michelson, L., & Wood, R. (1982). Development and psychometric properties of the Children's Assertive Behavior Scale. *Journal of Behavioral Assessment, 4*, 3–13.

Miller, L. C., Barrett, C. L., & Hampe, E. (1974). Phobias of childhood in a prescientific era. In A. Davids (Ed.), *Child personality and psychopathology: Current topics.* New York: John Wiley & Sons.

Miller, P. M. (1972). The use of visual imagery and muscle relaxation in the counter conditioning of a phobic child: A case study. *Journal of Nervous and Mental Disease, 154*, 457–460.

Mischel, W. (1974). Processes in delay of gratification. In L. Berkowitz (Ed.), *Advances in experimental social psychology,* Vol. 7. New York: Academic Press.

Mischel, W. (1981). A cognitive-social learning approach to assessment. In T. V. Merluzzi, C. R. Glass, & M. Genest (Eds.), *Cognitive assessment* (pp. 479–502). New York: Guilford Press.

Moreno, J. (1934). *Who shall survive? A new approach to the problem of human interrelations.* Washington, D.C.: Nervous and Mental Disease Publishing.

Morris, L. W., Brown, N. R., & Halbert, B. L. (1977). Effects of symbolic modeling on the arousal of cognitive and affective components of anxiety in preschool children. In C. D. Spielberger & I. G. Sarason (Eds.), *Stress and anxiety,* Vol. 4, (pp. 153–170). New York: John Wiley & Sons.

Morris, R. J., & Kratochwill, T. R. (1983). *Treating children's fears and phobias: A behavioral approach.* New York: Pergamon Press.

Muma, J. R. (1965). Peer evaluation and academic achievement performance. *Personnel Guidance Journal, 44*, 405–409.

Nasby, W., Hayden, B., & DePaulo, B. M. (1980). Attributional bias among aggressive boys to interpret unambiguous social stimuli as displays of hostility. *Journal of Abnormal Psychology, 89*, 459–548.

Neisser, U. (1967). *Cognitive Psychology.* New York: Appleton-Century-Crofts.

Nelson, W. M., III, & Finch, A. J., Jr. (1978). *The children's inventory of anger.* Unpublished manuscript, Xavier University.

Neitzel, M. T., & Bernstein, D. A. (1981). Assessment of anxiety and fear. In M. Hersen & A. A. Bellack (Eds.), *Behavioral assessment: A practical handbook* (2nd Ed.). New York: Pergamon Press.

Nowicki, S., & Strickland, B. R. (1973). A locus of control scale for children. *Journal of Consulting and Clinical Psychology, 40*, 148–155.

O'Brien, P. A. (1982). Construct validity of the Children's Depression Inventory: *A multi-trait, multi-method approach.* Paper presented at the 28th Annual Meeting of the Southeastern Psychological Association, New Orleans.

O'Connor, R. D. (1969). Modification of social withdrawal through symbolic modeling. *Journal of Applied Behavior Analysis, 2*, 15–22.

O'Connor, R. D. (1972). Relative efficacy of modeling, shaping and the combined procedures for modification of social withdrawal. *Journal of Abnormal Psychology, 79,* 327–334.

Oden, S., & Asher, S. (1977). Coaching children in skills for friendship making. *Child Development, 48*, 495–506.

O'Farrell, T. J., Hedlund, M. A., & Cutter, H. S. G. (1981). Desensitization for a severe phobia of a fourteen-year-old male. *Child Behavior Therapy, 3*, 67–77.

O'Keefe, E. (1975). Porteus Maze Q score as a measure of impulsivity. *Perceptual and Motor Skills, 41*, 675–678.

O'Leary, K. D., Becker, W. C., Evans, M. B., & Saudargas, R. A. (1969). A token reinforcement program in a public school: A replication and systematic analysis. *Journal of Applied Behavior Analysis, 2*, 3–13.

O'Leary, K. D., & O'Leary, S. G. (1972). *Classroom management: The successful use of behavior modification.* New York: Pergamon Press.

O'Leary, K. D. (1980). Pills or skills for hyperactive children. *Journal of Applied Behavior Analysis, 13*, 191–204.

Olexa, P. F., & Forman, S. G. (1984). Effects of social problem-solving training on classroom behavior of urban disadvantaged students. *Journal of School Psychology, 22*, 165–176.

Ollendick, T. H. (1984). *Outcome Expectancy Questionnaire-Children (R).* Unpublished test, Virginia Polytechnic Institute & State University, Blacksburg, Virginia.

Ollendick, T. H., Crowe, H. P., & Oswald, D. (November, 1986). *Self-efficacy in aggressive withdrawn and popular children.* Paper presented at the annual meeting of the Association for the Advancement of Behavior Therapy, Houston.

Ollendick, T. H., & Hersen, M. (1979). Social skills training for juvenile delinquents. *Behavior Research and Therapy, 17*, 547–554.

Ollendick, T. H., & Hersen, M. (1984). *Child behavioral assessment.* New York: Pergamon Press.

Ollendick, T. H., Oswald, I., & Crowe, H. P. (November, 1986). *The development of the Self-Efficacy Scale for Social Skills in children.* Paper presented at the annual meeting of the Association for the Advancement of Behavior Therapy, Houston.

Olweus, D. (1979). Stability of aggressive behavior patterns in males: A review. *Psychological Bulletin, 86*, 852–875.

Palkes, H., Stewart, M., & Freedman, J. (1972). Improvement in maze performance of hyperactive boys as a function of verbal training procedures. *Journal of Special Education, 5*, 337–342.

Palkes, H., Stewart, M., & Kahana, B. (1968). Porteus Maze performance of hyperactive boys after training in self-directed verbal commands. *Child Development, 39*, 817–826.

Palmer, D. J., Pfefferbaum, B., & Stowe, M. L. (1986). *A comparison of depressed and non-depressed disturbed children on measures of attributional style, hopelessness, life stress, and temperament.* Unpublished manuscript, Texas A&M University, College Station, Texas.

Palmer, D. J., & Rholes, W. S. (in press). Conceptual and methodological issues in the assessment of children's attributions. In J. Hughes & R. Hall (Eds.), *Cognitive-behavioral approaches in educational settings.* New York: Guilford Press.

Panella, D., & Henggeler, S. W. (1986). Peer interactions of conduct-disordered, anxious-withdrawn, and well-adjusted black adolescents. *Journal of Abnormal Child Psychology, 14*, 1–11.

Paris, S., Cross, D., & Lipson, M. (1984). Informed strategies for learning: A program to improve children's reading awareness and comprehension. *Journal of Educational Psychology, 76*, 1239–1252.

Parry, P. (1973). *The effect of reward on the performance of hyperactive children.* Unpublished doctoral dissertation, McGill University.

Parry, P., & Douglas, V. I. (1983). Effects of reinforcement on concept identification in hyperactive children. *Journal of Abnormal Child Psychology, 2*, 327–340.

Patterson, G. R., Reid, J. B., Jones, R. R., & Conger, R. E. (1975). *A social learning approach to family intervention,* Vol. 1. Eugene, OR: Castalia.

Peery, J. C. (1979). Popular, amiable, isolated, rejected: A reconceptualization of sociometric status in preschool children. *Child Development, 50*, 1231–1234.

Pellegrini, D. S. (1980). *The social-cognitive qualities of stress-resistant children.* Doctoral dissertation, University of Minnesota.

Pellegrini, D. S., & Urbain, E. S. (1985). An evaluation of cognitive problem-solving training with children. *Journal of Child Psychology and Psychiatry, 26*, 17–41.

Perry, D. G., Perry, L. C., & Rasmussen, P. (1986). Cognitive social learning mediators of aggression. *Child Development, 57*, 700–711.

Perry, M. A., & Furukawa, M. J. (1980). Modeling methods. In F. H. Kanfer & A. P. Goldstein (Eds.), *Helping people change* (2nd Ed.). New York: Pergamon Press.

Peterson, L., & Shigetomi C. (1981). The use of coping techniques in minimizing anxiety in hospitalized children. *Behavior Therapy, 12*, 1–14.

Petti, T. A., Bornstein, M., Delamater, A., & Conners, C. K. (1980). Evaluation and multimodality treatment of a depressed prepubertal girl. *Journal of the American Association of Child Psychiatry, 19*, 690–702.

Pfeffer, C. R., Solomon, G., Plutchik, R., Mizruchi, M. S., & Weiner, A. (1982). Suicidal behavior in latency-age psychiatric inpatients: A replication and cross-validation. *Journal of the American Academy of Child Psychiatry, 21*, 564–569.

Phillips, B. N. (1978). *School stress and anxiety: Theory research and intervention.* New York: Human Sciences Press.

Phillips, B. N., Martin, R. P., & Meyers, J. (1972). Interventions in relation to anxiety in school. In C. P. Spielberger (Ed.), *Anxiety: Current trends in theory and research.* Vol. 2. New York: Academic Press.

Piers, E. V., & Harris, D. S. (1964). Age and other correlates of self-concept in children. *Journal of Educational Psychology, 55*, 91–95.

Piers, E. V., & Harris, D. S. (1969). *The Piers-Harris Children's Self-Concept Scale.* Nashville: Counselor Recordings and Tests.

Platt, J. J., & Spivack, G. (1972). Social competence and effective problem-solving in psychiatric patients. *Journal of Clinical Psychology, 28*, 3–5.

Platt, J. J., & Spivack, G. (1975). *Manual for the Means-Ends Problem-Solving Procedure.* Department of Mental Health Sciences, Hahnemann University, Philadelphia, Pennsylvania.

Platt, J. J., Spivack, G., Altman, N., Altman, D., & Peizer, S. B. (1974). Adolescent problem solving thinking. *Journal of Consulting and Clinical Psychology, 42*, 787–793.

Porteus, S. (1955). *The maze test: Recent advances.* Palo Alto, CA: Pacific Books.

Poznanski, E. O., Grossman, J. A., Buchsbaum, Y., Banegas, M., Freeman, L., & Gibbons, R. (1984). Preliminary studies of the reliability and validity of the Children's Depression Rating Scale. *Journal of Child Psychiatry, 23*, 191–197.

President's Commission on Mental Health (1978). *Report to the President,* Vol. 1. Washington, DC: U.S. Government Printing Office.

Puig-Antich, J., & Chambers, W. (1978). *The Schedule for Affective Disorders and Schizophrenia for School-age children (Kiddie-SADS).* New York: New York State Psychiatric Institute.

Putallaz, M. (1983). Predicting children's sociometric status from their behavior. *Child Development, 54*, 1417–1426.

Putallaz, M., & Gottman, J. (1982). Conceptualizing social competence in children. In P. Karoly & J. J. Steffen (Eds.), *Improving children's social competence.* Lexington, MA: Lexington Books.

Quay, H. C. (1979). Classification. In H. C. Quay & J. S. Werry (Eds.), *Psychopathological disorders of childhood* (2nd Ed.). New York: John Wiley & Sons.

Quay, H. C., & Peterson, D. R. (1983). *Interim Manual for the Revised Behavior Problem Checklist.* University of Miami, Coral Gables, FL.

Raskind, L. T., & Nagle, R. J. (1980). Modeling effects on the intelligence performance of test anxious children. *Psychology in the School, 17*, 351–355.

Raven, J. C. (1965). *Standard Progressive Matrices Manual.* New York: Psychological Corporation.

Rehm, L. P. (1977). A self-control model of depression. *Behavior Therapy, 8*, 787–804.

Rehm, L. P., Kornblith, S. J., O'Hara, M. W., Lamparski, D. M., Romano, J. M., & Volkin, J. I. (1981). An evaluation of major components in a self-control therapy program for depression. *Behavior Modification, 5*, 459–489.

Renshaw, P. D. (1981). *Social knowledge and sociometric status: Children's goals and strategies for peer interaction.* Unpublished doctoral dissertation, University of Illinois.

Renshaw, P. D., & Asher, S. R. (1982). Social competence and peer status: The distinction between goals and strategies. In K. H. Rubin & H. S. Ross (Eds.), *Peer relationships and social skills in childhood.* New York: Springer-Verlag.

Reynolds, C. R. (1980). Concurrent validity of What I Think and Feel: The Revised Children's Manifest Anxiety Scale. *Journal of Consulting and Clinical Psychology, 48*, 774–775.

Reynolds, C. R. (1981). Long-term stability of scores on the revised children's manifest anxiety scale. *Perceptual and Motor Skills, 53*, 702.

Reynolds, C. R., & Gutkin, T. (1982) (Eds.). *The handbook of school psychology.* New York: Wiley.

Reynolds, C. R., & Paget, K. D. (1981). Factor analysis of the revised Children's Manifest Anxiety Scale for Blacks, Whites, Males, and Females with a national and innovative sample. *Journal of Consulting and Clinical Psychology, 49*, 352–359.

Reynolds, C. R., & Paget, K. D. (March, 1982). *National normative and reliability data for the Revised Children's Manifest Anxiety Scale.* Paper presented at the annual meeting of the National Association of School Psychologists, Toronto.

Reynolds, C. R., & Richmond, B. O. (1978). What I Think and Feel: A revised measure of children's manifest anxiety. *Journal of Abnormal Child Psychology, 6*, 271–280.

Reynolds, W. M. (1984). Depression in children and adolescents. Phenomenology evaluation and treatment. *School Psychology Review, 13*, 171–182.

Reynolds, W. M. (1985). Depression in childhood and adolescence: Diagnosis, assessment, intervention strategies and research. In T. R. Kratochwill (Ed.), *Advance in school psychology,* Vol. 4 (pp. 133–189). Hillsdale, NJ: Lawrence Erlbaum.

Reynolds, W. M. (1986). A model for the screening and identification of depressed children and adolescents in school settings. *Professional School Psychology, 1*, 117–129.

Reynolds, W. M. (1987a). *Assessment of depression: Manual for the Reynolds Adolescent Depression Scale.* Odessa, FL: Psychological Assessment Resources.

Reynolds, W. M. (1987b). *Reynolds Adolescent Depression Scale.* Odessa, FL: Psychological Assessment Resources.

Reynolds, W. M. (in press). *Child Depression Scale.* Odessa, FL: Psychological Assessment Resources.

Reynolds, W. M., Anderson, G., & Bartell, N. (1985). Measuring depression in children: A multimethod assessment investigation. *Journal of Abnormal child Psychology, 13*, 513–526.

Reynolds, W. M., & Coats, K. (July, 1982). *Depression in adolescents: Incidence, depth and correlates.* Paper presented at the 10th International Congress of the International Association for Child and Adolescent Psychiatry, Dublin, Ireland.

Reynolds, W. M., & Coats, K. I. (1986). A comparison of cognitive-behavioral therapy and relaxation training for the treatment of depression in adolescents. *Journal of Consulting and Clinical Psychology, 54*, 653–660.

Reynolds, W. M., & Stark, K. D. (1986). Self-control in children: A multi-method examination of treatment outcome measures. *Journal of Abnormal Child Psychology, 14*(1), 13–23.

Ribordy, S. C., Tracy, R. J., & Bernotas, T. D. (1981). The effects of an attentional training procedure on the performance of high and low test-anxious children. *Cognitive Therapy and Research, 5*, 19–28.

Richard, B. A., & Dodge, K. A. (1982). Social maladjustment and problem solving in school-aged children. *Journal of Consulting and Clinical Psychology, 50*, 226–233.

Rickel, A. U., & Burgio, J. C. (1982). Assessing social competencies in lower income preschool children. *American Journal of Community Psychology, 16*, 635–645.

Riddle, M. & Roberts, A. (1974). *The Porteus Mazes: A critical evaluation.* Report N. PR-74-3, Department of Psychiatry, University of Minnesota.

Roberts, M., Milich, R., Loney, J., & Caputo, J. (1981). A multi-trait, multi-method analysis of variance of teacher ratings of aggression, hyperactivity and inattention. *Journal of Abnormal Child Psychology, 9*(3), 371–380.

Roberts, M. C., & Peterson, L. C. (1984). Prevention models: Theoretical and practical implications. In M. C. Roberts & L. Peterson (Eds.), *Prevention of problems in childhood.* New York: John Wiley & Sons.

Roberts, R. N., & Nelson, R. O. (1984). Assessment issues and strategies in cognitive behavior therapy with children. In A. W. Meyers & W. E. Craighead (Eds.), *Cognitive behavior therapy with children* (pp. 99–128). New York: Plenum Press.

Robin, A., Fischel, J., & Brown, K. (1984). The measurement of self-control in children: Validation of the self-control rating scale. *Journal of Pediatric Psychology, 9*, 165–175.

Robin, A. L., Schneider, M., & Dolnick, M. (1976). The turtle technique: An extended case study of self-control in the classroom. *Psychology in the Schools, 13*, 449–453.

Robins, L. N. (1966). *Deviant children grown up.* Baltimore: Williams & Wilkins.

Robins, L. N. (1974). Antisocial behavior disturbances of childhood: Prevalence, prognosis, and prospects. In B. J. Anthony & C. Koupernik (Eds.), *The child and his family: Children at psychiatric risk.* New York: John Wiley & Sons.

Robins, L. N. (1979). Follow-up studies. In H. C. Quay & J. S. Werry (Eds.), *Psychopathological disorders of childhood.* New York: John Wiley & Sons.

Roff, J. D., & Wirt, R. D. (1984). Childhood aggression and social adjustment as antecedents of delinquency. *Journal of Abnormal Child Psychology, 12*, 111–126.

Roff, M. (1972). A two-factor approach to juvenile delinquency and the later histories of juvenile delinquents. In M. Roff, L. N. Robins, & M. Pollack (Eds.), *Life history research in psychopathology,* Vol. 2 (pp. 77–101). Minneapolis: University of Minnesota Press.

Roff, M., Sells, S. B., & Golden, M. M. (1972). *Social adjustment and personality development in children.* Minneapolis: University of Minnesota Press.

Roistacher, R. (1974). A microeconomic model of sociometric choice. *Sociometry, 37*, 219–238.

Rosenthal, R., & Allen, T. (1978). An examination of attention, arousal and learning dysfunctions of hyperkinetic children. *Psychological Bulletin, 85*(4), 689–715.

Ross, A. O. (1981). *Child behavior therapy: Principles, procedures, and empirical basis.* New York: John Wiley & Sons.

Ross, D., & Ross, S. (1982). *Hyperactivity: Current issues, research and theory.* New York: Wiley.

Routh, D. (1983). Attention deficit disorder: Its relationships with activity, aggression and achievement. In M. Wolraich (Ed.), *Advances in developmental and behavioral pediatrics,* 125–163. Greenwich, CT: JAI Press, Inc.

Rubin, K. H., & Daniels-Beirness, T. (1983). Concurrent and predictive correlates of sociometric status in kindergarten and grade 1 children. *Merrill-Palmer Quarterly, 29*, 337–351.

Rush, A. J., Beck, A. T., Kovacs, M., & Hollon, S. (1977). Comparative efficacy of cognitive therapy and pharmacotherapy in the treatment of depressed outpatients. *Cognitive Therapy and Research, 1*, 17–37.

Rush, A. J., Shaw, B., & Khatomi, M. (1980). *Cognitive Therapy and Research, 4*, 103–114.

Rush, A. J., & Watkins, J. T. (1981). Group versus individual cognitive therapy: A pilot study. *Cognitive Therapy and Research, 5*, 95–104.

Rutter, M. (1983). *Developmental Neuropsychiatry,* New York: Guilford.

Rutter, M., Tizard, J., & Whitmore, K. (Eds.) (1970). *Education, health, and behavior.* London: Longmans.

Ryan, E. B., Weed, K. A., & Short, E. J. (1987). Cognitive behavior modification: Promoting active, self-regulatory learning styles. In J. K. Torgesen & B. Y. L. Wong (Eds.), *Psychological and educational perspectives on learning disabilities: Some new perspectives* (pp. 367–397). New York: Academic Press.

Safer, D. (1971). Drugs for problem school children. *Journal of School Health, 41*, 32–35.

Safer, D., & Allen, R. (1976). *Hyperactive children: Diagnosis and management.* Baltimore, MD: University Park Press.

Salkind, N. (1979). *The development of norms for the Matching Familiar Figures Test.* Manuscript available from the author, University of Kansas.

Sarason, I. G. (1975). Anxiety and self-preoccupation. In I. G. Sarason & C. Spielberger (Eds.), *Stress and anxiety,* Vol. 2 (pp. 27–44). New York: John Wiley & Sons.

Sarason, I. G. (Ed.) (1980). *Test anxiety: theory research & applications.* Hillsdale, NJ: Lawrence Erlbaum.

Sarason, I. G., & Sarason, B. R. (1981). Teaching cognitive and social skills to high school students. *Journal of Consulting and Clinical Psychology, 49*, 908–918.

Sarason, S. B. (1981). *The culture of the school and the problem of change* (2nd Ed.). Boston: Allyn and Bacon.

Sarason, S. B., Davidson, K. S., Lighthall, F. F., Waite, R. R., & Ruebush, B. K. (1960). *Anxiety in elementary school children.* New York: John Wiley & Sons.

Saylor, C. F., Finch, A. J., Baskin, C. H., Furey, W., & Kelly, M. M. (1984). Construct validity for measures of childhood depression: Application of multitrait-multimethod methodology. *Journal of Consulting and Clinical Psychology, 52*, 977–985.

Saylor, C. F., Finch, A. J., Spirito, A., & Bennett, B. (1984). The children's Depression Inventory: A systematic evaluation of psychometric properties. *Journal of Consulting and Clinical Psychology, 52*, 955–967.

Scanlon, E. M., & Ollendick, T. H. (1986). Children's assertive behavior: The reliability and validity of three self-report measures. *Child and Family Behavior Therapy, 7*, 9–21.

Scarlett, W. G. (1980). Social isolation from agemates among nursery school children. *Journal of Child Psychology and Psychiatry, 12*, 231–240.

Schachar, R., Sandberg, S., & Rutter, M. (1986). Agreement between teachers' rating and observations of hyperactivity, inattentiveness and defiance. *Journal of Abnormal Child Psychology, 14*(2), 331–345.

Schinke, S. P., Blythe, B. J., & Gilchrist, L. D. (1981). Cognitive-behavioral prevention of adolescent pregnancy. *Journal of Counseling Psychology, 28*, 451–454.

Schmuck, R. A., & Schmuck, P. A. (1974). *A humanistic psychology of education.* Palo Alto, CA: National Press Books.

Schneider, M. (1974). Turtle technique in the classroom. *Teaching Exceptional Children, 8*, 22–24.

Schneider, M., & Robin, A. L. (1976). The turtle technique: A method for the self-control of impulsive behavior. In J. D. Krumboltz & C. E. Thoresen (Eds.), *Counseling methods.* New York: Holt, Rinehart, & Winston.

Schofield, J. W., & Whitley, B. E. (1983). Peer nomination versus rating scale measurement of children's peer preference. *Social Psychology Quarterly, 46*, 242–251.

Schrag, P., & Diroky, D. (1975). *The myth of the hyperactive child.* New York: Pantheon.

Schulterbrandt, J. G., & Raskin, A. (Eds.) (1977). *Depression in childhood: Diagnosis, treatment, and conceptual models.* New York: Raven Press.

Seligman, M. E. P. (1975). *Helplessness: On depression development, and death.* San Francisco: Freeman and Company.

Seligman, M. E. P., Kaslow, N. J., Allow, L. B., Peterson, C., Tannenbaum, R. L., & Abramson, L. Y. (1984). Attributional style and depressive symptoms in children. *Journal of Abnormal Psychology, 93*, 235–238.

Selman, R. L. (1980). *The growth of interpersonal understanding.* New York: Academic Press.

Selman, R. L., Jaquette, D., & Bruss-Saunders, E. (1979). *Assessing interpersonal understanding: An interview and scoring manual.* Harvard-Judge Baker Social Reasoning Project, Cambridge, Massachusetts.

Severson, H. H. (1984). Adolescent social drug use: School prevention program. *The School Psychology Review, 13*, 150–161.

Shure, M. B. (1979). Training children to solve interpersonal problems: A preventive mental health program. In R. F. Munoz, L. R. Snowden, & J. G. Kelly (Eds.), *Social and psychological research in community settings: Designing and conducting programs for social and personal well-being.* San Francisco: Jossey-Bass.

Shure, M. B. (1980). *Interpersonal problem-solving in ten-year-olds.* Washington, DC: National Institute of Mental Health.

Shure, M. B. (1981). Social competence as a problem-solving skill. In J. D. Wine & M. D. Smye (Eds.), *Social competence* (pp. 158–185). New York: Guilford.

Shure, M. B., & Spivack, G. (1972). Means-ends thinking, adjustment and social class among elementary school-age children. *Journal of Consulting and Clinical Psychology, 38*, 348–353.

Shure, M. B., & Spivack, G. (1974). *The PIPS Test manual.* Philadelphia: Department of Mental Health Sciences, Hahnemann Medical College.

Shure, M. B., & Spivack, G. (1978). *Problem solving techniques in childrearing.* San Francisco: Jossey-Bass.

Shure, M. B., & Spivack, G. (1980). Interpersonal problem-solving as a mediator of behavioral adjustment in preschool and kindergarten children. *Journal of Applied Developmental Psychology, 1*, 29–43.

Shure, M. B., & Spivack, G. (1982). Interpersonal problem-solving in young children: A cognitive approach to prevention. *American Journal of Community Psychology, 10*, 341–356.

Skinner, B. F. (1953). *Science and human behavior.* New York: Free Press.

Skinner, B. F. (1971). *Beyond freedom and dignity.* New York: Knopf.

Smucker, M. R., Craighead, W. E., Craighead, L. W., & Green, B. J. (1986). Normative and reliability data for the Children's Depression Inventory. *Journal of Abnormal Child Psychology, 14*, 25–39.

Spivack, G., Platt, J. J., & Shure, M. B. (1976). *The problem solving approach to adjustment.* San Francisco: Jossey-Bass.

Spivack, G., & Shure, M. B. (1974). *Social adjustment of young children: A cognitive approach to solving real-life problems.* San Francisco: Jossey-Bass.

Spivack, G., & Shure, M. B. (1982). The cognition of social adjustment: Interpersonal cognitive problem-solving thinking. In B. B. Lahey & A. E. Kazdin (Eds.), *Advances in clinical child psychology,* Vol. 5 (pp. 323–372). New York: Plenum Press.

Spivack, G., Shure, M. B., & Platt, J. J. (1985). *Means-ends problem solving stimuli and scoring procedures supplement.* Philadelphia: Hahnemann University, Department of Mental Health Sciences.

Sprague, R., Christensen, D., & Werry, J. (1974). Experimental psychology and stimulant drugs. In K. Conners (Ed.), *Clinical use of stimulant drugs in children.* The Hague: Exerpta Medica.

Sprague, R., & Sleator, E. (1973). Effects of psychopharmacological agents on learning disorders. *Pediatric Clinics of North America, 20*, 719–735.

Stark, K. D., Reynolds, W. M., & Kaslow, N. J. (1987). A comparison of the relative efficacy of self-control therapy and a behavioral problem-solving therapy for depression in children. *Journal of Abnormal Child Psychology, 15*, 91–113.

Steinberg, M. D., & Dodge, K. A. (1983). Attributional bias in aggressive adolescent boys and girls. *Journal of Social and Clinical Psychology, 1*, 312–321.

Stephens, T. M. (1981). *Technical information: social behavior assessment.* Columbus, OH: Cedars.

Stevens, R., & Pihl, R. (1983). Learning to cope with school: A study of the effects of a coping skill training program with test vulnerable 7th grade students. *Cognitive Therapy and Research, 1*, 155–158.

Strauss, C., Forehand, R., Frame, C., & Smith, K. (1984). Characteristics of children with extreme scores on the Children's Depression Inventory. *Journal of Clinical Child Psychology, 13*, 227–231.

Strober, M., Green, J., & Carlson, G. (1981). Utility of the Beck Depression Inventory with psychiatrically hospitalized adolescents. *Journal of Consulting and Clinical Psychology, 49*, 482–485.

Stuart, R. B. (1967). Behavioral control over eating. *Behavior Research and Therapy, 5*, 357–365.

Sweeney, P. D., Anderson, K., & Bailey, S. (1986). Attributional style in depression: A meta-analytic review. *Journal of Personality and Social Psychology, 50*, 974–991.

Tarplay, B. S., & Sandargas, R. A. (1981). An intervention for a withdrawn child based on teacher recorded levels of social interaction. *School Psychology Review, 3*, 409–412.

Taylor, D. W. (1972). Treatment of excessive frequency of urination by desensitization. *Journal of Behavior Therapy and Experimental Psychiatry, 3*, 311–313.

Taylor, E., & Sandberg, S. (1984). Hyperactive behavior in English school children: A questionnaire survey. *Journal of Abnormal Child Psychology, 12*(1), 143–156.

Teri, L. (1982). The use of the Beck Depression Inventory with adolescents. *Journal of Abnormal Child Psychology, 10*, 277–284.

Thoresen, C. E., & Mahoney, M. J. (1974). *Behavioral self-control.* New York: Holt, Rinehart, & Winston.

Trickett, E. J., & Moos, R. H. (1973). The social environment of junior high and high school classrooms. *Journal of Educational Psychology, 65*, 93–102.

Ullmann, C. A. (1957). Teachers, peers, and tests as predictors of adjustment. *Journal of Educational Psychology, 48*, 257–267.

Ullman, R., Sleator, E., & Sprague, R. (1985). A change of mind: The Conners Abbreviated Rating Scales reconsidered. *Journal of Abnormal Child Psychology, 13*(4), 553–565.

Uphoff, J. W., Smith, C. L., & Stewart, B. J. (August, 1983). *Perspective-taking and social behavior in behaviorally disordered boys.* Paper presented at the meeting of the American Psychological Association, Anaheim, California.

Urbain, E. S., & Kendall, P. C. (1980). Review of social-cognitive problem-solving interventions with children. *Psychological Bulletin, 88*, 109–143.

Urbain, E. S., & Kendall, P. C. (1981). *Interpersonal problem-solving, social perspective-taking, and behavioral contingencies: A comparison of group approaches with impulsive-aggressive children.* Unpublished manuscript, University of Minnesota.

Urbain, E. S., & Savage, P. (in press). Interpersonal cognitive problem-solving training with children in the schools. In J. Hughes & R. Hall (Eds.), *Cognitive-behavioral approaches in educational settings.* New York: Guilford Press.

Vaal, J. J. (1973). Applying contingency contracting to a school phobic: A case study. *Journal of Behavior Therapy and Experimental Psychiatry, 4*, 371–373.

Vallis, T. M., & Bucher, B. (1986). Self-efficacy as a predictor of behavior change: Interaction with type of training for pain tolerance. *Cognitive Therapy and Research, 10*, 79–94.

Van Alstnyne, D., & Hattwick, L. A. (1939). A follow-up study of the behavior of nursery school children. *Child Development, 10*, 43–72.

Vygotsky, L. (1962). *Thought and language.* New York: John Wiley & Sons.

Waddell, K. (1984). The self concept and social adaptation of hyperactive children in adolescence. *Journal of Clinical Child Psychology, 13*(1), 50–55.

Waksman, S. A. (1985). The development and psychometric properties of a rating scale for children's social skills. *Journal of Psychoeducational Assessment, 3*, 111–121.

Waldman, I. (August, 1986). *Social perceptual deficits and biases in aggressive children and in children who demonstrate information processing deficits.* Paper presented at the annual meeting of the American Psychological Association, Washington, DC.

Waldrop, M. F., & Halverson, L. F., Jr. (1975). Intensive and extensive peer behavior: Longitudinal and cross-sectional analyses. *Child Development, 46*, 19–26.

Walker, H. M. (1976). *Walker Problem Behavior Identification Checklist Manual.* Los Angeles: Western Psychological Services.

Walker, H. M., Greenwood, C. R., Hops, H., & Todd, N. M. (1979). Differential effects of reinforcing topographic components of social interaction. *Behavior Modification, 3*, 291–321.

Waterman, J. B., Sobesky, W. E., Silvern, L., Aoki, B., & McCaulay, M. (1981). Social perspective-taking and adjustment in emotionally disturbed, learning disabled, and normal children. *Journal of Abnormal Child Psychology, 9*, 133–148.

Watson, J. B. (1924). *Behaviorism.* Chicago: University of Chicago Press.

Watson, J. B., & Rayner, R. (1920). Conditioned emotional reactions. *Journal of experimental Psychology, 3*, 1–14.

Watt, N. F. (1978). Patterns of childhood social development in adult schizophrenics. *Archives of General Psychiatry, 35*, 160–170.

Weinrott, M. R., Corson, J. A., & Wilchesky, M. (1979). Teacher mediated treatment of social withdrawl. *Behavior Therapy, 10*, 281–294.

Weiss, G., & Hechtman, L. (1986). *Hyperactive children grown up: Empirical findings and theoretical considerations.* New York: Guilford Press.

Weiss, G., Minder, K., Werry, J., Douglas, V., & Nemeth, E. (1971). Studies on the hyperactive child: VIII. Five year follow-up. *Archives of General Psychiatry, 24*, 409–414.

Weissberg, R., Gesten, E., Carnrike, C., Toro, P., Rapkin, B., Davidson, E., & Cowen, E. (1981a). Social problem solving training: A competence building intervention with second to fourth grade children. *American Journal of Community Psychology, 9*, 411–423.

Weissberg, R. P., Gesten, E. L., Rapkin, B. D., Cowen, E. L., Davidson, E., De Apodaca, R. F., & McKim, B. (1981b). Evaluation of a social problem-solving training program for suburban and inner-city third-grade children. *Journal of Consulting and Clinical Psychology, 49*, 251–261.

Werry, J., & Sprague, R. (1974). Methylphenidate in children: Effects of dosage. *Australian and New Zealand Journal of Psychiatry, 8*, 9–19.

Whalen, C., Henker, B., & Henshaw, S. (1985). Cognitive-behavioral therapies for hyperactive children: Premises, problems, and prospects. *Journal of Abnormal Child Psychology, 13*, 391–410.

Wheeler, V. A., & Ladd, G. W. (1982). Assessment of children's self-efficacy for social interaction with peers. *Developmental Psychology, 18*, 795–805.

White, J., & Poteat, G. M. (1983). Improving kindergarten students' social skills through consultation and teacher directed activities. *School Psychology Review, 12*, 476–480.

Whitehead, M., Hersen, M., & Bellack, A. S. (1980). Conversation skills training for socially isolated children. *Behavior Research and Therapy, 18*, 217–225.

Whitman, T., Burgio, L., & Johnston, M. (1984). Cognitive behavioral interventions with mentally retarded children. In A. W. Meyers & W. E. Craighead (Eds.), *Cognitive behavior therapy with children* (pp. 193–227). New York: Plenum Press.

Williams, M., & Lahey, B. (1977). The functional independence of response latency and accuracy: Implications for the concept of cognitive tempo. *Journal of Abnormal Child Psychology, 5*, 371–378.

Wilson, G. T. (1978). Cognitive behavior therapy: Paradigm shift or passing phase? In J. P. Foley & D. P. Rathjen (Eds.), *Cognitive behavior therapy: Research and applications.* New York: Plenum Press.

Wine, J. I. (1971). Test anxiety and direction of attention. *Psychological Bulletin, 76*, 92–104.

Winer, J. I., Hilpert, P. L., Gesten, E. L., Cowen, E. L., & Schubin, W. E. (1982). The evaluation of a kindergarten social problem solving program. *Journal of Primary Prevention, 2*, 205–216.

Winnett, R. A., & Winkler, R. C. (1972). Current behavior modification in the classroom: Be still, be docile. *Journal of Applied Behavior Analysis, 3*, 499–504.

Witt, J., Elliott, S., & Gresham, F. (1987). *Handbook of behavior therapy in education.* New York: Plenum Press.

Wolf, M. M. (1978). Social validity: The case for subjective measurement or how applied behavior analysis is finding its heart. *Journal of Applied Behavior Analysis, 11*, 203–214.

Wolpe, J. (1958). *Reciprocal inhibition therapy.* Stanford, CA: Stanford University Press.

Wong, B. Y. L. (1985). Issues in cognitive-behavioral interventions in academic skill areas. *Journal of Abnormal Child Psychology, 13*, 425–442.

Yarrow, L. J. (1960). Interviewing children. In P. H. Mussen (Ed.), *Handbook of research methods in child development* (pp. 561–602). New York: John Wiley & Sons.

Zatz, S. L., & Chassin, L. (1983). Cognitions of test anxious children. *Journal of Consulting and Clinical Psychology, 51*, 526–534.

Zatz, S. L., & Chassin, L. (1985). Cognitions of test-anxious children under naturalistic test-taking conditions. *Journal of Consulting and Clinical Psychology, 53*, 393–401.

Author Index

Subject Index

bout the Author

an N. Hughes, Ph.D., currently an associate professor in the Department f Educational Psychology at Texas A&M University, was recently ppointed to the chair of the department's school psychology doctoral rogram. Dr. Hughes served as director of the department's Counseling and ssessment Clinic from 1984 to 1987. Before coming to Texas A&M, Dr. lughes taught in the Department of Psychology, as associate professor, at adford University from 1976 to 1984, chairing the school psychology rogram from 1978 to 1984. As a licensed psychologist in Virginia (1978 to 984) and then in Texas, Dr. Hughes has maintained an active private ractice in child and school psychology and has provided consultative ervices to numerous schools and child-centered agencies during the last 10 ears. Dr. Hughes has also served in positions of national leadership in the chool Psychology Division of the American Psychological Association and ne National Association of School Psychologists. The author of numerous nonographs and articles on cognitive-behavioral approaches with children,)r. Hughes serves on the editorial board of *Professional School Psychology* nd the *School Psychology Review*.

Pergamon General Psychology Series

Editors: Arnold P. Goldstein, Syracuse University
Leonard Krasner, Stanford University &
SUNY at Stony Brook

Vol. 1. WOLPE—*The Practice of Behavior Therapy, Third Edition*
Vol. 2. MAGOON *et al.*—*Mental Health Counselors at Work**
Vol. 3. McDANIEL—*Physical Disability and Human Behavior, Second Edition**
Vol. 4. KAPLAN *et al.*—*The Structural Approach in Psychological Testing*
Vol. 5. LaFAUCI & RICHTER—*Team Teaching at the College Level**
Vol. 6. PEPINSKY *et al.*—*People and Information**
Vol. 7. SIEGMAN & POPE—*Studies in Dyadic Communication*
Vol. 8. JOHNSON—*Existential Man: The Challenge of Psychotherapy*
Vol. 9. TAYLOR—*Climate for Creativity*
Vol. 10. RICKARD—*Behavioral Intervention in Human Problems**
Vol. 14. GOLDSTEIN—*Psychotherapeutic Attraction*
Vol. 15. HALPERN—*Survival: Black/White*
Vol. 16. SALZINGER & FELDMAN—*Studies in Verbal Behavior: An Empirical Approach*
Vol. 19. LIBERMAN—*A Guide to Behavioral Analysis and Therapy*
Vol. 22. PEPINSKY & PATTON—*The Psychological Experiment: A Practical Accomplishment**
Vol. 23. YOUNG—*New Sources of Self*
Vol. 24. WATSON—*Child Behavior Modification: A Manual for Teachers, Nurses and Parents*
Vol. 25. NEWBOLD—*The Psychiatric Programming of People: Neo-Behavioral Orthomolecular Psychiatry*
Vol. 26. ROSSI—*Dreams and the Growth of Personality: Expanding Awareness in Psychotherapy**
Vol. 27. O'LEARY & O'LEARY—*Classroom Management: The Successful Use of Behavior Modification, Second Edition*
Vol. 28. FELDMAN—*College and Student: Selected Readings in the Social Psychology of Higher Education*
Vol. 29. ASHEM & POSER—*Adaptive Learning: Behavior Modification with Children*
Vol. 30. BURCK *et al.*—*Counseling and Accountability: Methods and Critique**
Vol. 31. FREDERIKSEN *et al.*—*Prediction of Organizational Behavior*
Vol. 32. CATTELL—*A New Morality from Science: Beyondism*
Vol. 33. WEINER—*Personality: The Human Potential*
Vol. 34. LIEBERT & SPRAFKIN—*The Early Window: Effects of Television on Children and Youth, Third Edition*
Vol. 35. COHEN *et al.*—*Psych City: A Simulated Community*
Vol. 36. GRAZIANO—*Child Without Tomorrow*
Vol. 37. MORRIS—*Perspectives in Abnormal Behavior*
Vol. 38. BALLER—*Bed Wetting: Origins and Treatment**
Vol. 40. KAHN, CAMERON & GRIFFEN—*Methods and Evaluation in Clinical and Counseling Psychology*
Vol. 41. SEGALL—*Human Behavior and Public Policy: A Political Psychology*
Vol. 42. FAIRWEATHER *et al.*—*Creating Change in Mental Health Organizations*

Vol. 43. KATZ & ZLUTNICK—*Behavior Therapy and Health Care: Principles and Applications*
Vol. 44. EVANS & CLAIBORN—*Mental Health Issues and the Urban Poor*
Vol. 46. BARBER, SPANOS & CHAVES—*Hypnosis, Imagination and Human Potentialities*
Vol. 47. POPE—*The Mental Health Interview: Research and Application*
Vol. 48. PELTON—*The Psychology of Nonviolence**
Vol. 49. COLBY—*Artificial Paranoia—A Computer Simulation of Paranoid Processes*
Vol. 50. GELFAND & HARTMANN—*Child Behavior Analysis and Therapy, Second Edition*
Vol. 51. WOLPE—*Theme and Variations: A Behavior Therapy Casebook*
Vol. 52. KANFER & GOLDSTEIN—*Helping People Change: A Textbook of Methods, Third Edition*
Vol. 53. DANZIGER—*Interpersonal Communication*
Vol. 55. GOLDSTEIN & STEIN—*Prescriptive Psychotherapies*
Vol. 56. BARLOW & HERSEN—*Single-Case Experimental Designs: Strategies for Studying Behavior Changes, Second Edition*
Vol. 57. MONAHAN—*Community Mental Health and the Criminal Justice System*
Vol. 58. WAHLER, HOUSE & STAMBAUGH—*Ecological Assessment of Child Problem Behavior: A Clinical Package for Home, School and Institutional Settings*
Vol. 59. MAGARO—*The Construction of Madness: Emerging Conceptions and Interventions into the Psychotic Process*
Vol. 60. MILLER—*Behavioral Treatment of Alcoholism**
Vol. 61. FOREYT—*Behavioral Treatments of Obesity*
Vol. 62. WANDERSMAN, POPPEN & RICKS—*Humanism and Behaviorism: Dialogue and Growth*
Vol. 63. NIETZEL, WINETT, MACDONALD & DAVIDSON—*Behavioral Approaches to Community Psychology*
Vol. 64. FISHER & GOCHROS—*Handbook of Behavior Therapy with Sexual Problems. Vol. I: General Procedures. Vol. II: Approaches to Specific Problems*
Vol. 65. BELLACK & HERSEN—*Behavioral Assessment: A Practical Handbook, Third Edition*
Vol. 66. LEFKOWITZ, ERON, WALDER & HUESMANN—*Growing Up to Be Violent: A Longitudinal Study of the Development of Aggression*
Vol. 67. BARBER—*Pitfalls in Human Research: Ten Pivotal Points*
Vol. 68. SILVERMAN—*The Human Subject in the Psychological Laboratory*
Vol. 69. FAIRWEATHER & TORNATZKY—*Experimental Methods for Social Policy Research**
Vol. 70. GURMAN & RAZIN—*Effective Psychotherapy: A Handbook of Research**
Vol. 71. MOSES & BYHAM—*Applying the Assessment Center Method*
Vol. 72. GOLDSTEIN—*Prescriptions for Child Mental Health and Education*
Vol. 73. KEAT—*Multimodal Therapy with Children*
Vol. 74. SHERMAN—*Personality: Inquiry & Application*
Vol. 75. GATCHEL & PRICE—*Clinical Applications of Biofeedback: Appraisal and Status*

Vol. 76. CATALANO—*Health, Behavior and the Community: An Ecological Perspective*
Vol. 77. NIETZEL—*Crime and Its Modification: A Social Learning Perspective*
Vol. 78. GOLDSTEIN, HOYER & MONTI—*Police and the Elderly*
Vol. 79. MIRON & GOLDSTEIN—*Hostage*
Vol. 80. GOLDSTEIN *et al.*—*Police Crisis Intervention*
Vol. 81. UPPER & CAUTELA—*Covert Conditioning*
Vol. 82. MORELL—*Program Evaluation in Social Research*
Vol. 83. TEGER—*Too Much Invested to Quit*
Vol. 84. MONJAN & GASSNER—*Critical Issues in Competency-Based Education*
Vol. 85. KRASNER—*Environmental Design and Human Behavior: A Psychology of the Individual in Society*
Vol. 86. TAMIR—*Communication and the Aging Process: Interaction Throughout the Life Cycle*
Vol. 87. WEBSTER, KONSTANTAREAS, OXMAN & MACK—*Autism: New Directions in Research and Education*
Vol. 89. CARTLEDGE & MILBURN—*Teaching Social Skills to Children: Innovative Approaches, Second Edition*
Vol. 90. SARBIN & MANCUSO—*Schizophrenia—Medical Diagnosis or Moral Verdict?**
Vol. 91. RATHJEN & FOREYT—*Social Competence: Interventions for Children and Adults*
Vol. 92. VAN DE RIET, KORB & GORRELL—*Gestalt Therapy: An Introduction*
Vol. 93. MARSELLA & PEDERSEN—*Cross-Cultural Counseling and Psychotherapy*
Vol. 94. BRISLIN—*Cross-Cultural Encounters: Face-to-Face Interaction*
Vol. 95. SCHWARTZ & JOHNSON—*Psychopathology of Childhood: A Clinical-Experimental Approach, Second Edition*
Vol. 96. HEILBRUN—*Human Sex-Role Behavior*
Vol. 97. DAVIDSON, KOCH, LEWIS, WRESINSKI—*Evaluation Strategies in Criminal Justice*
Vol. 98. GOLDSTEIN, CARR, DAVIDSON, WEHR—*In Response to Aggression: Methods of Control and Prosocial Alternatives*
Vol. 99. GOLDSTEIN—*Psychological Skill Training: The Structured Learning Technique*
Vol. 100. WALKER—*Clinical Practice of Psychology: A Guide for Mental Health Professionals*
Vol. 101. ANCHIN & KIESLER—*Handbook of Interpersonal Psychotherapy*
Vol. 102. GELLER, WINNETT EVERETT—*Preserving the Environment: New Strategies for Behavior Change*
Vol. 103. JENKINS—*The Psychology of the Afro-American: A Humanistic Approach*
Vol. 104. APTER—*Troubled Children/Troubled Systems*
Vol. 105. BRENNER—*The Effective Psychotherapist: Conclusions from Practice and Research*
Vol. 106. KAROLY & KANFER—*Self-Management and Behavior Change: From Theory to Practice*
Vol. 107. O'BRIEN, DICKINSON, ROSOW—*Industrial Behavior Modification: A Management Handbook*

Vol. 108. AMABILE & STUBBS—*Psychological Research in the Classroom: Issues for Educators and Researchers**
Vol. 110. DiMATTEO & DiNICOLA—*Achieving Patient Compliance: The Psychology of the Medical Practitioner's Role*
Vol. 111. CONOLEY & CONOLEY—*School Consultation: A Guide to Practice and Training*
Vol. 112. PAPAJOHN—*Intensive Behavior Therapy: The Behavioral Treatment of Complex Emotional Disorders*
Vol. 113. KAROLY, STEFFEN, O'GRADY—*Child Health Psychology: Concepts and Issues*
Vol. 114. MORRIS & KRATOCHWILL—*Treating Children's Fears and Phobias: A Behavioral Approach*
Vol. 115. GOLDSTEIN & SEGALL—*Aggression in Global Perspective*
Vol. 116. LANDIS & BRISLIN—*Handbook of Intercultural Training*
Vol. 117. FARBER—*Stress and Burnout in the Human Service Professions*
Vol. 118. BEUTLER—*Eclectic Psychotherapy: A Systematic Approach*
Vol. 119. HARRIS—*Families of the Developmentally Disabled: A Guide to Behavioral Intervention*
Vol. 120. HERSEN, KAZDIN, BELLACK—*The Clinical Psychology Handbook*
Vol. 121. MATSON & MULICK—*Handbook of Mental Retardation*
Vol. 122. FELNER, JASON, MORITSUGU, FARBER—*Preventive Psychology: Theory Research and Practice*
Vol. 123. CENTER FOR RESEARCH ON AGGRESSION—*Prevention and Control of Aggression*
Vol. 124. MORRIS & KRATOCHWILL—*The Practice of Child Therapy*
Vol. 125. VARNI—*Clinical Behavioral Pediatrics: An Interdisciplinary Biobehavioral Approach*
Vol. 126. RAMIREZ—*Psychology of the Americas: Mestizo Perspectives on Personality and Mental Health*
Vol. 127. LEWINSOHN & TERI—*Clinical Geropsychology: New Directions in Assessment and Treatment*
Vol. 128. BARLOW, HAYES, NELSON—*The Scientist Practitioner: Research and Accountability in Clinical and Educational Settings*
Vol. 129. OLLENDICK & HERSEN—*Child Behavioral Assessment: Principles and Procedures*
Vol. 130. BELLACK & HERSEN—*Research Methods in Clinical Psychology*
Vol. 131. GOLDSTEIN & HERSEN—*Handbook of Psychological Assessment*
Vol. 132. BELLACK & HERSEN—*Dictionary of Behavior Therapy Techniques*
Vol. 133. COOK—*Psychological Androgyny*
Vol. 134. DREW & HARDMAN—*Designing and Conducting Behavioral Research*
Vol. 135. APTER & GOLDSTEIN—*Youth Violence: Programs and Prospects*
Vol. 136. HOLZMAN & TURK—*Pain Management: A Handbook of Psychological Treatment Approaches*
Vol. 137. MORRIS & BLATT—*Special Education: Research and Trends*
Vol. 138. JOHNSON, RASBURY, SIEGEL—*Approaches to Child Treatment: Introduction to Theory, Research and Practice*
Vol. 139. RYBASH, HOYER & ROODIN—*Adult Cognition and Aging: Developmental Changes in Processing, Knowing and Thinking*
Vol. 140. WIELKIEWICZ—*Behavior Management in the Schools: Principles and Procedures*

Vol. 141. PLAS—*Systems Psychology in the Schools*
Vol. 142. VAN HASSELT & HERSEN—*Handbook of Adolescent Psychology*
Vol. 143. BRASSARD, GERMAIN & HART—*Psychological Maltreatment of Children and Youth*
Vol. 144. HERSHENSON & POWER—*Mental Health Counseling: Theory and Practice*
Vol. 145. GOLDSTEIN & KRASNER—*Modern Applied Psychology*
Vol. 146. CARSTENSEN & EDELSTEIN—*Handbook of Clinical Gerontology*
Vol. 147. HERSEN & BELLACK—*Dictionary of Behavioral Assessment Techniques*
Vol. 148. VAN HASSELT, STRAIN & HERSEN—*Handbook of Developmental and Physical Disabilities*
Vol. 149. BLECHMAN & BROWNELL—*Handbook of Behavioral Medicine for Women*
Vol. 150. MAHER & ZINS—*Psychoeducational Interventions in Schools: Methods and Procedures for Enhancing Student Competence*
Vol. 151. LAST & HERSEN—*Handbook of Anxiety Disorders*
Vol. 152. KAZDIN—*Child Psychotherapy: Developing and Identifying Effective Treatments*
Vol. 153. RUSSELL—*Stress Management for Chronic Disease*
Vol. 154. HIGGINBOTHAM, WEST & FORSYTH—*Psychotherapy and Behavior Change: Social, Cultural and Methodological Perspectives*
Vol. 155. HUGHES—*Cognitive Behavior Therapy with Children in Schools*

Out of print in original format. Available in custom reprint edition.